IMAGES
*of America*

# SAXAPAHAW

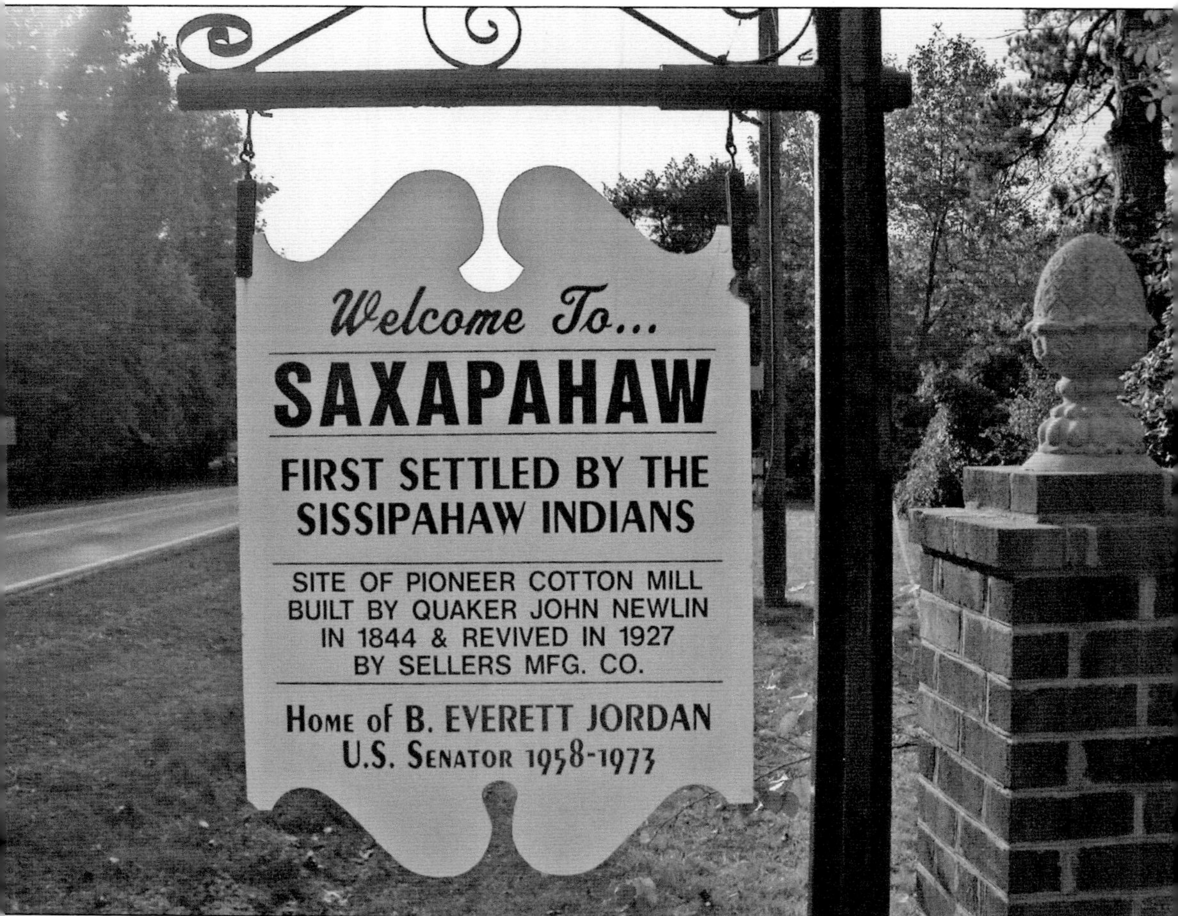


The "Welcome to Saxapahaw" landmark appears on each roadside leading into Saxapahaw. (Photograph by the author.)

**ON THE COVER:** This is a very appropriate photograph chosen to represent the village of Saxapahaw. It is North Carolina's former U.S. senator and Saxapahaw's longtime friend, boss, and mentor, the late Benjamin Everett Jordan. When B. Everett Jordan's uncle Charles V. Sellars (after whom the mill was named) asked Everett to come to Saxapahaw to co-own and manage the mill and develop the village, Everett and his wife, Katherine, took that very seriously and very dear to their hearts. Katherine told Everett, "You work on the Mill and I will work on the village," and that they did. When Everett Jordan was asked by his friend Edgar Cashwell, head of the Saxapahaw Community Center, if he would donate toward lighting the Saxapahaw ball field adjacent to Saxapahaw Elementary (now known as B. Everett Jordan Elementary), B. Everett Jordan replied by offering to match dollar for dollar the amount of money raised by the community as a whole. B. Everett Jordan is captured as he gives the dedication speech before the first ball is thrown for the first night game. (Courtesy of Edgar Cashwell.)

IMAGES
*of America*

# SAXAPAHAW

Heather Leigh Wallace

ARCADIA
PUBLISHING

ISBN 978-0-7385-6801-0

Published by Arcadia Publishing
Charleston, South Carolina

Printed in the United States of America

Library of Congress Control Number: 2008938822

For all general information contact Arcadia Publishing at:
Telephone 843-853-2070
Fax 843-853-0044
E-mail sales@arcadiapublishing.com
For customer service and orders:
Toll-Free 1-888-313-2665

Visit us on the Internet at www.arcadiapublishing.com

*For my father, Donald L. Wallace Sr.,*
*for teaching me to respect, love, and laugh at history.*
*And for my son, Keith F. Kosman,*
*who told me, "If you write it; they will come."*

# Contents

# Acknowledgments

The outpouring of love and the photographs and stories that came to life from so many people made this book possible.

I am indebted to my new friend John Jordan for spending countless hours sharing stories with me and his devotion to ensuring all the right people were interviewed. Thank you, Mac Jordan, for trusting me with the most prized photographic collection of the mill. Thank you, Margaret Jordan, for your grace and patience.

My dear friend Edgar Cashwell, your big heart and time meant a great deal to me.

Thanks to Ben F. Bulla, Saxapahaw's first historian, for expressing his feelings and in-depth research about Saxapahaw so eloquently since 1949, which provided a beacon of light for this book.

Thanks to the lovely Clara Alston, who gave me the biggest hug when we first met. No wonder Senator and Katherine Jordan hired you to tend to their vacation home; you are a warm and wonderful woman.

Thanks to the darling couple Frances and Crayton Hardin. I was touched when I saw Frances and Clara Alston holding hands at the mill reunion. May I also be so lucky to have such wonderful, long-lasting friendships based upon altruistic meanings.

A very special thank-you goes to Gary Johnson and his daughter Margaret Ann Johnson for opening their hearts and their home and for providing the oldest photographs.

Monique de Latour provided several of her real-photo cards from her collection sold in stores.

The heart-warming, tear-invoking Olympic photographs would not have been accessible without Cheryl Treworgy of www.prettysporty.com and her personal and professional media connections.

Thanks to the amazing, prejudice-free Frankie Hayes, whose newfound friendship was essential in introducing me to a whole new circle of wonderful Saxapahaw locals ("conservatives, rednecks, and loose as a goose").

Thank you to my sister, Donna Heron, for her expert writing advice. Your years of experience before me have always paved the perfect road.

Special mention should be made of the Seals, Harwood, and Mues families for making the world a better and brighter place. A kind thank-you to Nelson Rex Paris and his charming wife, Rachel Paris, for sharing the untold stories about Saxapahaw and for providing the priceless photograph of the much loved Jack Paris.

Finally, I must acknowledge my editor, Lindsay Harris, for her instant fondness of Saxapahaw and her patience, time, and dedication to seeing this project to fruition.

# Introduction

Saxapahaw is a beautiful historic mill village located on the banks of the Haw River, minutes from Chapel Hill. In the center of the village, along the riverside trail, is the newly restored Saxapahaw Cotton Mill, now called the Saxapahaw Rivermill. This picturesque little place is finding new life as a sustainable "green" bedroom community. Within walking distance of the rolling hillsides of the Rivermill is a 5 mile hiking trail, a bed and breakfast, a canoe and kayak company, a vineyard, a yoga center, a lake spanning over 300 acres, two environmental schools (high school and grammar), and the Saxapahaw General Store, which has everything from gourmet wines and cheeses to fishing tackle. Saxapahaw is that place you dream about with only a quick commute from everywhere you need to be and everywhere you want to be without the traffic, noise, and congestion. This is a village where all walks of life still get together to roast s'mores and weenies over a bon fire, and some bring their own instruments to play bluegrass and back porch music.

Saxapahaw was first settled by the Sissipahaw Indians. The Sissipahaw Indians (a presumed Siouan tribe) was a hunting and farming tribe and was believed to be affluent due to their acquiring of prime lands nestled on the Haw River. The Sissipahaw Indians were visited by Juan Pardo in 1569, who referred to their village as "Sauxpa." Then, around 1700, John Lawson, an early English historian and explorer, visited the Sissipahaw area along the Haw River. Mr. Lawson referred to the area as the "flower of Carolina." In his journals, he describes the land as being extraordinarily fertile and capable of supporting thousands of families. He found the Indian tribe to be well fed and very friendly.

Around 1715, the Sissipahaw Indians joined other area tribes (possibly the Catawba and the Occoneechi Band of Saponi Nations) to fight against the invading English, who had a desire for the immensely rich land. It is also believed that the people of the Haw were severely weakened by European disease spread through trading contacts with the coast. The Saxapahaw area was later settled by the Northern Quakers and the Pennsylvania Dutch around 1740. It is said that, for a time, the Haw River was called the Saxapahaw River after the Indian tribe; however, due to linguistic manipulation being what it is, the title soon was shortened into something easier to say.

John Newlin, a Quaker, began construction of the Saxapahaw Cotton Mill in 1844 using slaves. Newlin did not agree with slavery, however. He paid the laborers for their work, and when the mill was finished, Newlin's sons took the slaves up North and freed them. The Newlin family owned the mill, which is said to have supplied textiles to the Confederate army until it was sold to Edwin Holt in 1873. Edwin Holt's sons-in-law—Capt. James W. White and John L. Williamson—joined him, forming Holt, White, and Williamson. When Edwin Holt died, the mill was changed to White-Williamson and Company. The White-Williamson's prospered, then lost everything due to a recession and abandoned the mill in 1924.

In 1927, Mr. Charles V. Sellars purchased the Mill and enlisted the much needed help of his nephew B. Everett Jordan to manage the mill. After learning that the village of Saxapahaw had been neglected for four years, B. Everett Jordan and his wife, Katherine, drove the former dirt road into Saxapahaw to their new home and made a promise to one another that Everett would take care of everything related to the mill, and Katherine would take care of the village. At the height of the Great Depression, Katherine recorded in her diaries accounts of her husband working through the night trying to get a machine to run and days during the summer when drought dried up the Haw River, causing loss of power that shut the mill down and darkened the village homes. Katherine, being an avid gardener, planted hundreds of Redbud trees and flowers along the roadsides. She took food to the ill and made sure everyone kept their yards clean and maintained. B. Everett Jordan believed that young children needed something positive to do to prevent them from throwing rocks through the mill windows, so the Jordans built a community recreation center and asked friend Edgar Cashwell to be the director. They also enlisted friend Ben F. Bulla to create a Scout troop (Troop 65). Additionally, the Jordan's donated 30 acres of land for a school to be built called Saxapahaw Elementary School and a community baseball field, which are both now renamed in honor of B. Everett Jordan.

In the South, there is a saying that you always want to leave the wood pile higher than you found it. B. Everett Jordan and his wife, Katherine, believed in the Golden Rule of doing unto others as you would have them do unto you. B. Everett Jordan delved into the political scene as a means to help make a better life for North Carolina and the Saxapahaw community. He became a senator in 1958 and held the seat for nearly 15 years before his passing in 1974.

After Senator Jordan's passing, the mill was sold in 1978 to Dixie Yarns, and Jordan's son John purchased the surrounding land and 66 mill village homes, continuing to live out his father's dream and passion for making Saxapahaw the best place to live. John Jordan is the benevolent visionary benefactor. He is a real estate artist with Saxapahaw as his easel. John sold off the 33 homes on the south side of the Haw River at a cost of $10,000 to $20,000 and renovated the 33 homes on the north side of the river into energy efficient rental cottages complete with wood stoves, natural gas appliances, and neighborhood garden spots. In the early 1980s, John established a foundation in his name with six local churches—two black and one white—to implement Jesus' teaching as outlined in Matthew 25:35-45, helping individuals who could not help themselves. Electricity bills were paid up to two times, and glasses and clothing were purchased for the less fortunate. The fund continued for 20 years. John Jordan pays to have the roads leading to Saxapahaw mowed and maintained (even though this is the State's job) and to have all the trash picked up weekly, so the village remains spotless. Jordan continues to work 12 hours a day and has also been very generous with local Elon University, so much so that the university named a gym and a dorm in his and his father's honor.

On Palm Sunday 1994, a tornado ripped through Saxapahaw. Miraculously, the twister spared homes and lives, but it uprooted trees as it left a path on the south side of the river before hitting the lower mill. The storm peeled the roof off the west end of the spinning mill and cotton shed, blew the metal top off the elevated water tower, and completely demolished Jordan Properties hay barn No. 2. After 150 years in operation, the Saxapahaw Cotton Mill closed its doors forever. To the families who had spent their lives working in the mill and to the community whose jobs were lost, having the mill close was like a death in the family. But for Mac Jordan, the tragedy presented an opportunity to realize a dream—the dream of renovating the mill into something totally new.

In spite of reservations and warnings from others, Mac Jordan urged his father, John Jordan, to buy back the mill property from Dixie Yarns. After a year and a half of negotiations, the Jordans closed on the industrial complex, which spanned 31 acres and more than 250,000 square feet. Mac, charged by his father to take care of the mill, enlisted the help of his brother Carter to begin a revitalization process. A few years later, the historic mill received recognition in the National Register of Historic Places.

Hurricane Fran significantly flooded the mill project in 1996, an air compressor exploded and caught the mill on fire in 2004, and significant delays in funding seemed endless, but none of these things stopped Mac and his brother Carter from seeing the first phase of the Rivermill project to fruition in 2005. The former spinning mill currently includes 75 quaint living spaces—many with breathtaking views overlooking the Haw River—with 14- to 16-foot ceilings, 10-foot windows, and antique hardwood floors. Condos and other sustainable businesses are on the horizon.

Through fire and flood, the history of Saxapahaw and the Jordan family continues with the help of a new group of investors as Mac and Carter work to finish the revitalization of their grandfather's mill. Once done, a village will be complete, and a wood pile a little higher.

# *One*

# Saxapahaw Cotton Mill

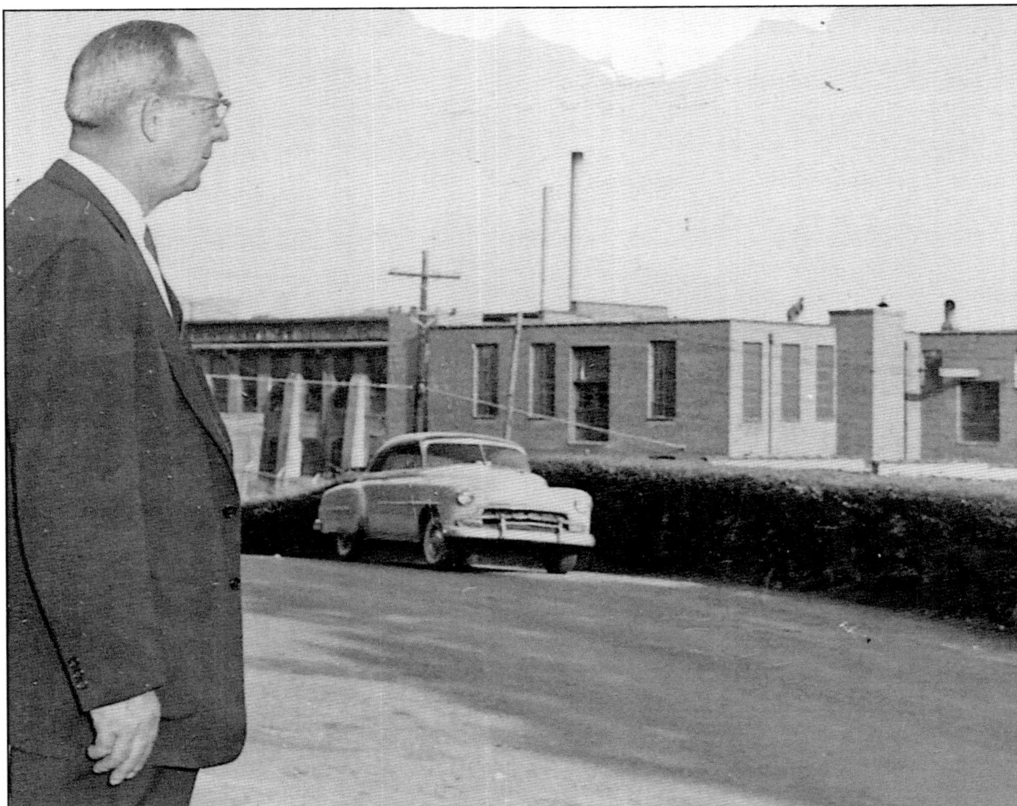

On May 2, 1958, the day he was appointed as U.S. senator for North Carolina after W. Kerr Scott's death, Benjamin Everett Jordan said goodbye to Saxapahaw and his cotton mill. The newly appointed U.S. senator was the picture of self-confidence and was fully prepared to assume his role. . He owned four mills—two in Saxapahaw, one in Wake Forest, and one in Cedar Falls—but felt secure as he looked over at the mill pictured here that his son Ben E. Jordan Jr. would successfully run his mills as the president in his absence. (Courtesy of the Textile Heritage Museum, Glencoe, North Carolina.)

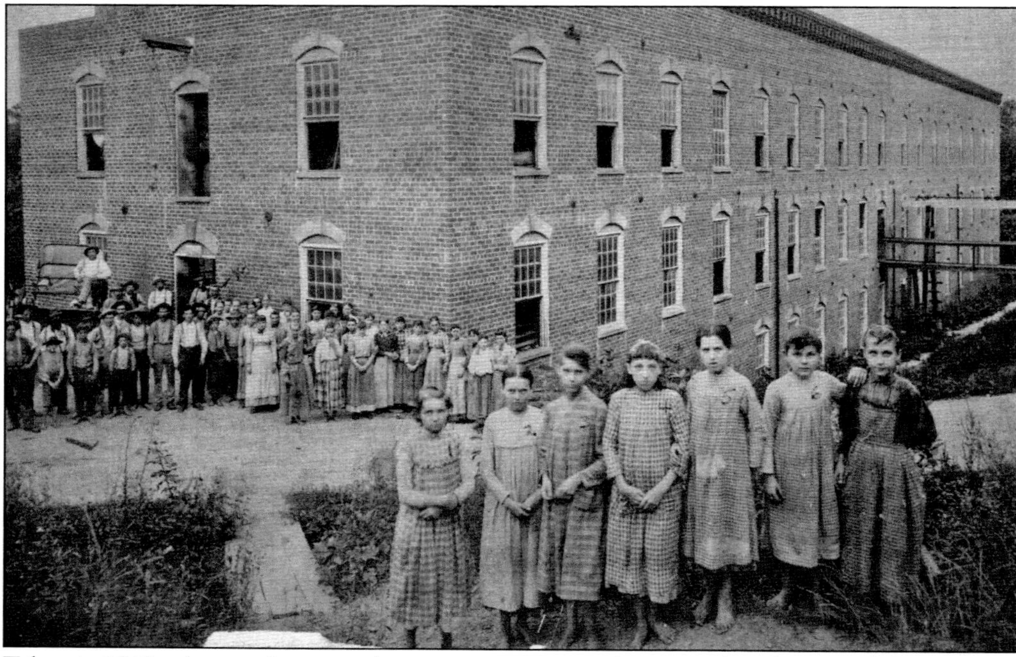

Taken in 1848, when underage workers were common in America, this photograph hangs in the Textile Heritage Museum. At a time when most companies were trying to hide their child laborers and the conditions they worked under, the village of Saxapahaw did not. If these children were not working in the protected environment of the mill, they would have been sent to work in the farm fields. These children, who earned more money than most farmers in the area, made enough to support themselves and their parents and never wanted to be known as victims. Children of the same age who farmed had to begin their work in harsh weather conditions from before light until dark, while the children in the warm factory finished their day at 3:00 p.m. From left to right are (first row) Sally Dodson Guthrie, Molly Crutchfield Morrow, unidentified, Mattie Cheek, Ella McVey Pickard, Leona Dodson Lashley, and "Vonie" Johnson Crutchfield. The children in the background are unidentified. (Courtesy of Mac Jordan.)

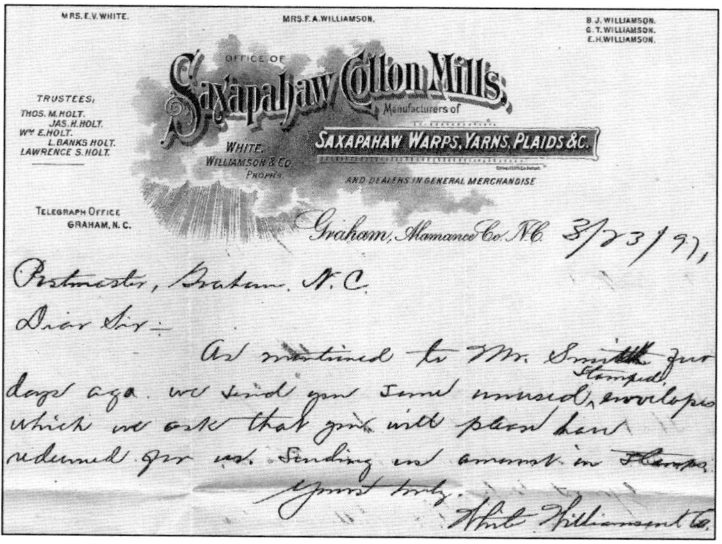

MRS. E.V. WHITE. MRS. F.A. WILLIAMSON. B.J. WILLIAMSON. G.T. WILLIAMSON. E.H. WILLIAMSON.

OFFICE OF Saxapahaw Cotton Mills; Manufacturers of SAXAPAHAW WARPS, YARNS, PLAIDS &C. AND DEALERS IN GENERAL MERCHANDISE

TRUSTEES: THOS. M. HOLT. JAS. H. HOLT. WM. E. HOLT. L. BANKS HOLT. LAWRENCE S. HOLT.

WHITE, WILLIAMSON & CO. PROPRS.

TELEGRAPH OFFICE GRAHAM, N.C.

Graham, Alamance Co. N.C. 3/23/97,

Postmaster, Graham, N.C.

Dear Sir:-

As mentioned to Mr. Smith few days ago we send you some unused stamped envelopes which we ask that you will please have redeemed for us. Sending us amount in stamps.

Yours truly,

White Williamson & Co.

In 1886, White-Williamson and Company had several registered businesses in Saxapahaw: the cotton factory, general store, cotton gin, gristmill, and blacksmith shop. This letterhead is from 1897. Williamson eventually lost everything and became a beggar in front of the Saxapahaw Post Office. (Courtesy of the author.)

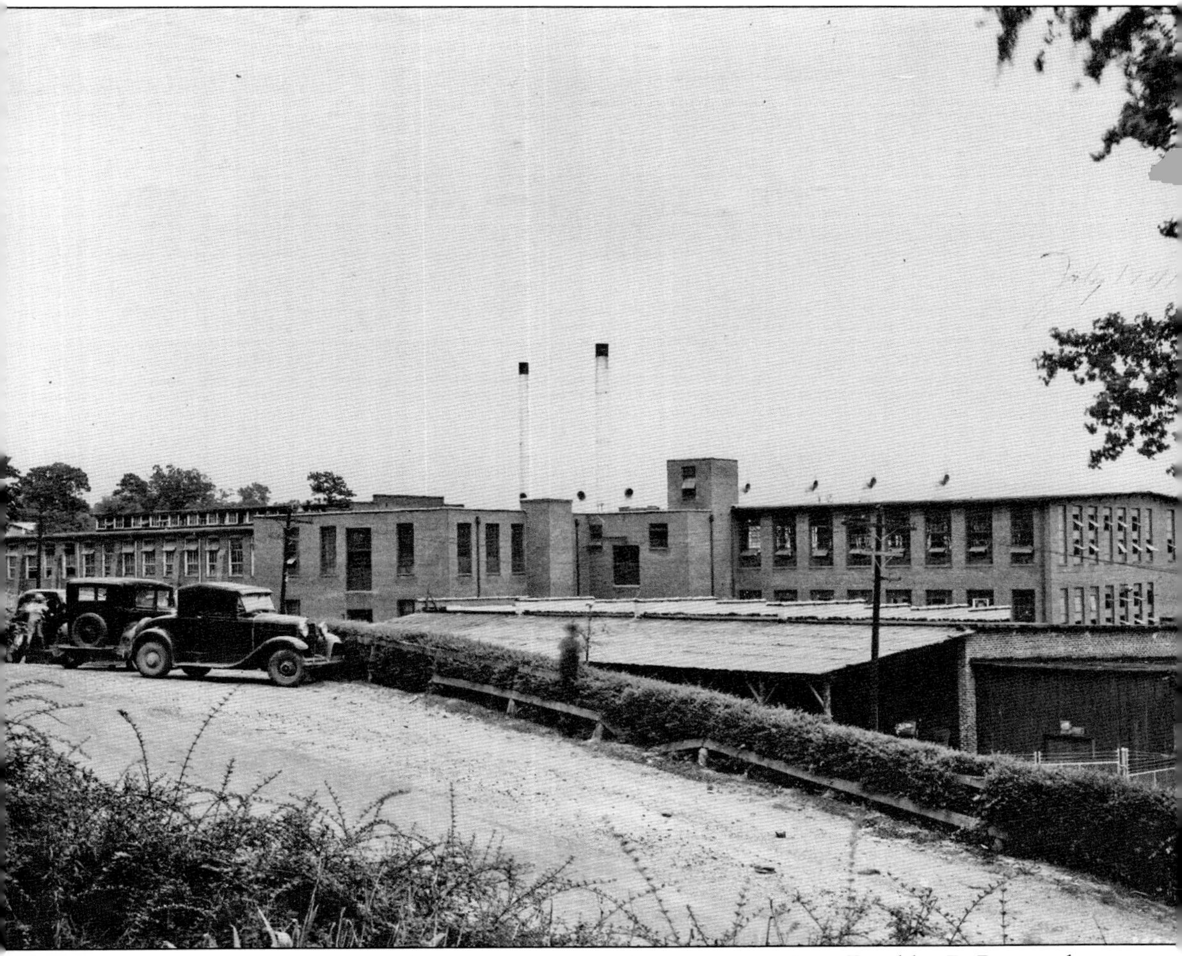

This is the Saxapahaw Cotton Mill. In 1932, during the Depression, Pres. Franklin D. Roosevelt created the New Deal for the protection of textile workers, requesting that mill employees be paid at least $12 a week and have the right to organize. Mill workers grew restless that the New Deal was taking too long to come to fruition. This led to determined attempts by the workers to organize and join the Textile Workers Union and the largest single labor conflict in American history, a strike of 400,000 textile workers. In order to speed the process, the union organized groups of members to go to each mill, attempting to close them down. These groups were called the Flying Squadrons. Roger Gant Jr., son-in-law of Senator Jordan, stated during a Southern Oral History Project interview with Ben F. Bulla that he remembered the situation was so severe that B. Everett Jordan called upon the National Guard, who placed machine guns on the corners of the roof of the mill with sandbags to protect the mill from the vandalism. To lessen the burden on the employees, mill cottages were provided at $1 per week. (Courtesy of Mac Jordan.)

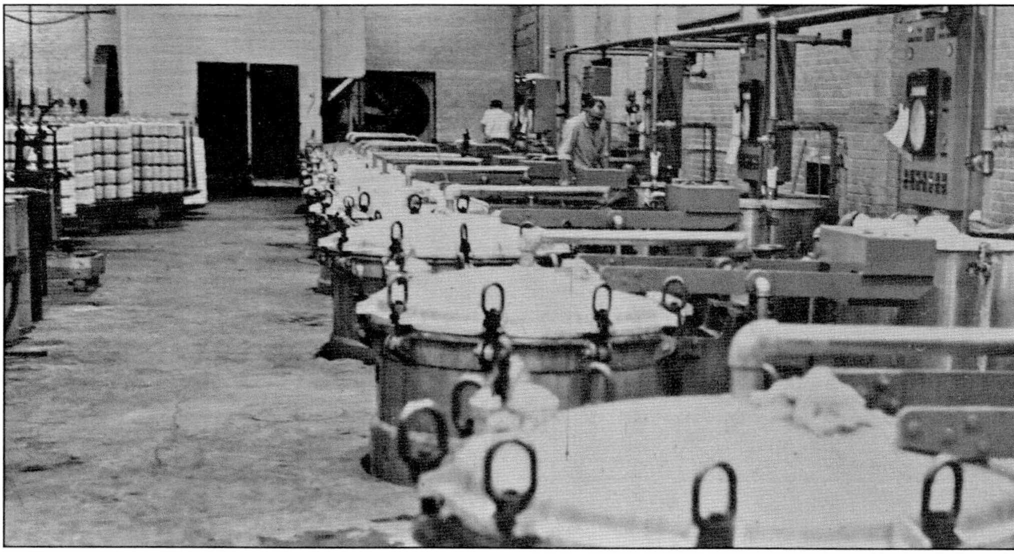

These are the large "dye kier vats" that were used to dye the cotton in 1944. The mill also purchased cotton from Egypt and Perugia to produce T-shirts and shorts. The mill created most of its power from its own power plant that resided next to them alongside the Haw River. Diesel power, including the engine from a submarine, was used to provide backup power during periodic droughts. Leroy Hudson is shown operating a kier vat. (Courtesy of Mac Jordan.)

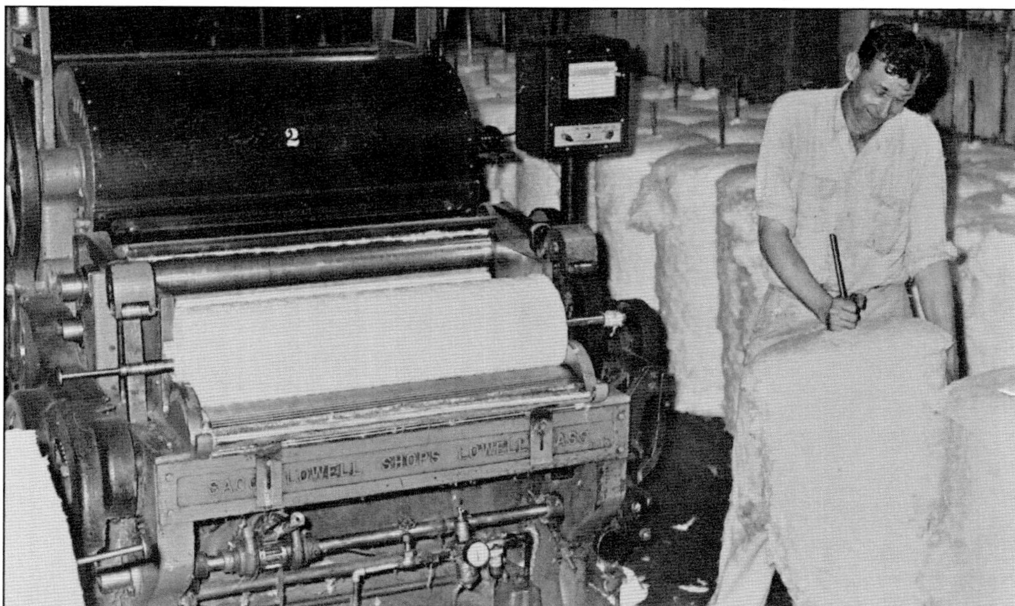


Ed Rickman was a "picker." He walked 6 miles in the dark every night to work the third shift. One evening, John Jordan was walking through the mill at 10:30 p.m. and found a foot sticking up in the air. Jordan found Rickman sleeping and warming up inside of a hopper full of cotton before he started his shift. This machine, which picked the cotton with metal teeth, was the most dangerous machine in the mill. The Saxapahaw Cotton Mill was known for being accident-free. (Courtesy of Mac Jordan.)

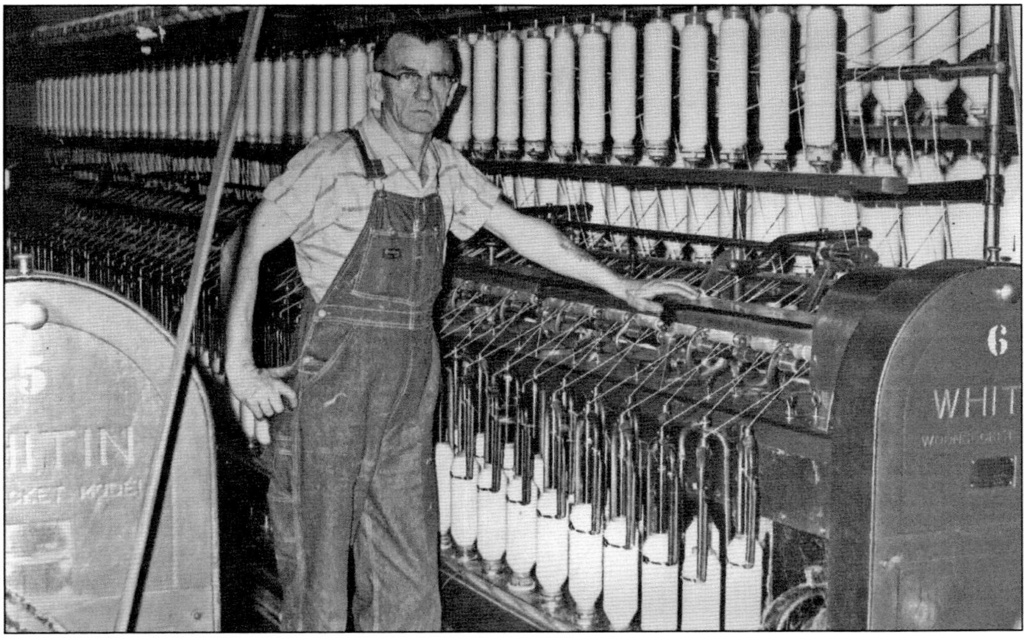


Orval Boley is shown in the Saxapahaw Cotton Mill around 1940. When the mill first opened, there were only a couple thousand yarn spindles. Later the mill grew to acquire more than 16,000 spindles. The mill workers were encouraged to go to church and live in the village within one of the rental properties provided by the mill. Management employees were not encouraged but required to live in Saxapahaw. The men all hunted and fished together. Most of the families would go to church together. There was great camaraderie among management and mill workers. Almost all of the machines at the mill were run 24 hours a day, 6 days a week during the three working shifts and would often break down. For religious reasons, the mill never ran on Sundays. (Both courtesy of Mac Jordan.)

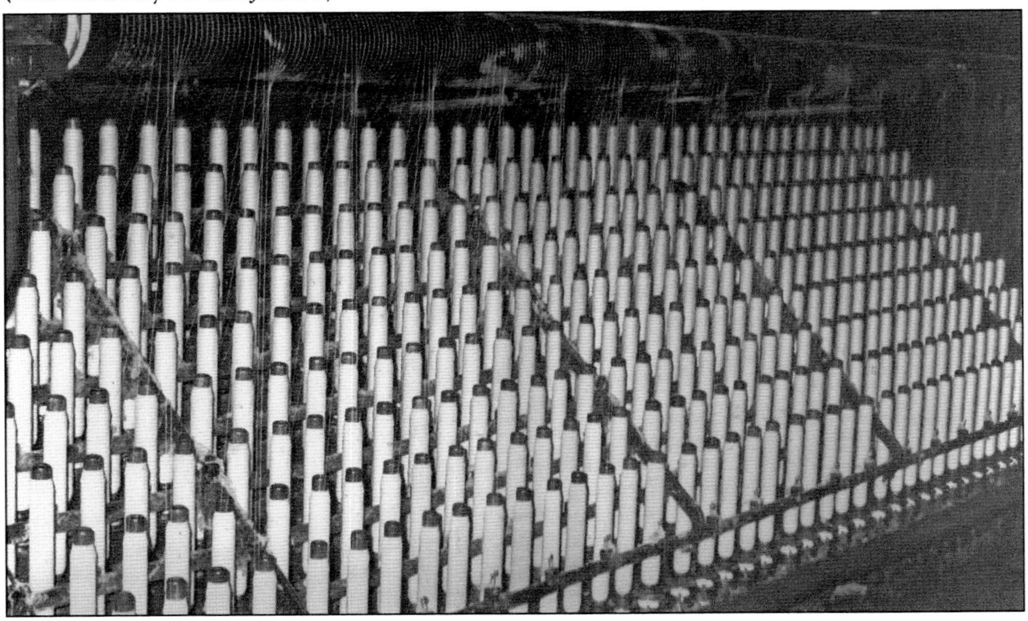

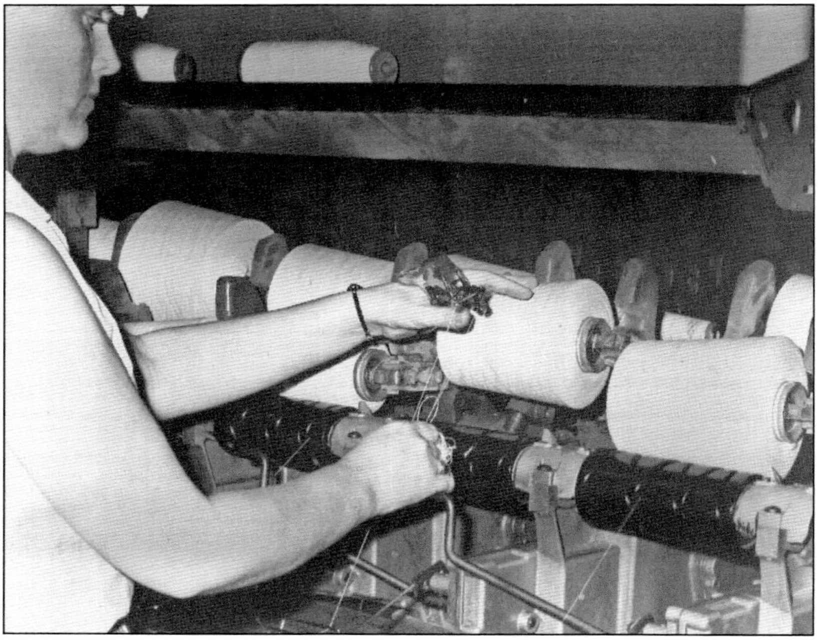

The "winder-tender" is seen in the above photograph with the winder and cones. The bobbin was dropped into a pocket, and knots were tied to the end of the cone using a one-handed tool called the knotter. One of the female employees was able to do twice the amount of work than any other person working the machine. Management decided to watch the employee to find out how she was able to finish so much work in half the time. It was simple: her major advantage was her shorter female stature, which made it easier for her to reach and see what she was doing. Women became very valuable and respected at the mill. (Both courtesy of Jordan Properties Archives.)

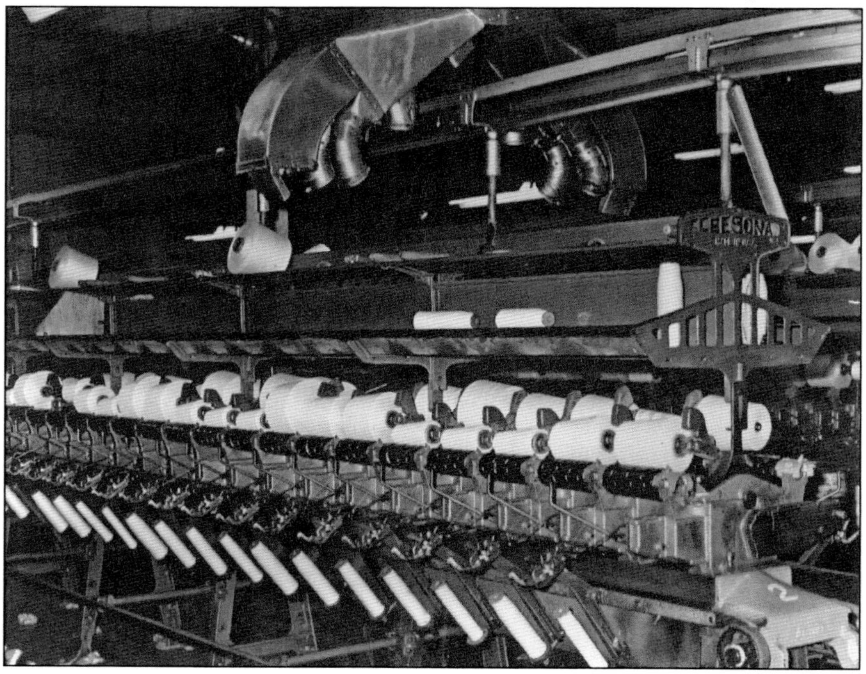

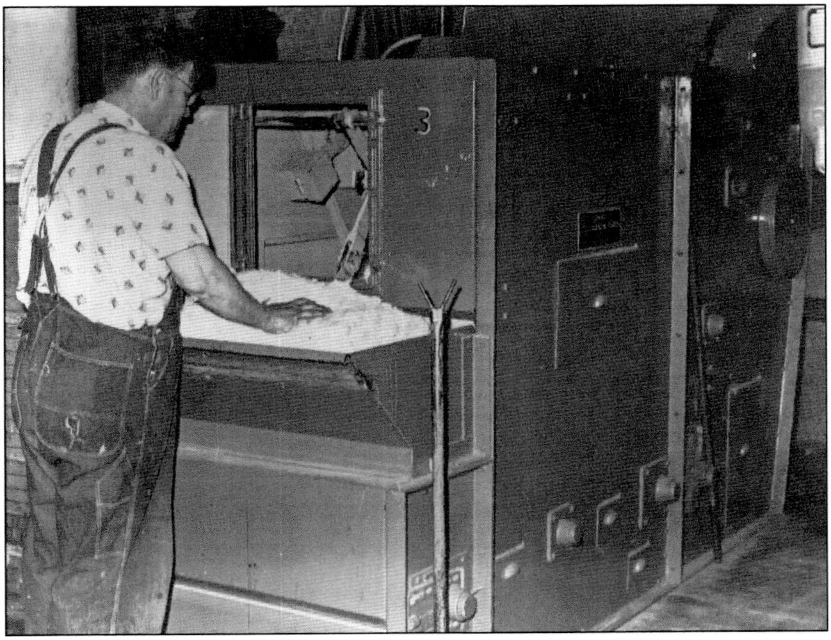

During the 1930s, the Saxapahaw Mill went through a complete renovation. The old looms, which once produced cloth for the Confederate army, were discarded, and the mill was equipped to spin and mercerize combed yarn to supply to the knitting industry. In those days, Alamance County was the "hosiery capital." The Saxapahaw Mill was the prime supplier for that market as well as the underwear market for other parts of the country. In 1952, the Saxapahaw Mill built their dyeing operation (known as Sellers Dyeing Company) to furnish dyed yarn to the fast-developing hosiery and knit outerwear trade. During the rest of the 1950s, this plant supplied men's argyle hosiery. (Both courtesy of Mac Jordan.)

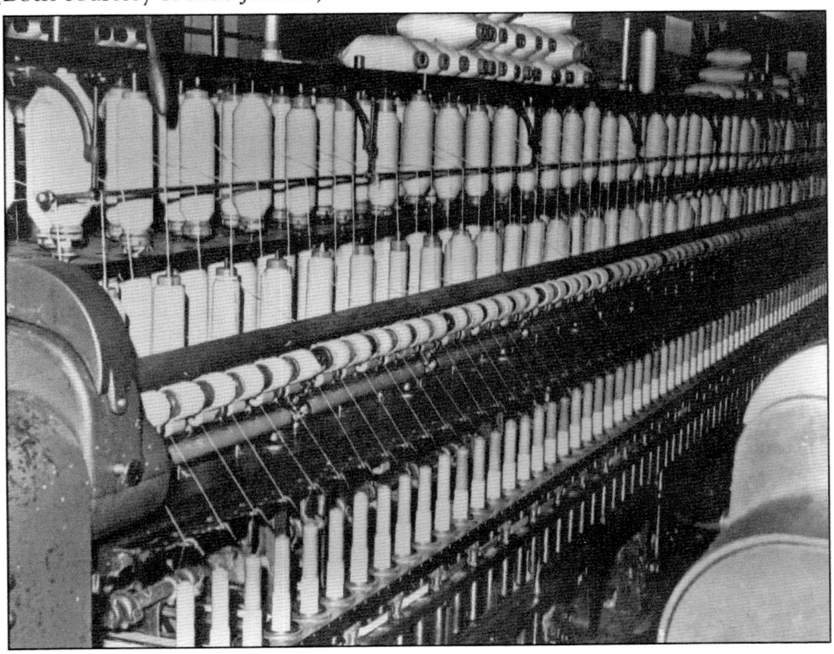

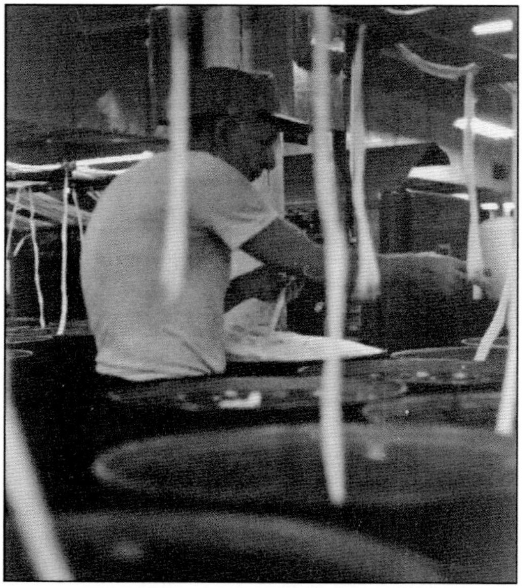

Joe King was in charge of "creeling slubbers," a job that required constant attention and proper timing. This task makes roving, a length of softly wound cotton. Each spindle produced a thread, and this was the result of the two rovings being stretched and then twisted together. The rovings were cylindrical packages containing a considerable length of roving, and as the contents were used up, the empty or almost empty package had to be replaced by a full one. The roving packages were arranged in racks, behind and above the spindles, and these racks were known as creels, so the act of replenishing the roving was known as creeling. (Courtesy of John Jordan.)

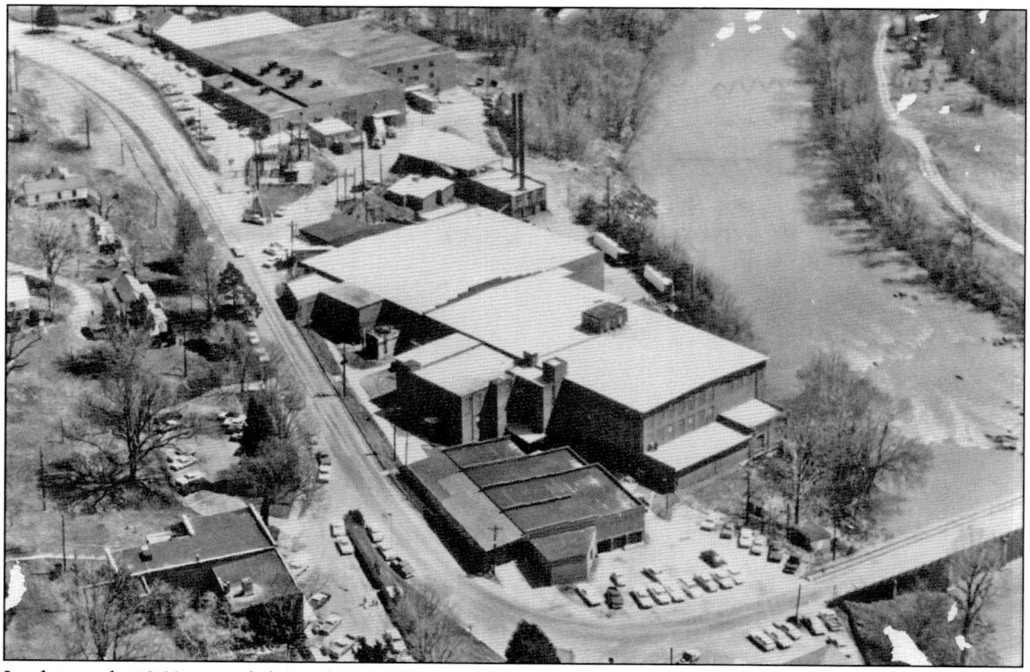

In this early 1960s aerial shot of the mill, the original smokestacks can be seen. They were removed when the gas company convinced B. Everett Jordan gas was cleaner and cheaper than coal and diesel fuel. John Jordan donated one of the homes on the left to the local fire department so they could practice putting out fires. The east wing of the mill was built in 1906 and the west wing in 1930. The total complex was comprised of 80 dwellings among 6 acres, including 51 mill homes, 2 I-houses, 1 log dwelling, 2 mill owners' homes, 1 church, 1 civic building, 2 former mill complexes, 1 cotton shed, 1 powerhouse, 2 structures, and 16 secondary outbuildings. According to the Securities and Exchange Commission in 1994, the mill was 264,000 square feet. (Courtesy of John Jordan.)

To the right is Clara Alston working as the spooler tender at the mill. She remembers getting only 10 minutes for lunch. It was just enough time to eat, laugh with her friends, and get back to work. She did not live in a mill house, so her walk home was even further than those who did. Clara Alston put in more than 10 years of service before she missed a day of work. She retired after 25 years of gaining respect and friendships that would last a lifetime. (Courtesy of Jordan Properties Archives.)

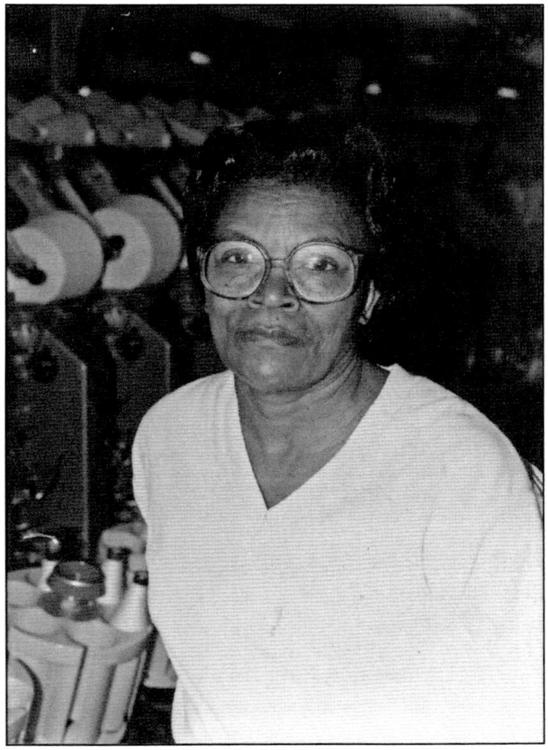

Below is a 1977 issue of the *Four-Most Spinners* paper, the Saxapahaw Cotton Mill newsletter. This newsletter replaced the old-school paper version called the *Saxapahaw Pow-Wow* that was hand-typed and mimeographed back in the 1940s and 1950s. The new name was voted on by the mill employees and is named from the association of the Saxapahaw Mill with three other spinning mills. (Courtesy of Margaret Jordan.)

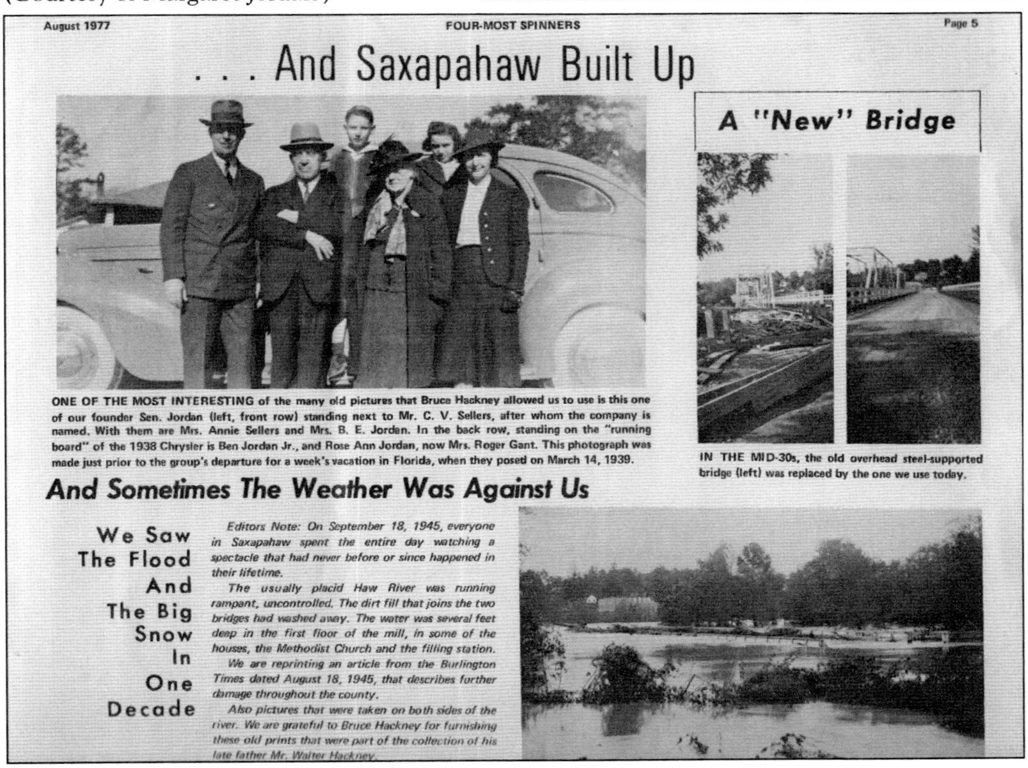

August 1977 FOUR-MOST SPINNERS Page 5

. . . And Saxapahaw Built Up

ONE OF THE MOST INTERESTING of the many old pictures that Bruce Hackney allowed us to use is this one of our founder Sen. Jordan (left, front row) standing next to Mr. C. V. Sellers, after whom the company is named. With them are Mrs. Annie Sellers and Mrs. B. E. Jordan. In the back row, standing on the "running board" of the 1938 Chrysler is Ben Jordan Jr., and Rose Ann Jordan, now Mrs. Roger Gant. This photograph was made just prior to the group's departure for a week's vacation in Florida, when they posed on March 14, 1939.

A "New" Bridge

IN THE MID-30s, the old overhead steel-supported bridge (left) was replaced by the one we use today.

And Sometimes The Weather Was Against Us

We Saw The Flood And The Big Snow In One Decade

*Editors Note: On September 18, 1945, everyone in Saxapahaw spent the entire day watching a spectacle that had never before or since happened in their lifetime.*

*The usually placid Haw River was running rampant, uncontrolled. The dirt fill that joins the two bridges had washed away. The water was several feet deep in the first floor of the mill, in some of the houses, the Methodist Church and the filling station.*

*We are reprinting an article from the Burlington Times dated August 18, 1945, that describes further damage throughout the county.*

*Also pictures that were taken on both sides of the river. We are grateful to Bruce Hackney for furnishing these old prints that were part of the collection of his late father Mr. Walter Hackney.*

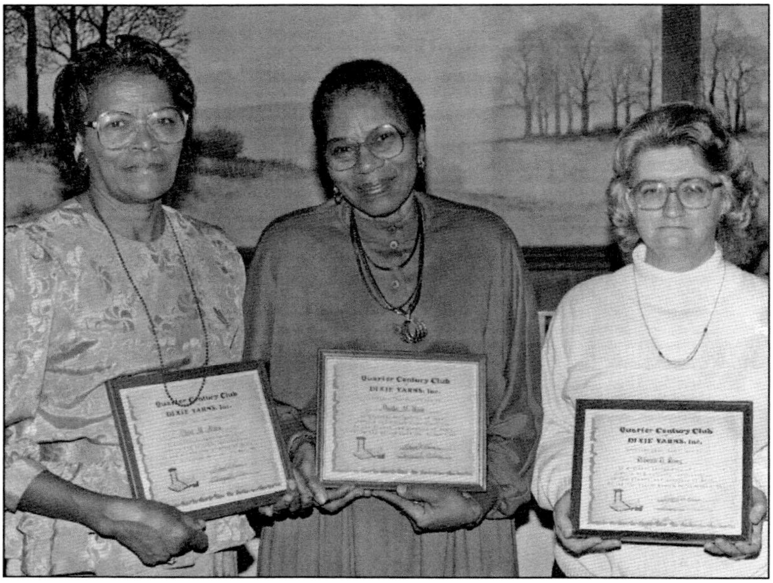

Above, with 25 years of service at the cotton mill, are Clara Alston (left), Martha Wade (center), and Rebecca Brewer Roney. In 1965, Clara Alston was the first black woman to work at the Saxapahaw Cotton Mill. She was a spooler and unicone attendant. Clara was also the housekeeper for Senator Jordan and his wife, Katherine, at their vacation home in Montreat, North Carolina. Clara proved to be a model employee by working 10 straight years before she missed a day of work. On a cold and icy day, Clara completed her shift but was asked to stay to work the evening shift because many people did not show up for work. The ice continued to lay on the ground so slick that when Clara finally left work late in the evening, she had to crawl up the Saxapahaw Bethlehem Church Road hill toward Mineral Springs Road on her hands and knees. Paul Parrish found her and helped her to his car to drive her home. Below are Clara and Danny Beardon, the plant superintendant of Dixie Yarns. Dixie Yarns owned the Saxapahaw Cotton Mill from 1978 to 1994. (Both courtesy of Clara Alston.)

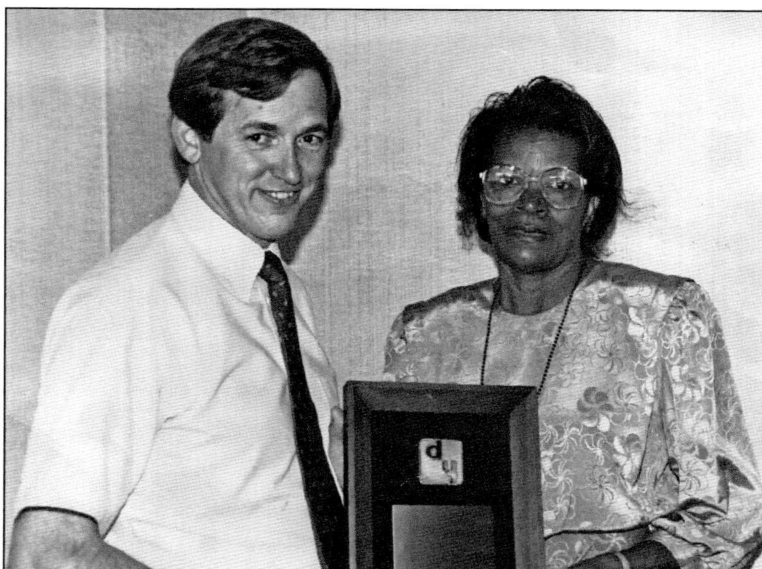

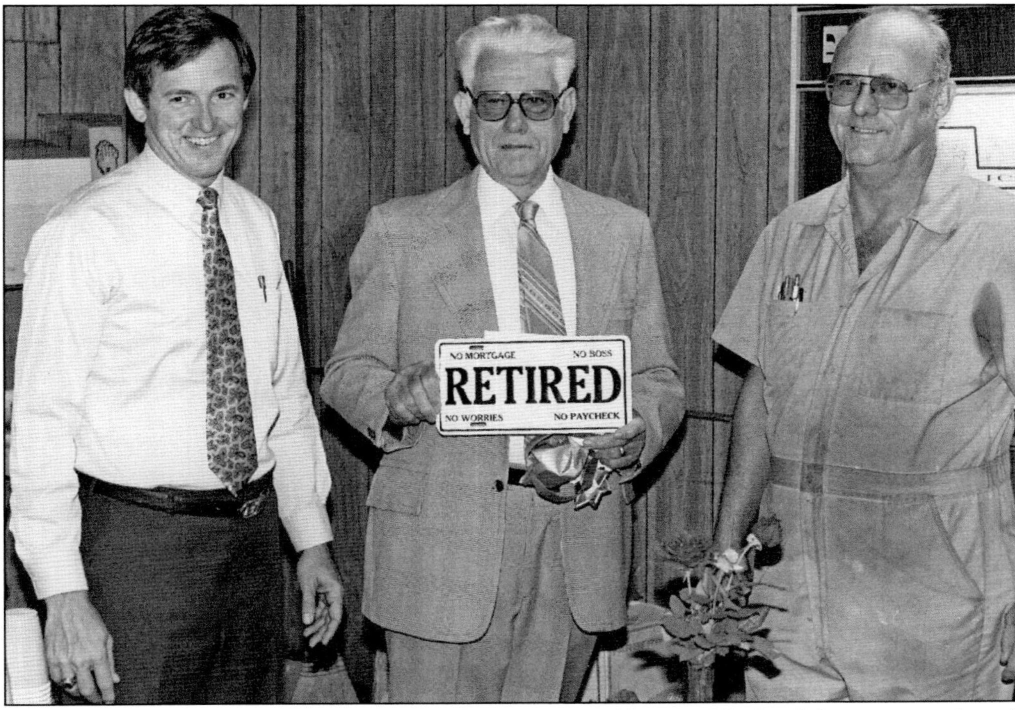


Picture from left to right are Danny Beardon, Leon Madden, and Jackie Johnson upon Leon's retirement. Leon Madden married "the little blonde from the mountains," Eula Mae, who taught him how to quill. He moved their family to Saxapahaw in 1928 into one of the original Newlin-built homes and worked at the Saxapahaw Cotton Mill for 54 years, from February 1940 to March 27, 1994 (the day the tornado tore part of the mill's roof off). He was the shop manager and took a few years' sabbatical when he joined the air force and was sent to the Boeing Manufacturing plant to assist with refurbishing engines for World War II. After retirement, Leon continued to work at the mill part-time. Jackie Johnson took Leon's full-time spot at the mill. (Courtesy of Leon Madden.)

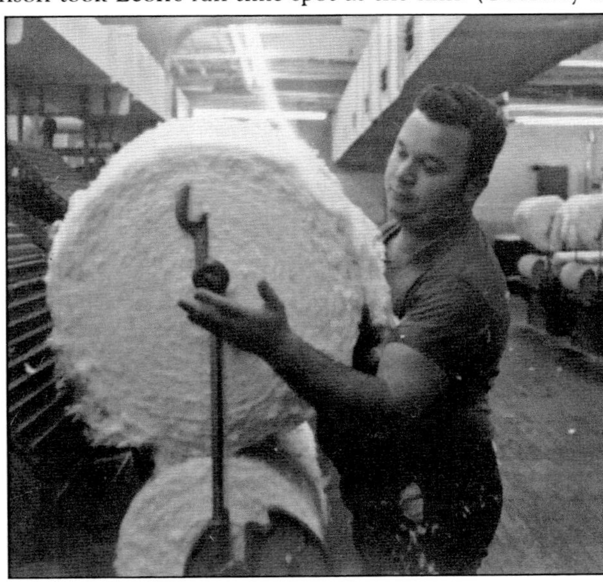

The finisher picker, Ennis Marshall, receives partially cleaned cotton in the form of LAP from the breaker picker and completes the cleaning and fluffing process. LAP is a general term used to designate wide sheets of loosely matted cotton. The cotton is next processed by a carding machine, where dirt and short fibers are removed; other fibers are laid parallel and formed into a ropelike strand called sliver. Subsequent processing depends on whether better grade (combed) yarn or lower grade (carded) yarn is desired. (Courtesy of Jordan Properties Archives.)

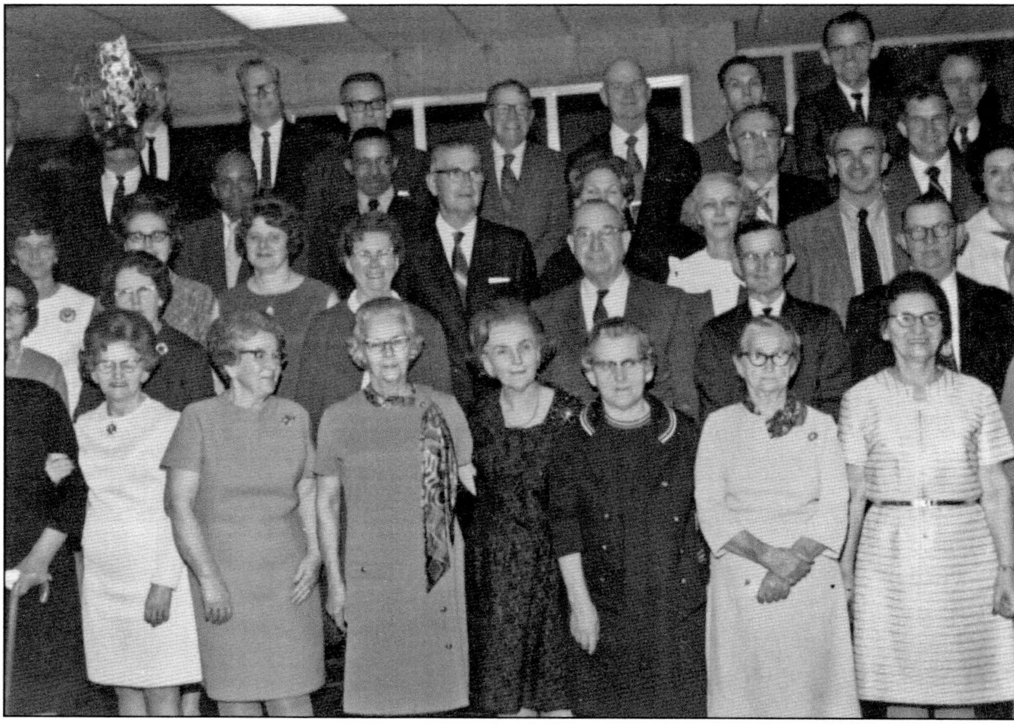

The Jordan family wanted to thank their longtime mill employees, so they started the Old Timers Club and held a yearly appreciation dinner. Only a portion of the club's members are shown above. The people in this photograph had been with the mill for more than 25 years. (Courtesy of Jordan Properties Archives.)

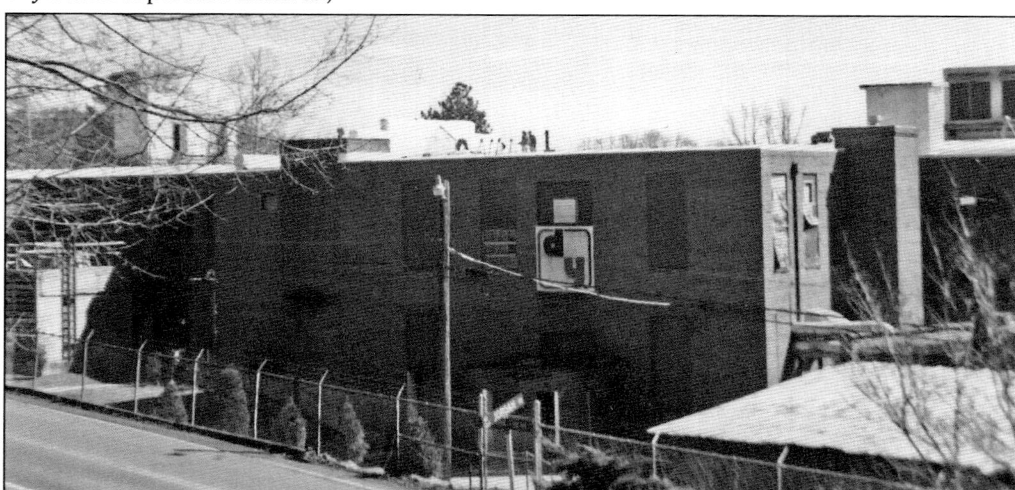

The Jordan family sold the Saxapahaw Cotton Mill to Dixie Yarns in 1978, which closed its doors in 1994 when a tornado damaged the structure. The damage from the tornado was too expensive to repair, and 168 people were left without jobs. The closing ended 150 years of manufacturing at the mill, which served as a key industry and center of activity for the community of mill houses around Saxapahaw. In 1995, the Jordan family saw an opportunity and bought the mill back. (Courtesy of Jordan Properties Archives.)

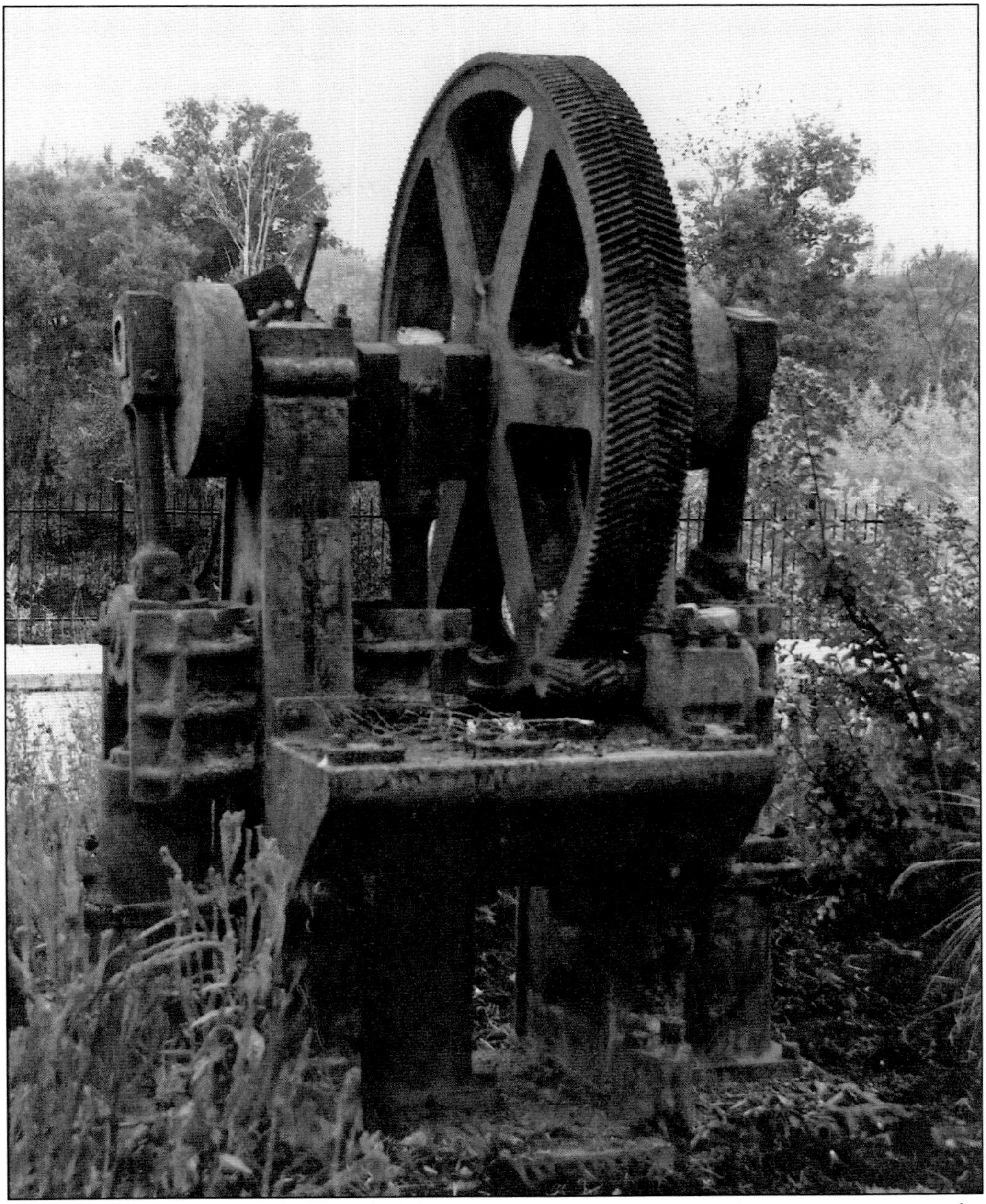

The jockey fire pump still sits behind the mill in the garden. It was used to pump water into the sprinklers in case of fire. While participating in the Southern Oral History Program, B. Everett Jordan shared a story with Roger Gant Jr. about A. T. Davis, who was working in the pump house in the 1940s. Jordan was looking for Davis and found him standing in water next to a motor in the pump house. Jordan heard Davis making a "croaking sound" from his throat. Realizing that Davis had grounded a current from the motor, Jordan ran down and flipped off the power. Davis turned to Jordan and said, "What took you so long; I have been hollering at you for five minutes!" This photograph is one in a series of postcard photographs sold in stores by artist and designer Monique de Latour. (Courtesy of Monique de Latour.)

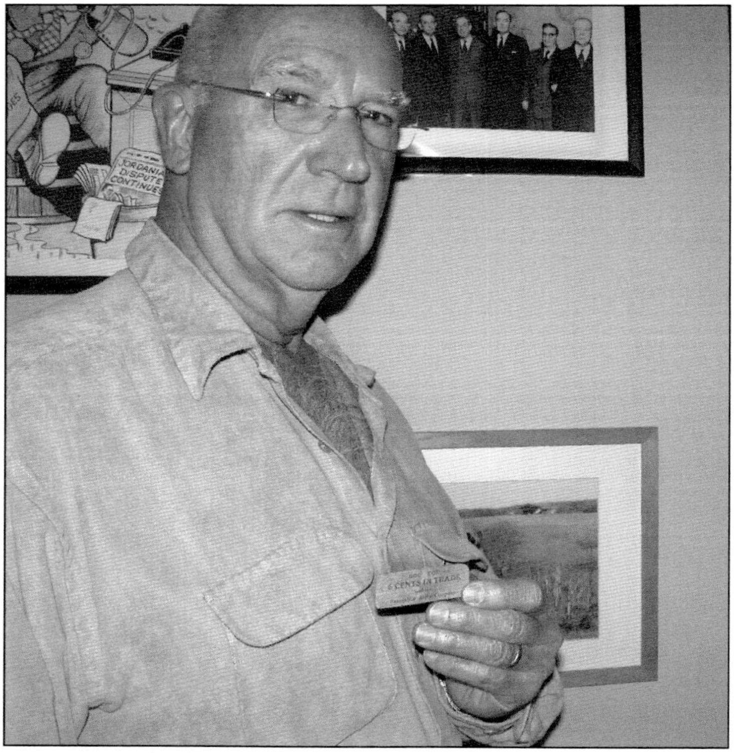

John Jordan is holding a "ducat" or "dukie." This was pasteboard money that substituted for cash at the general store during the recession and Depression in the 1920s and 1930s. This ducat is believed to be the last ducat. It belongs to Kent Miller, longtime dedicated employee of the Jordan family. Throughout Europe before World War I, the ducat was a gold coin used as a trade currency. The term, derived from the Latin word for duke, is still used as slang for a unit of currency. The Saxapahaw ducat was used in exchange for food, gas, and even alcohol. (Photograph by the author.)

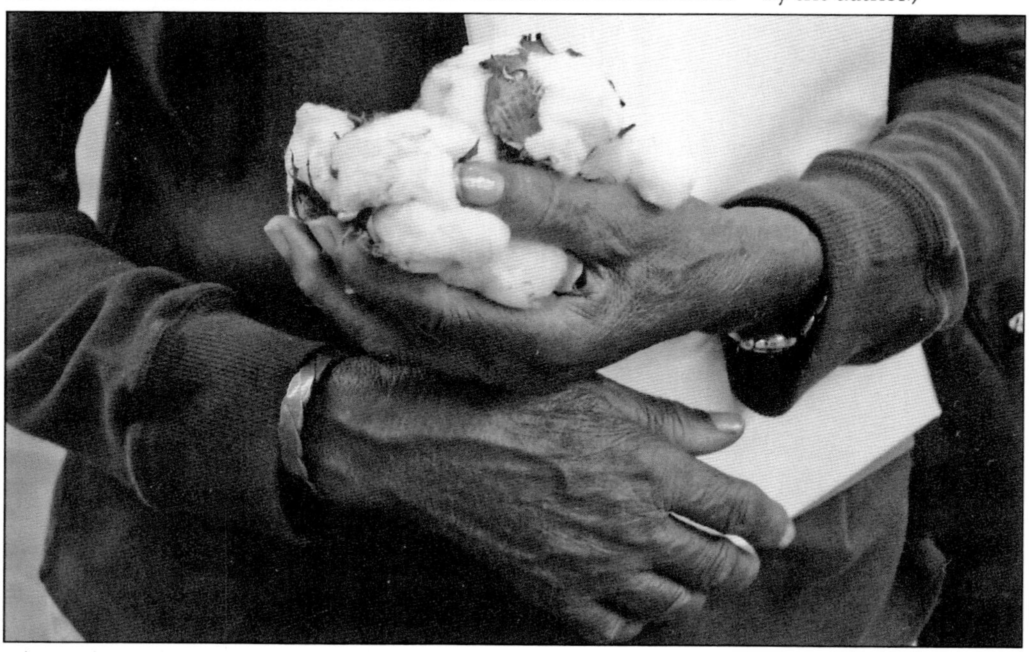

Clara Alston displays cotton for a photo opportunity during a mill reunion party. "Miss Clara" is a treasured Saxapahaw resident. This photograph is one in a series of photograph postcards and folding cards sold in stores and created by graphic artist Monique de Latour. (Courtesy of Monique de Latour.)

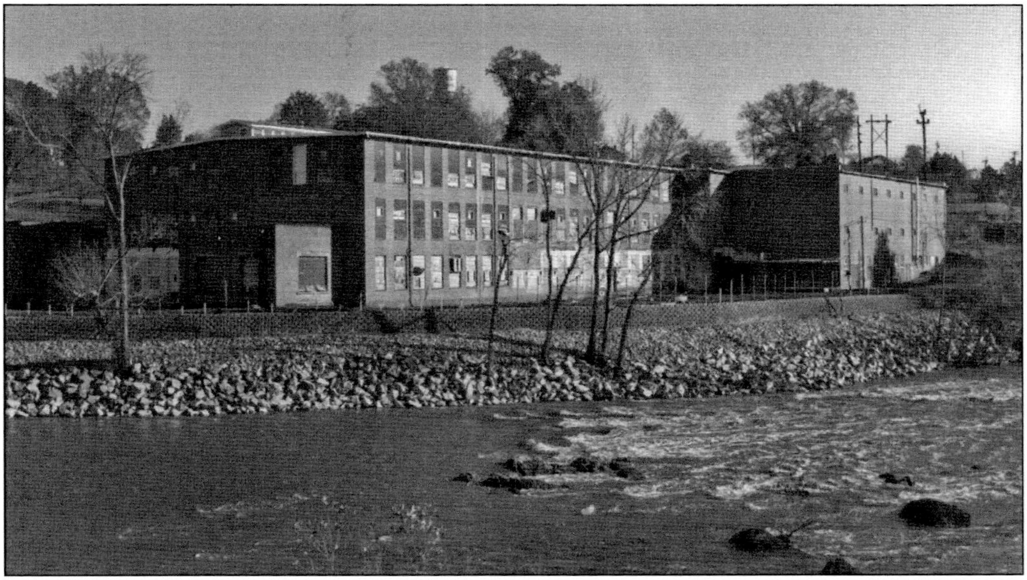

Above is the last photograph taken before the historic former cotton and spinning mill began renovation. Below is the Saxapahaw Rivermill, a beautifully restored cotton mill on the banks of the Haw River. Located in picturesque Saxapahaw, just a short drive from Chapel Hill, the Rivermill offers a unique blend of history and nature while providing for every modern necessity. There are 75 loft apartments with gorgeous river views; spacious floor plans; beautiful natural light; 14- to 16-foot ceilings; 10-foot windows; antique hardwood floors; skylights; exposed brick; modern amenities; individual washers and dryers; private and semi-private courtyards; high-speed cable and Internet access; a fitness center offering pilates, dance, massage therapy, weight training, cardio, and group exercises; and large covered garages. (Above courtesy of Jordan Properties Archives; below photograph by the author.)

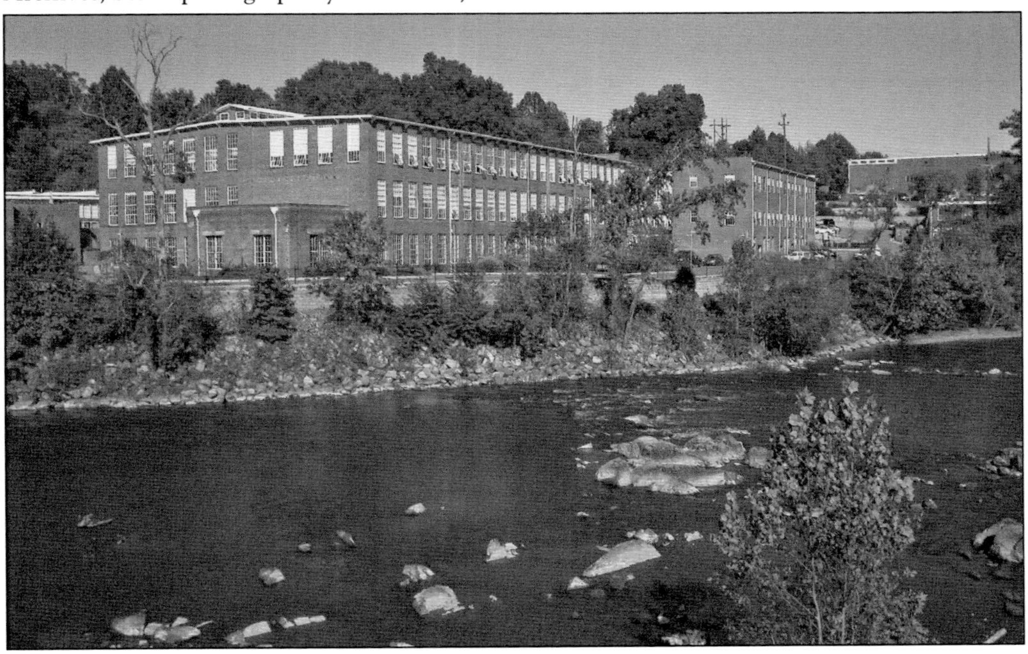

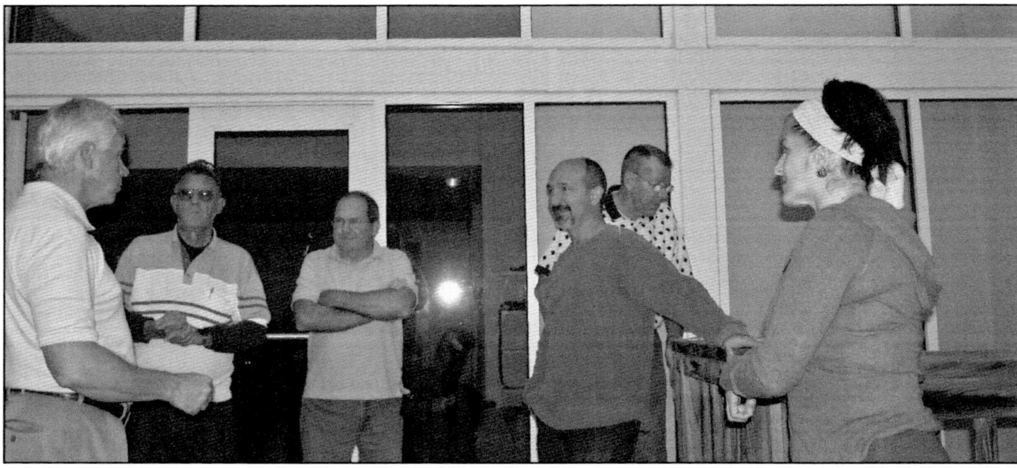

Above is the inside of the Saxapahaw Rivermill today. In 1990, Mac Jordan's thesis at North Carolina State University School of Architecture was about converting the Saxapahaw upper mill into a new village center including residential and commercial space. Almost five years later, that dream became reality when the Jordan family repurchased the mill in 1995. Planning and renovations for what has become the reinvention of Saxapahaw currently includes 75 living spaces, one of which can be seen here (below, right) from the back overlooking the Haw River with its expansive windows on a back deck. Mac Jordan (above, right, with his hand on the rail) is giving a tour of the sample loft during Textile Heritage Day. Also pictured are, from left to right, former mill employees Donald Beal, Melvin Walters, Harry Ferguson, and O. D. Thrift, along with Monique de Latour, a highly respected teacher at the Hawbridge Environmental High School, which is housed in the dye house in the upper mill. Below is a real-photo postcard of the Saxapahaw Rivermill. (Above photograph by the author; below courtesy of John Jordan.)

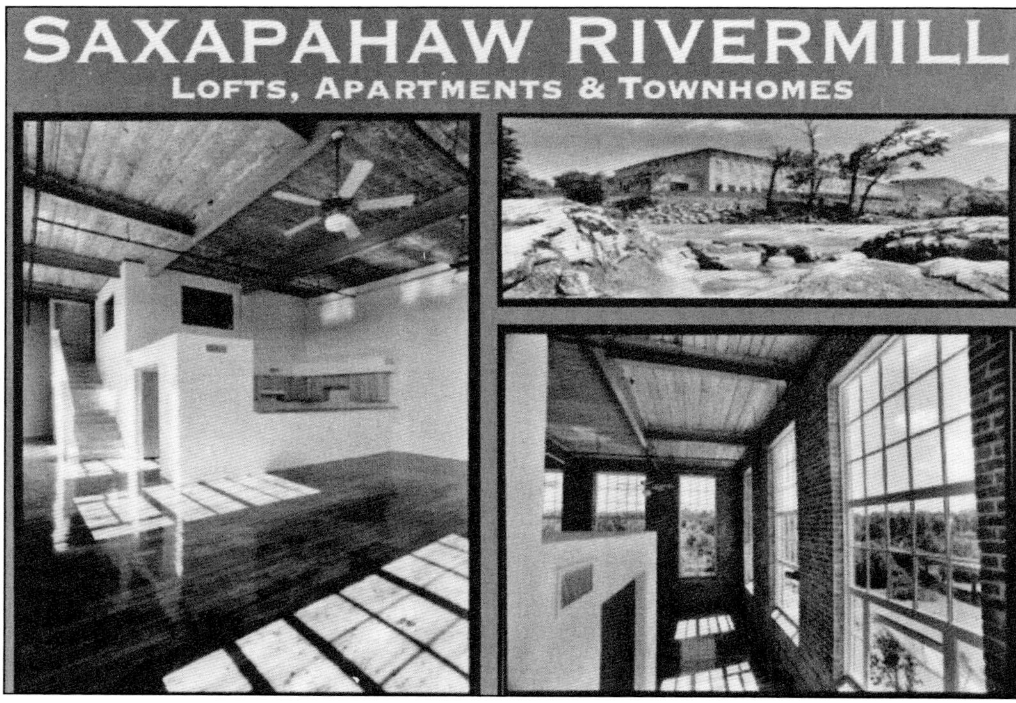

# *Two*

# Sen. B. Everett Jordan

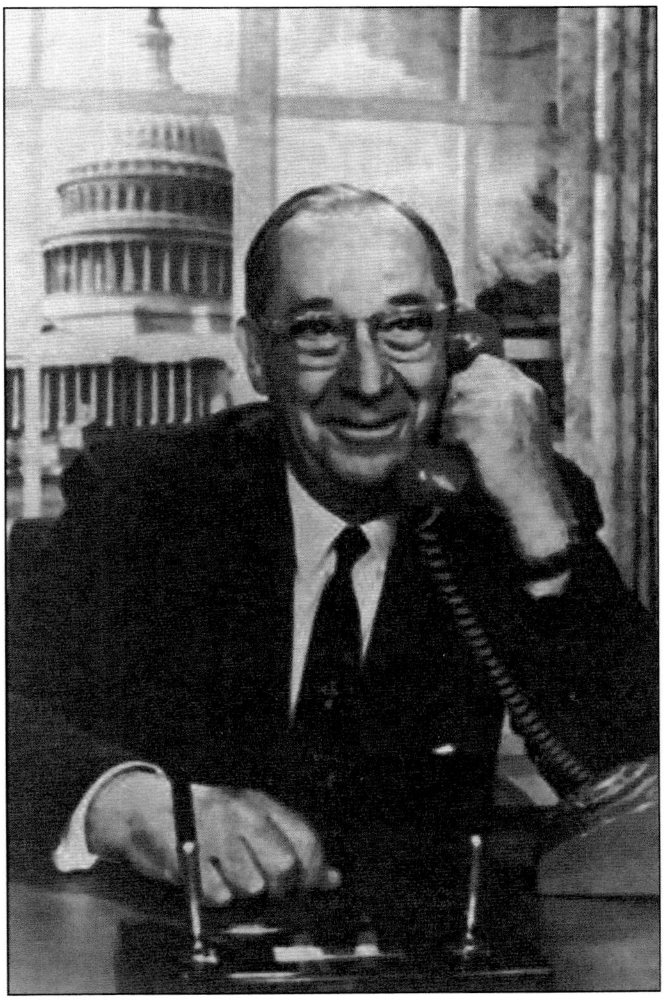

U.S. senator Benjamin Everett Jordan served from 1958 to 1973. B. Everett Jordan was born on September 8, 1896, and called Saxapahaw home from 1927 to his passing in 1974. He served overseas in the army during World War I. In 1927, his uncle Charles V. Sellars asked him if he would help him own and run a mill in Saxapahaw. Eventually, Jordan bought the mill and ran it successfully for decades, turning management over to his sons, Ben E. Jordan Jr. as president and John M. Jordan as vice president, while attending to his duties in the senate. Senator Jordan often voted for what was best for his constituents and countrymen, even if it meant going against his own party's beliefs. (Courtesy of Ben F. Bulla.)

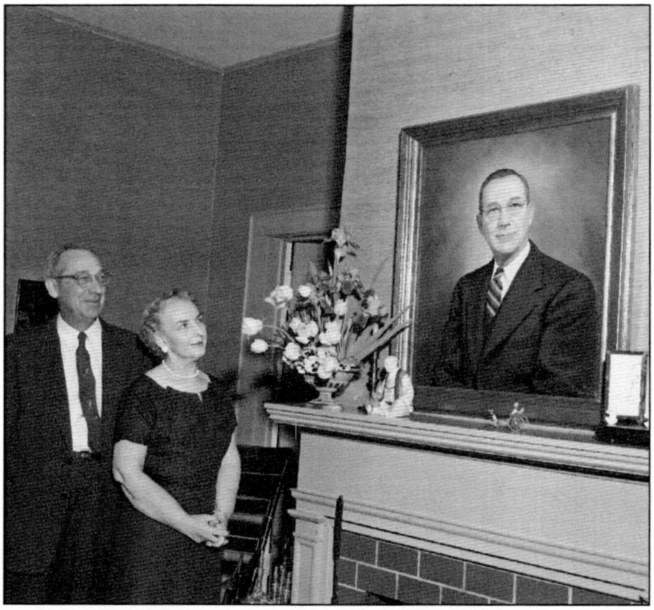

When B. Everett and Katherine Jordan moved to Saxapahaw in 1927, they agreed he would take care of everything in the mill and she would take care of everything in the village, including taking food to shut-ins. Katherine planted grass and dogwood and redbud trees throughout the village to help with the red mud problem. Everett taught adult Sunday school at Saxapahaw Methodist Church. The Jordans are seen here in their home before leaving for Washington in 1958 for Everett's appointment as a U.S. senator. (Courtesy of the North Carolina Collection Photographic Archives, Wilson Library, UNC–Chapel Hill.)

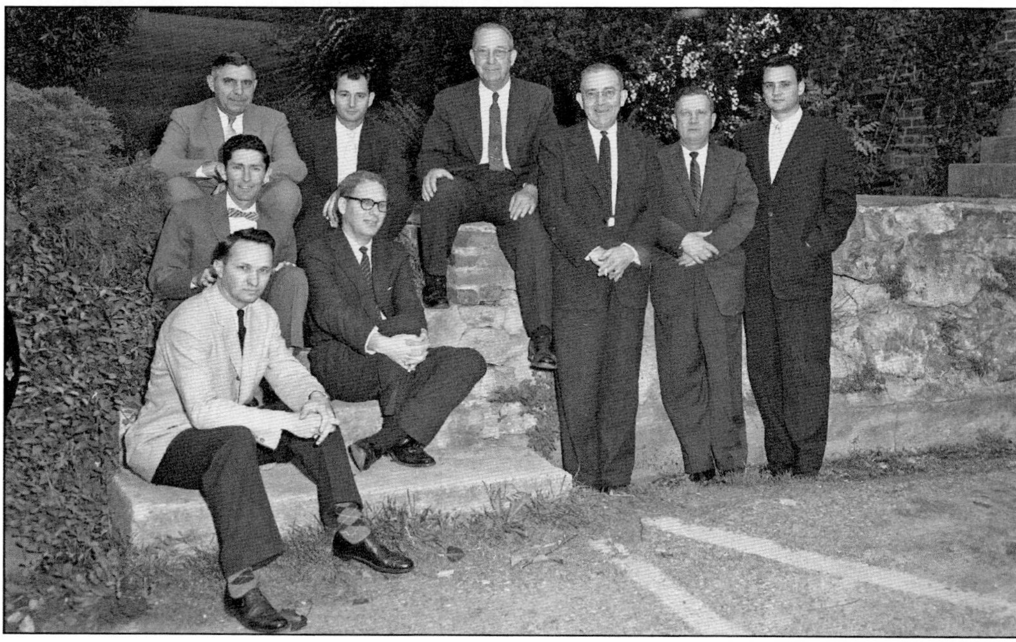

In 1958, Sen. B. Everett Jordan (center) sits on the steps to the Saxapahaw Post Office off the side of his home. Seated to the left of Senator Jordan are, from left to right, (first row) Ben F. Bulla; (second row) J. W. "Jake" Miller and Phil Doroughty; (third row) Frank Longerier and Ben E. Jordan Jr. Standing to the right of the senator are, from left to right, his brother Henry Jordan, Joe M. Neel, and Alton B. Smith. This was the day Ben E. Jordan Jr. assumed his position as president of the mill as his father left for his appointment to the Senate. Senator Jordan tried to come home almost every weekend. He felt Saxapahaw was a "retreat" for him and told his family that visiting Saxapahaw recharged his batteries. (Courtesy of the North Carolina Collection Photographic Archives, Wilson Library, UNC–Chapel Hill.)

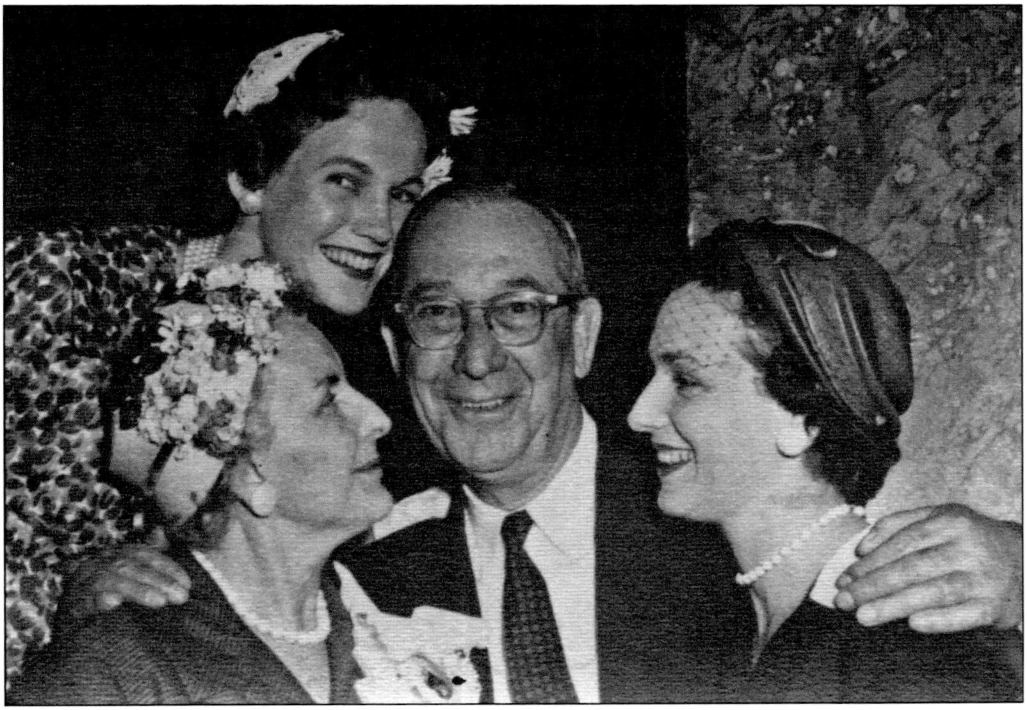

Senator Jordan and "his ladies" are pictured after he officially won the senate appointment in 1960. From left to right, the ladies are Katherine Jordan (his wife), Ellen Jordan (daughter-in-law), and Rose Ann Jordan Gant (his daughter). (Courtesy of Margaret Jordan.)

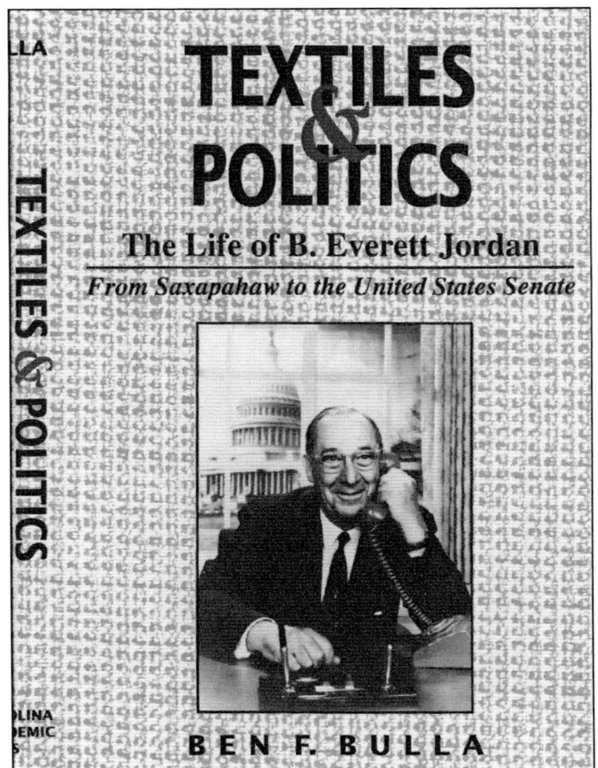


Ben F. Bulla, longtime Saxapahaw Mill employee and good friend of the Jordan family, wrote a fascinating book about Senator Jordan's journey from mill operator to the Senate. A quote on the back cover from Sen. Jesse Helms reads, "Senator Jordan is remembered here for his acumen, his dedication, and his unfailing cheerfulness. His friendship was special and I am honored to occupy the seat that he held for so many years." (Courtesy of the author.)

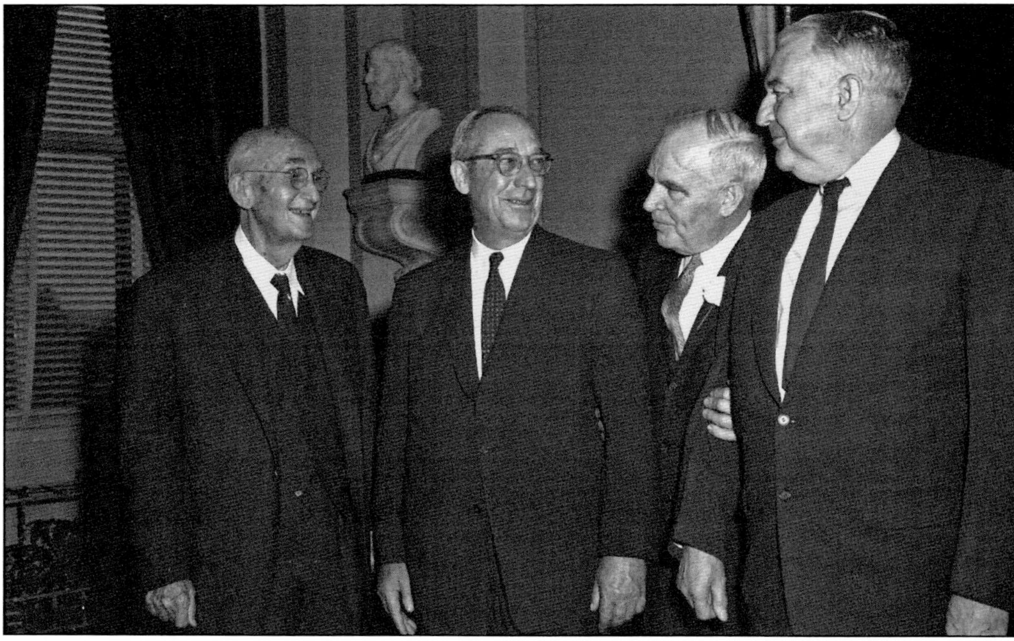

In 1958, shown from left to right are unidentified, B. Everett Jordan, Gov. Luther Hodges, and Sen. Sam Ervin before B. Everett Jordan is sworn in as senator of North Carolina. He filled the vacancy that was left behind by the passing of Sen. W. Kerr Scott. Senator Jordan would hold this position for almost 15 years. Senator Jordan's life positively influenced and changed the culture and history of Saxapahaw. (Courtesy of the North Carolina Collection Photographic Archives, Wilson Library, UNC–Chapel Hill.)

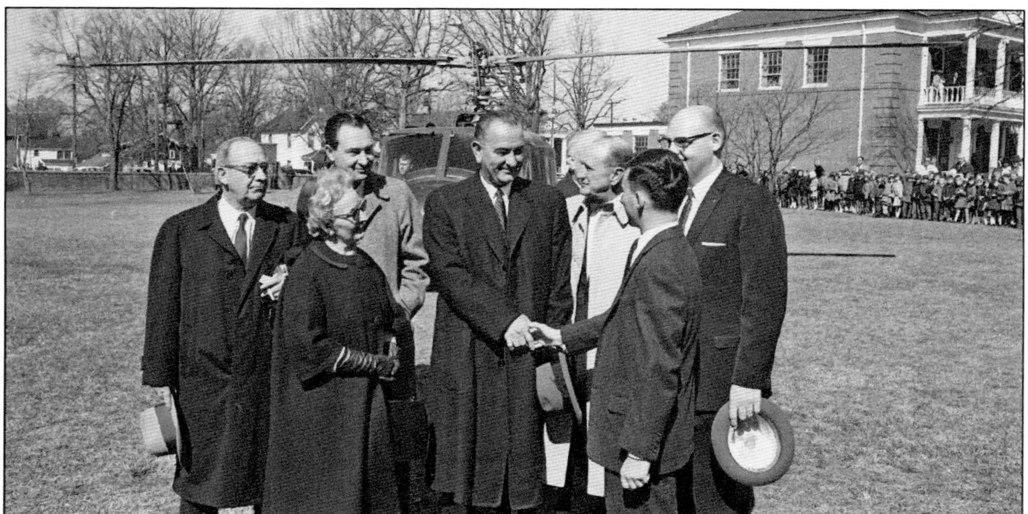

U.S. vice president Lyndon B. Johnson arrived at Elon University by helicopter on March 8, 1962, for the Founder's Day celebration. In attendance are Sen. B. Everett and Katherine Jordan (far left) and, in no particular order, U.S. Representative (6th District–N.C.) Horace Kornegay, U.S. Senator Sam Ervin, Elon College President James Earl Danieley, and two unidentified young men. (Courtesy of the North Carolina Collection Photographic Archives, Wilson Library, UNC–Chapel Hill.)

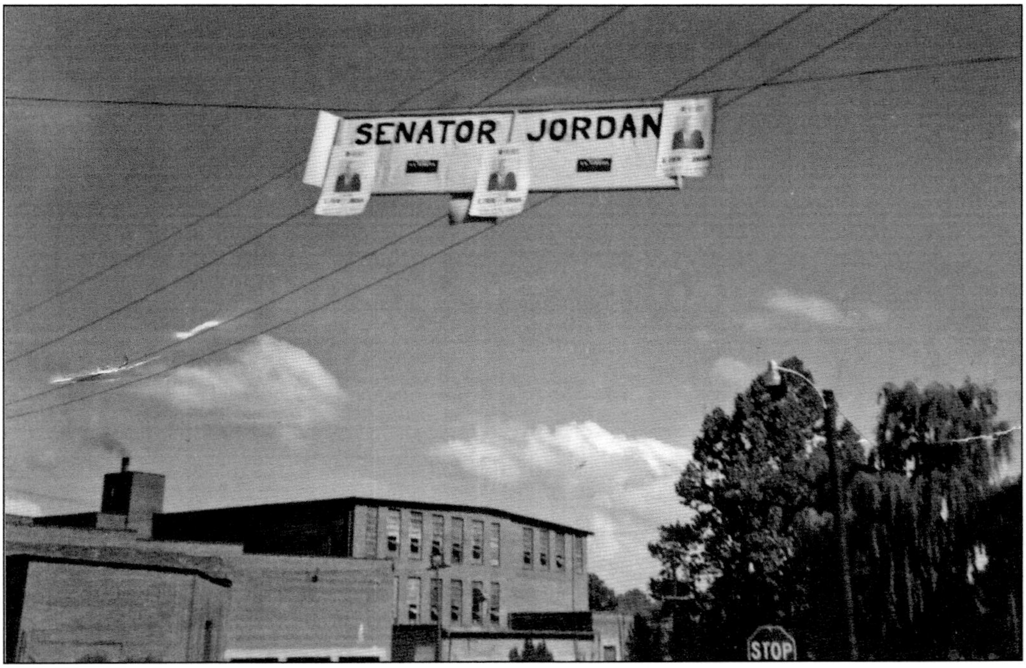


Here are the "Vote for Senator Jordan" signs in 1960 over the streets of Saxapahaw next to the cotton mill. B. Everett Jordan said he entered politics to help bring progress to the small village of Saxapahaw and turn it into a full town. When B. Everett Jordan came to Saxapahaw in 1927, the mill was abandoned, dirt roads were the only way in or out, there were no operating telephones, and there was no electric power except for what the mill's water turbine generated from a wooden damn. Pictured below are Senator and Katherine Jordan. (Both courtesy of the Jordan family albums.)

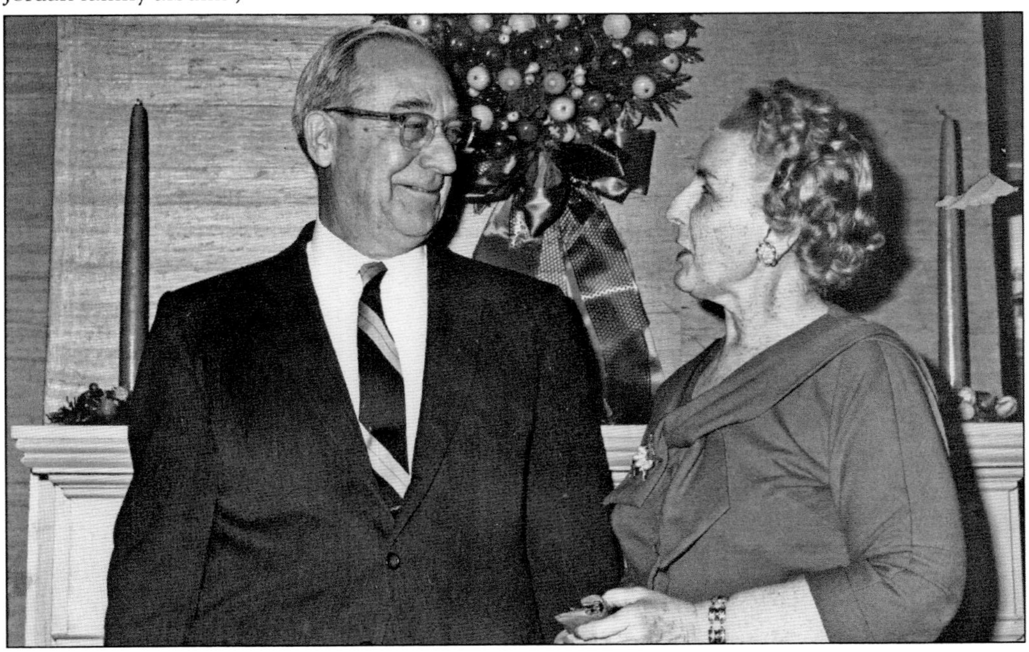

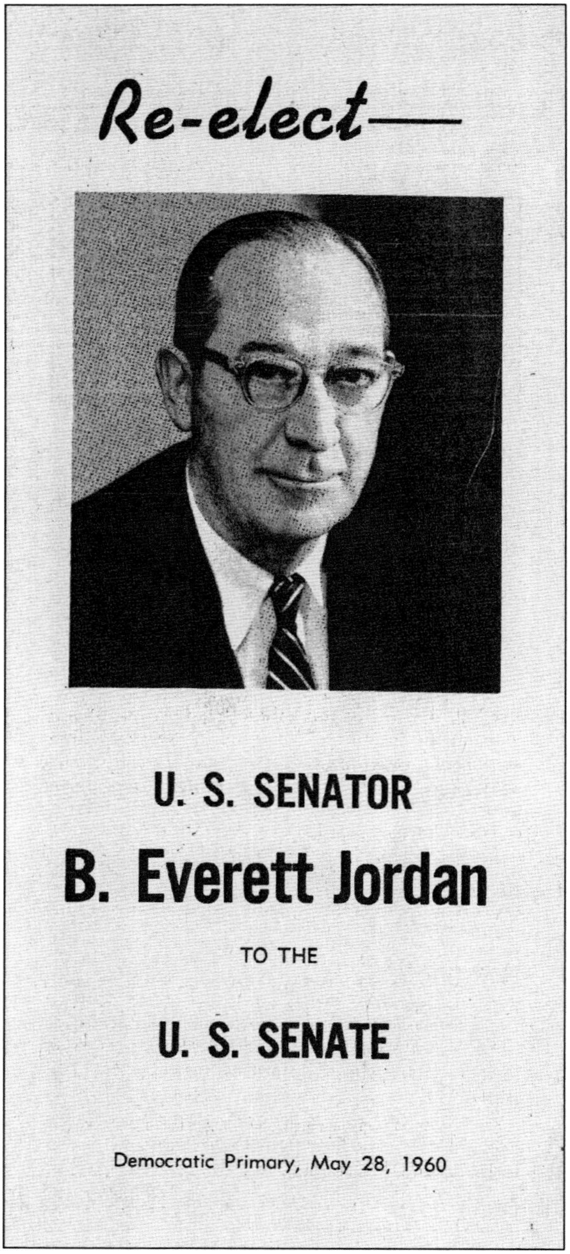


Voters reelected Senator Jordan in 1960. Per the voting brochure, Senator Jordan's stance on defense was as follows: "We must keep our military strength at such a level that no nation would dare attack the United States or any of our allies." Senator Jordan says on imports, "Imports have been increasing in recent years at a rate, which, if allowed to continue, will ruin many of our basic industries, including textiles, commercial fishing, and many others that provide jobs for a large segment of our people." Senator Jordan supported research in medical science, agriculture, industrial uses of farm products, water, missile development, and the mysteries of outer space. Senator Jordan was the author of the Cotton Allotment Transfer Bill to assist farmers with small allotments. (Courtesy of the Jordan family albums.)

# *Three*

# The Jordan Family Legacy Continues

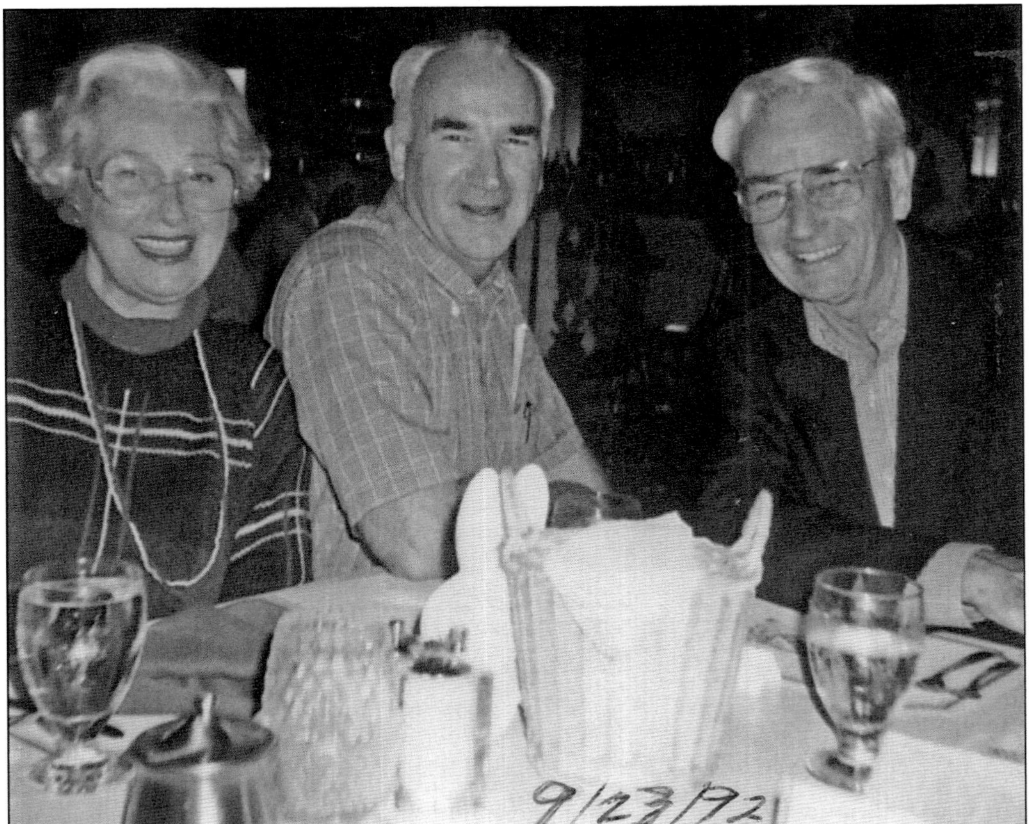


Senator Jordan's three children are, from left to right, Rose Ann Jordan Gant, John M. Jordan, and Ben E. Jordan Jr. After the passing of the late senator, his estate was split into three divisions in each of his three children's names. Ben E. Jordan Jr. handles the affairs for both Rose Ann and himself and, along with John Jordan, established Jordan Properties across from the original Saxapahaw Cotton Mill. (Courtesy of John Jordan.)

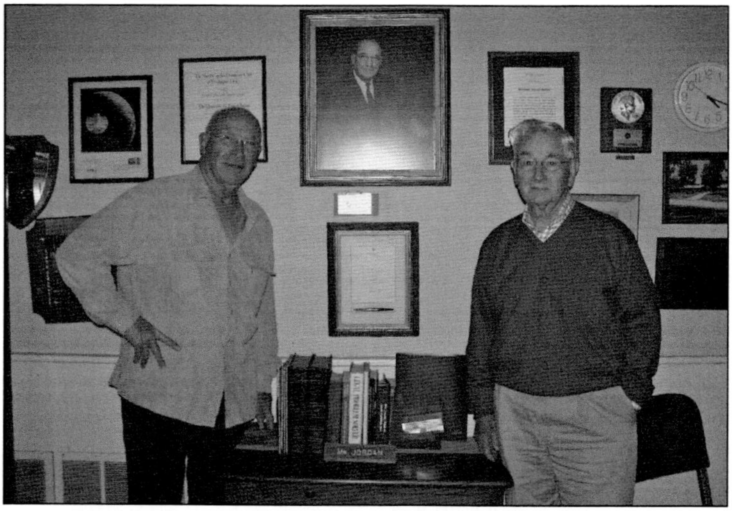

John Jordan (left) and Ben E. Jordan Jr. pose with their father's portrait between them. Former senator B. Everett Jordan's office is now occupied by his son Ben E. Jordan Jr., who took over as president of the Saxapahaw Cotton Mill when his father left for Washington, D.C., to become a U.S. senator. (Photograph by the author.)

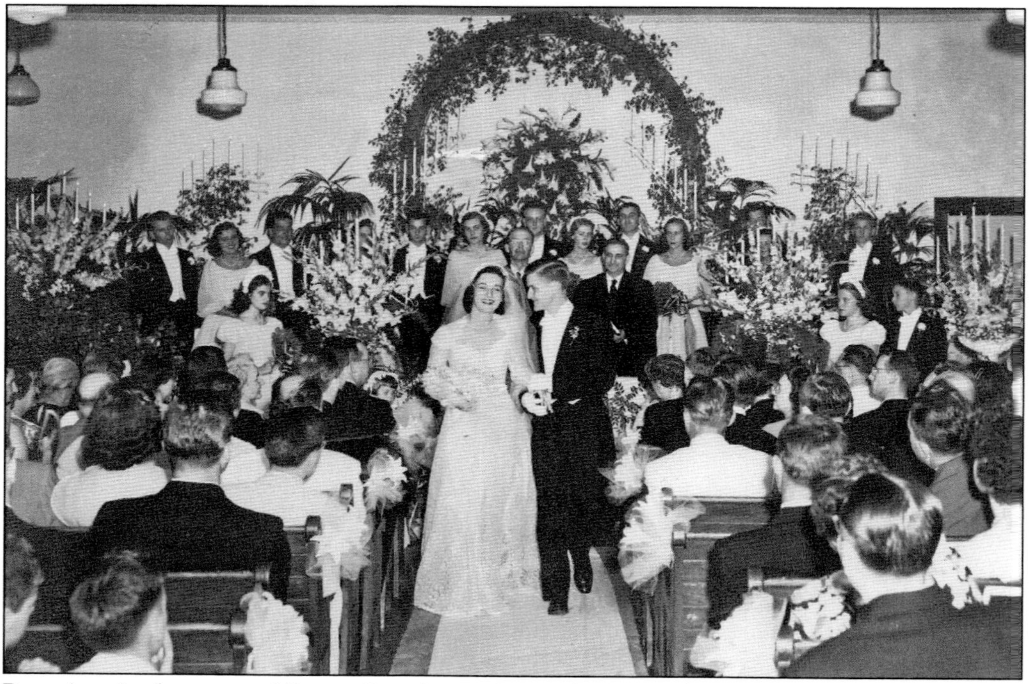

Rose Ann Jordan married Roger Gant Jr. in 1949 at the Saxapahaw United Methodist Church. Roger Gant Jr. retired as president of the Glen Raven Mill. The Glen Raven Mill, formerly co-owned by Roger Gant Sr., was the first mill to dye an awning in 1908 and the first mill to produce and receive a patent for seamless hosiery in 1952. In 1960, they launched the first Sunbrella, a 100-percent acrylic awning fabric. They began to develop and supply fabrics to the Disney Corporation used for the decorative umbrellas and awnings in their parks. The material for the flag that was planted on the moon in 1969 was developed at Glen Raven. Roger Gant Jr. was named president in 1972. In 2008, Glen Guard FR fabric was designed to result in protective garments that exceed safety standards and are more comfortable, more durable, and more colorfast than any other protective apparel available in the market. More information can be found in Margaret Elizabeth Gant's *The Raven's Story*. (Courtesy of John Jordan.)

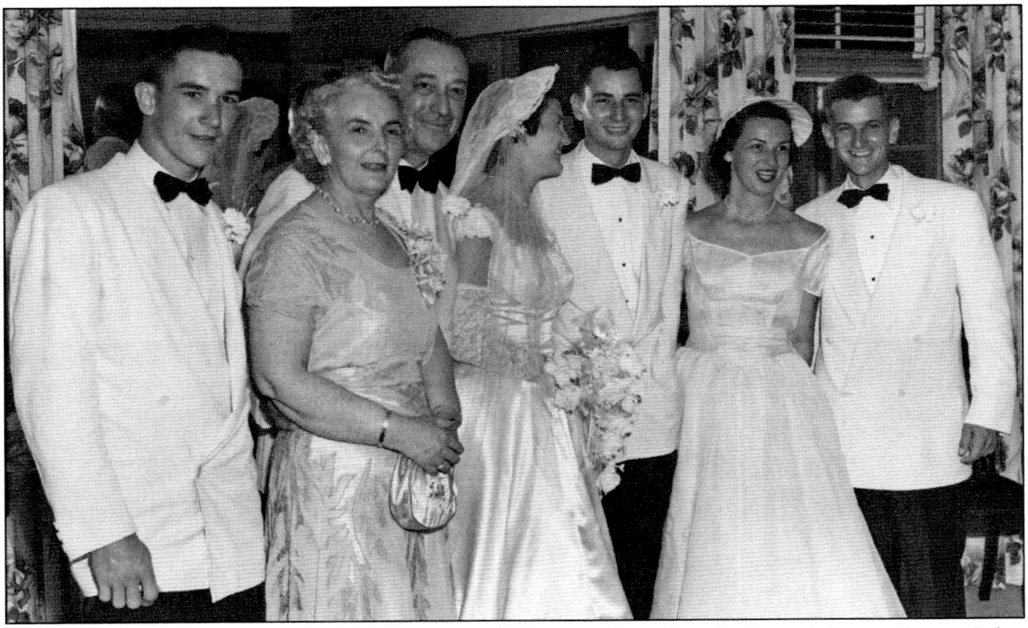

At Ben E. Jordan Jr.'s wedding is a gathering of the immediate family. From left to right are John M. Jordan, Katherine Jordan, Senator Jordan, Ellen Jordan, Ben E. Jordan Jr., Rose Ann Jordan Gant, and Roger Gant Jr. (Courtesy of Ben E. Jordan Jr.)

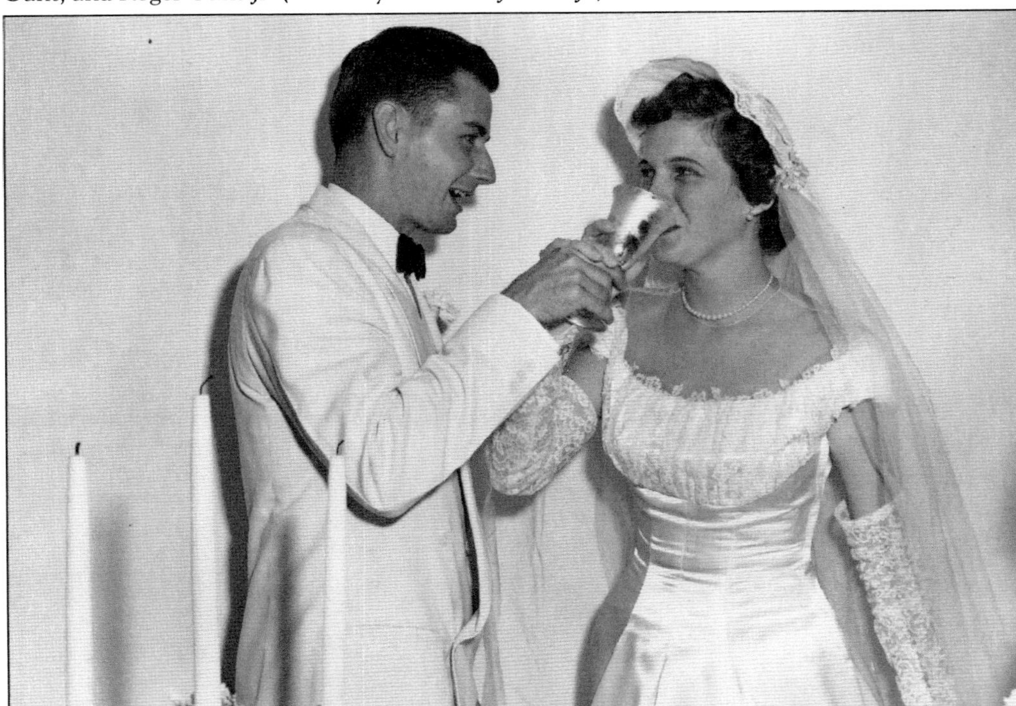

Ben E. Jordan Jr. and Ellen Jordan are pictured on their wedding day in 1951. Ellen did not drink alcohol, so she pretended to be drinking for this photograph, which is the reason she appears to be laughing. (Courtesy of Ben E. Jordan Jr.)

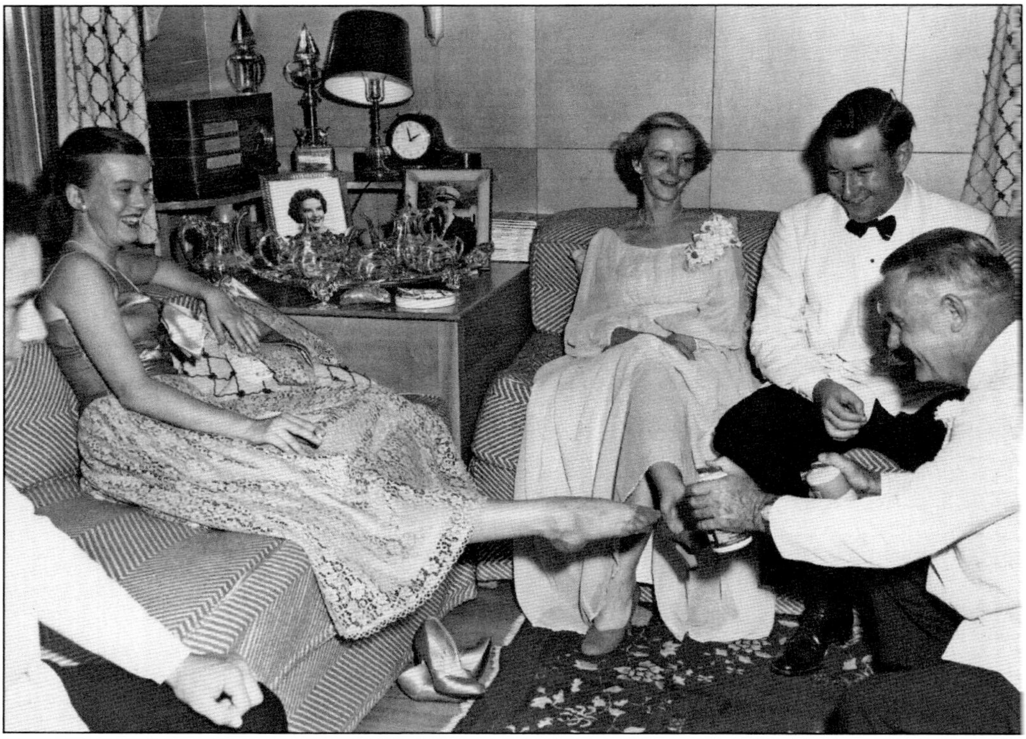

Ben E. Jr. and Ellen Jordan's wedding day is shown here. The mosquitoes were so bad that the bridesmaids had to have their legs and feet sprayed with repellent. From left to right are Jane Hanes, Alice McLean, P. Frank Hanes Jr., and L. L. McMasters. (Courtesy of Ben E. Jordan Jr.)

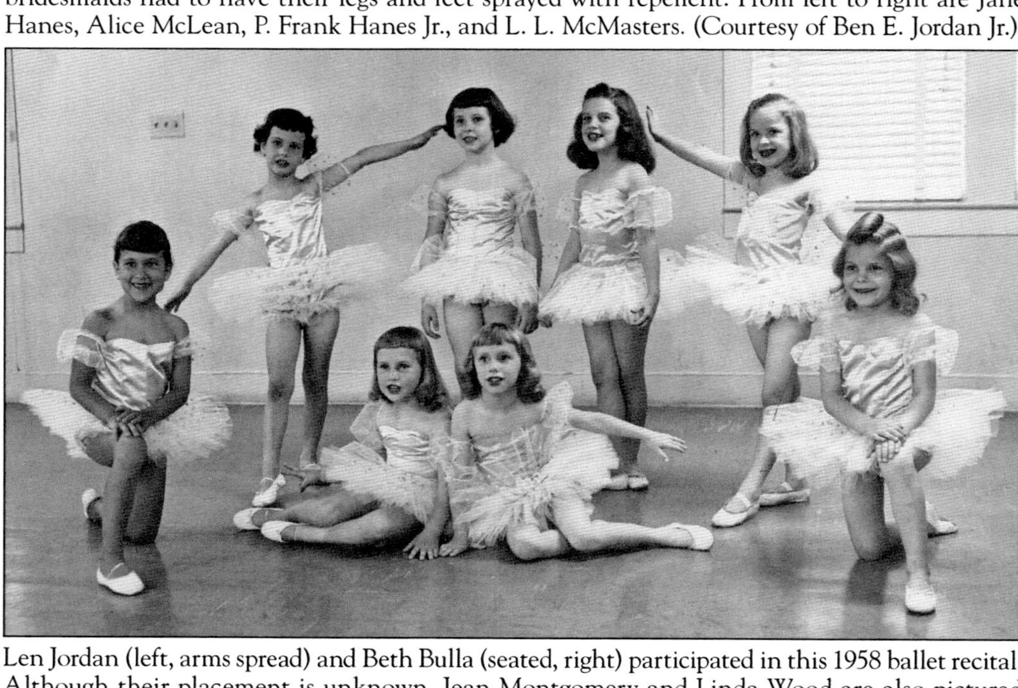

Len Jordan (left, arms spread) and Beth Bulla (seated, right) participated in this 1958 ballet recital. Although their placement is unknown, Jean Montgomery and Linda Wood are also pictured among the other unidentified Saxapahaw girls. (Courtesy of Ben E. Jordan Jr.)

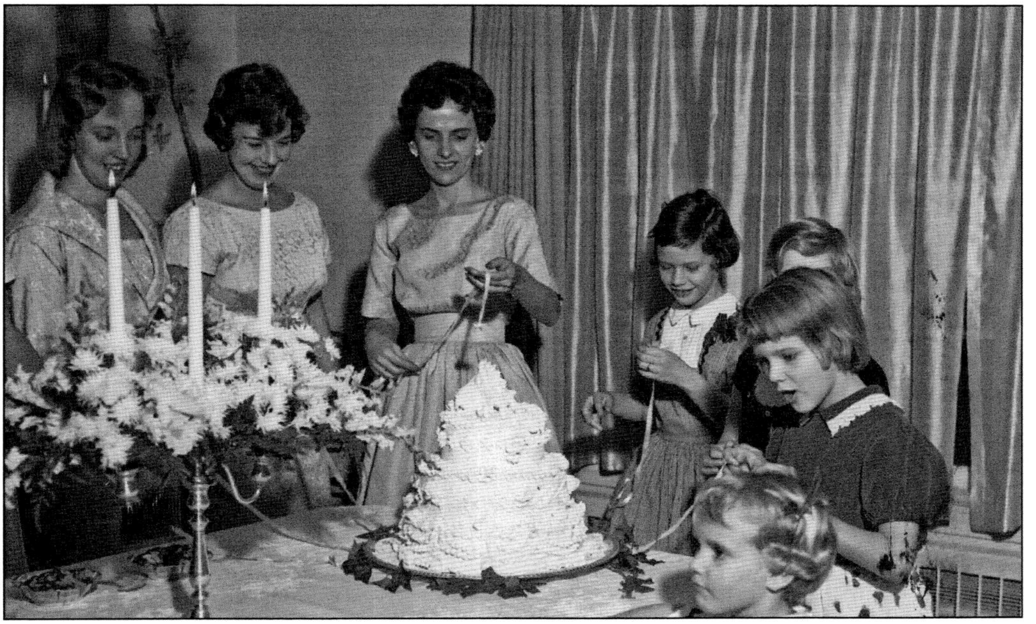

Ben E. Jordan Jr.'s daughters are pictured at John and Margaret Jordan's wedding. From left to right are three unidentified bridesmaids, Ellen "Len" Jordan, Katherine "Kathy" Jordan, Alice Gant, and Barbara "Barbie" Jordan. (Courtesy of Ben E. Jordan Jr.)

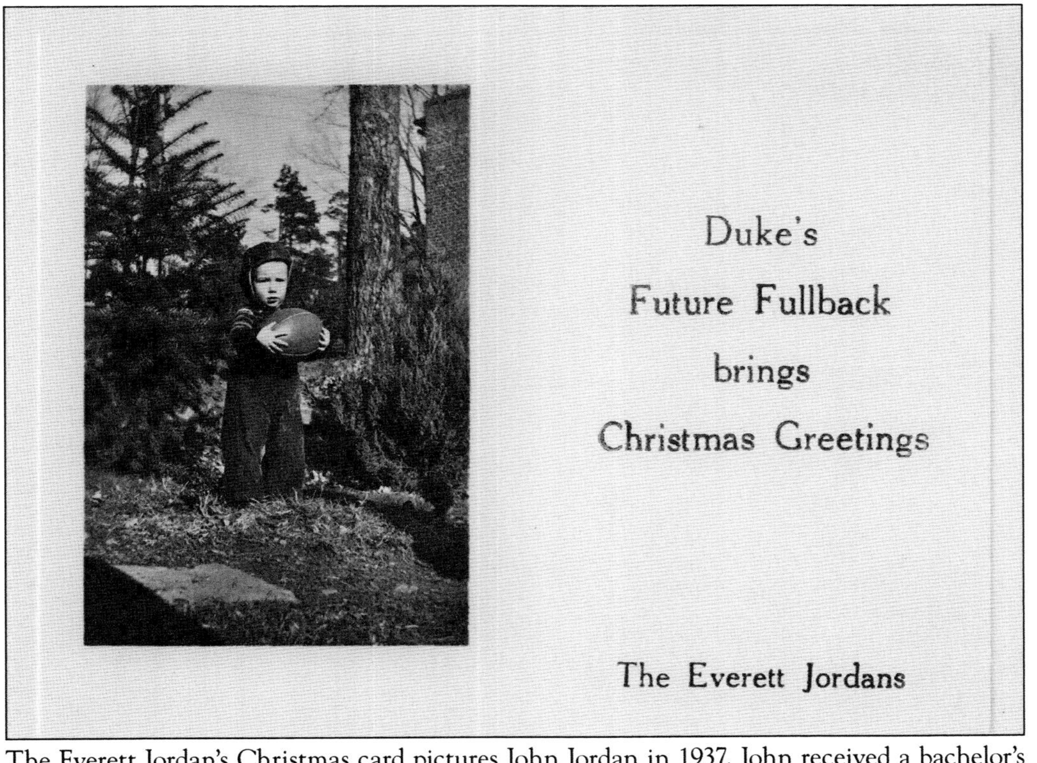


The Everett Jordan's Christmas card pictures John Jordan in 1937. John received a bachelor's degree in business administration from Duke University. (Courtesy of Margaret Jordan.)

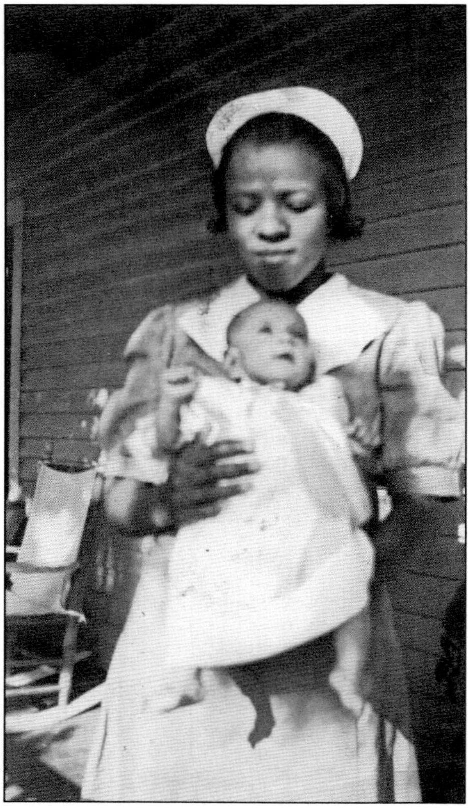

Shown here in 1938 is Bessie Wilson (Mrs. Odell Wilson), employee of Thomas and Louise Carter. Bessie is holding Margaret Carter, who married John Jordan. Seventy years later, Margaret Carter Jordan still visits with Bessie, who currently lives in Mebane, North Carolina. (Courtesy of Margaret Jordan.)

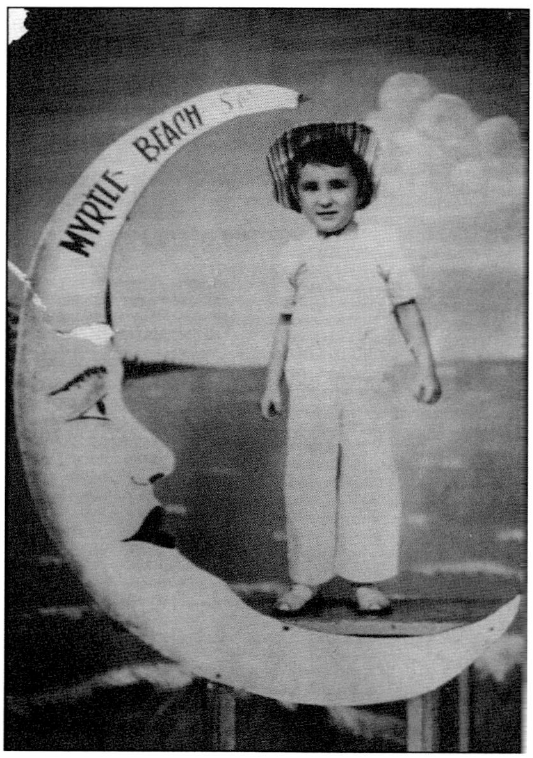


A 1941 photograph shows Margaret Carter. Myrtle Beach has always been a popular summer spot for vacationers in North Carolina. Margaret Carter Jordan and her family went to Myrtle Beach every summer. According to Margaret and John's son Mac, "It was the place to go." (Courtesy of Margaret Jordan.)

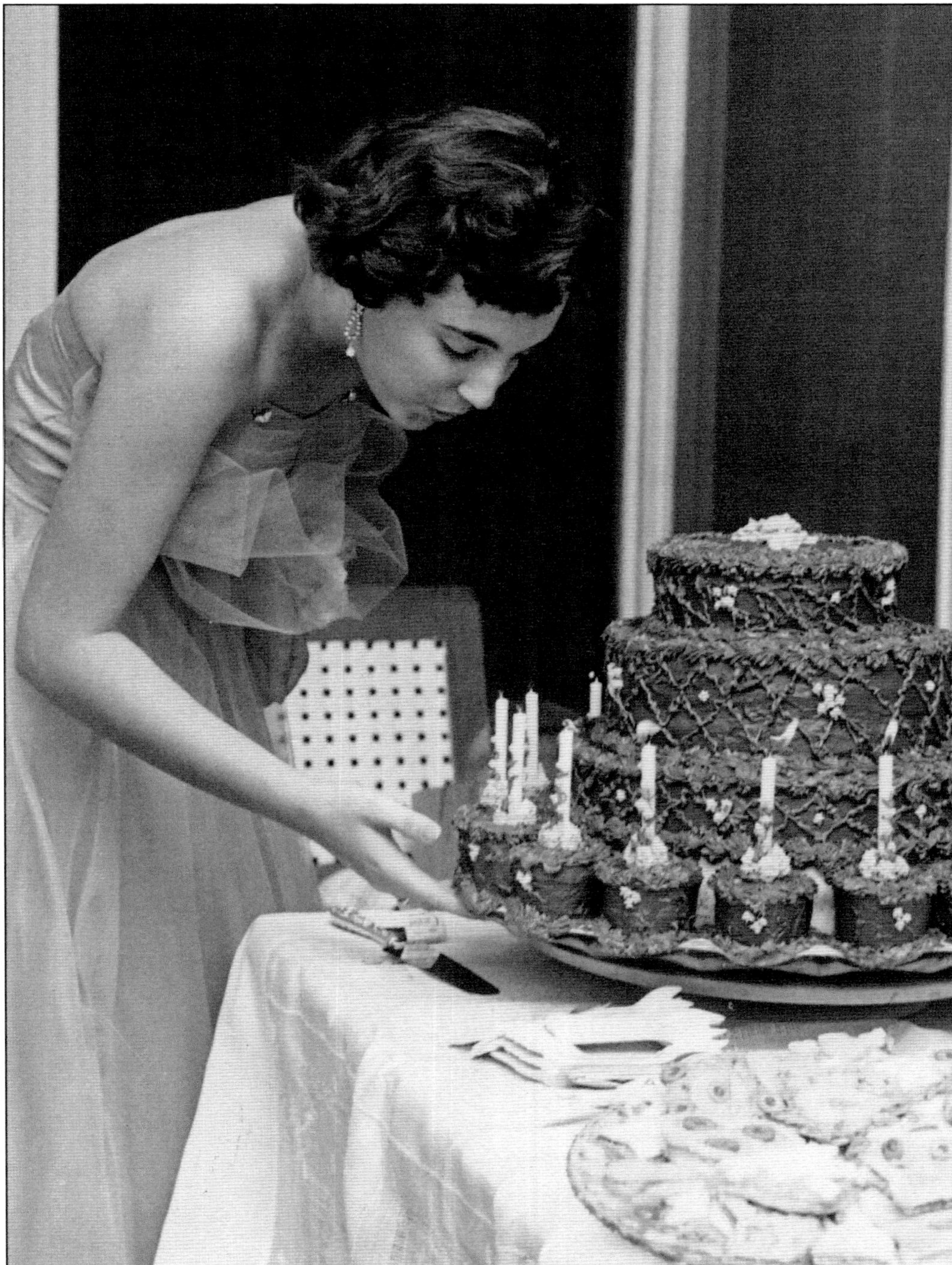

In 1954, Margaret Carter blows out the candles on her 16th birthday. Her family had a party for her. It is tradition to have a Sweet 16 birthday party. Margaret married John Jordan on November 25, 1960. She was a Girl Scout leader for 13 years, a choir director for 40 years, and PTA president. She has always remained very active at the Saxapahaw United Methodist Church and within the Saxapahaw community. (Courtesy of the Jordan family albums.)

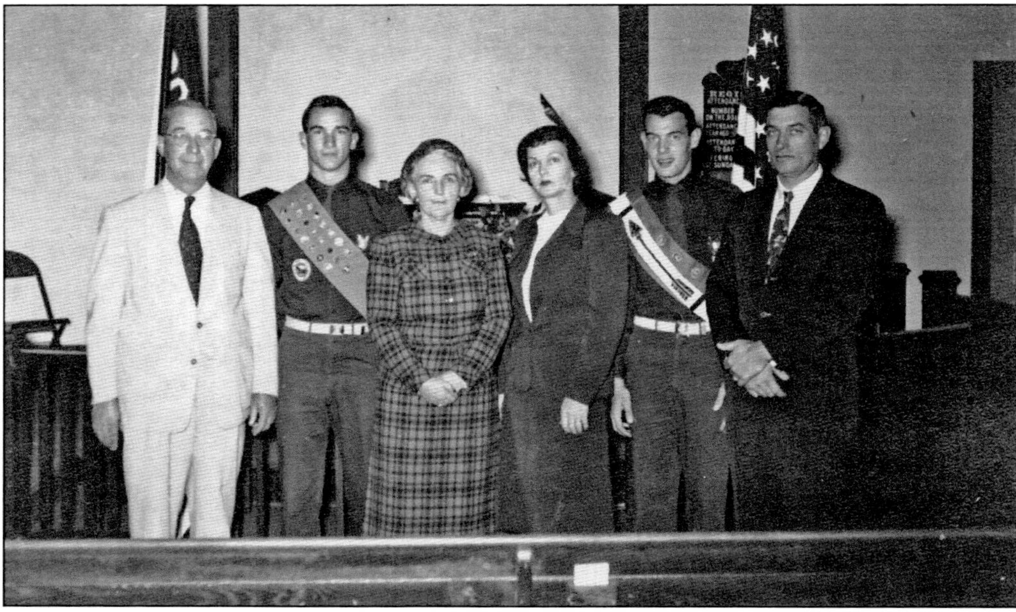

This is the Eagle Scout presentation for John Jordan and Delmer Crisson, John Jordan's very best friend. Delmer joined the army, and while at Fort Jackson, it began to storm one day. Delmer ran under a tree for protection and was struck and killed by lightning. From left to right are Senator Jordan, John Jordan, Katherine Jordan, Elsie Crisson, Delmer Crisson, and Grover Crisson. (Courtesy of Margaret Jordan.)

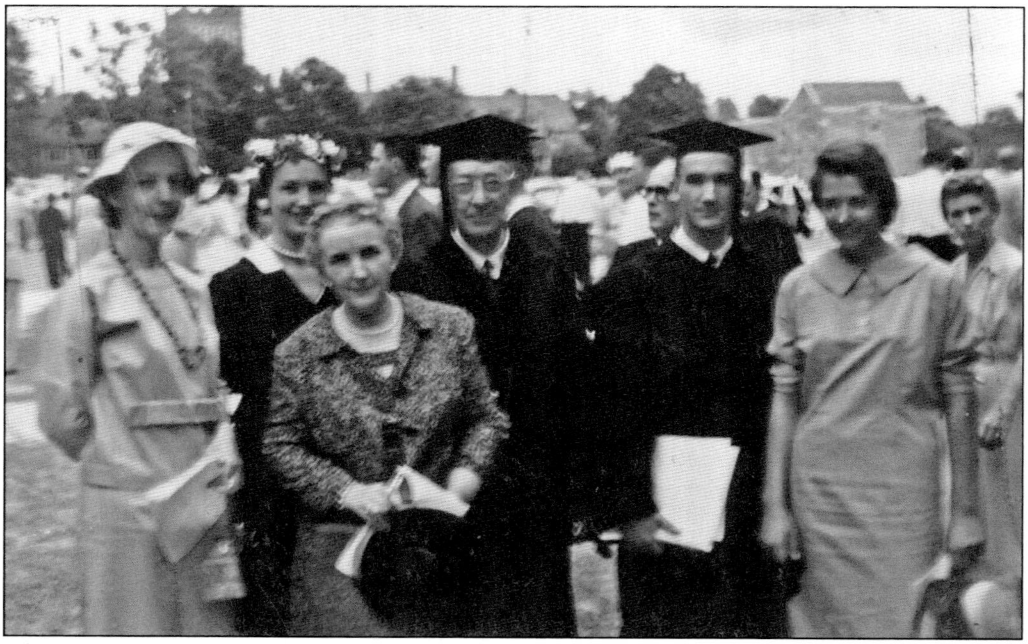

John Jordan's graduation day from Duke University is pictured here. His father and uncle were on the board of trustees at Duke. Senator Jordan received an honorary doctorate degree from Duke. From left to right are Alice McLean, Rose Ann Jordan Gant, Katherine McLean Jordan, Senator Jordan, John McLean Jordan, and John's girlfriend. (Courtesy of Margaret Jordan.)

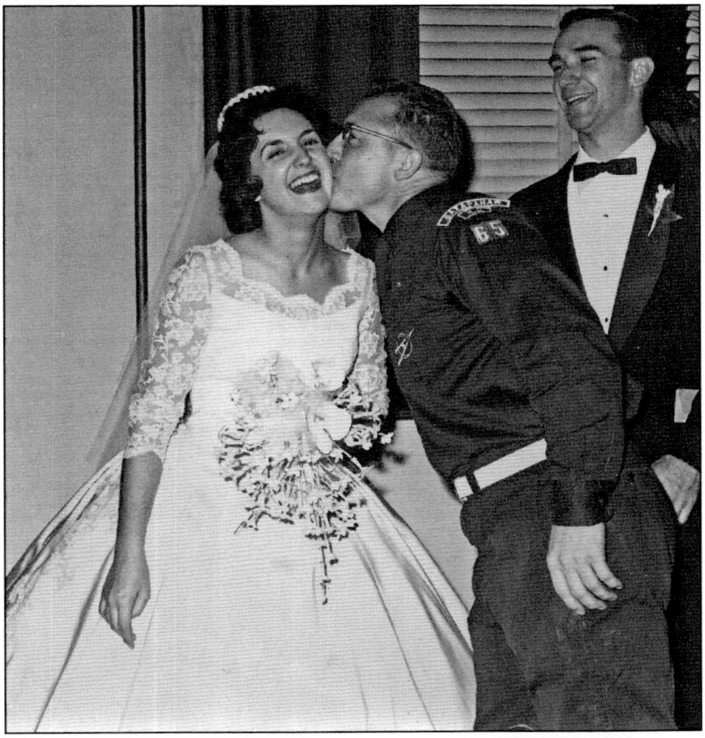

Margaret Jordan is being kissed by Bernard Hodgin on her wedding day in 1960. That same year, Bernard was the oldest person to become an Eagle Scout in the United States. Afterward, the U.S. Scouting Association changed the rule that Eagle must be made by the age of 18. Bernard Hodgin was 45 years old at the time. (Courtesy of Margaret Jordan.)

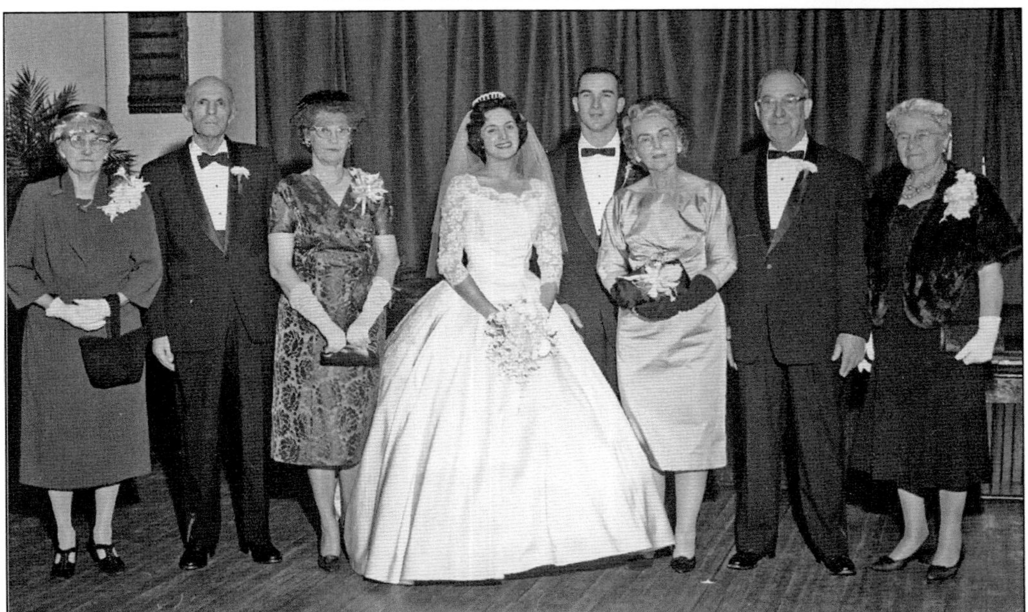

Here is one of John and Margaret Jordan's wedding photographs. Shown from left to right are Margaret's grandmother, Mrs. Margaret Young; Margaret's parents, Thomas Carter (lawyer) and Louise Carter (piano teacher); Margaret Carter Jordan; John McLean Jordan; John's parents, Katherine and B. Everett Jordan; and John's grandmother, Mrs. Edith McLean. (Courtesy of Margaret Jordan.)

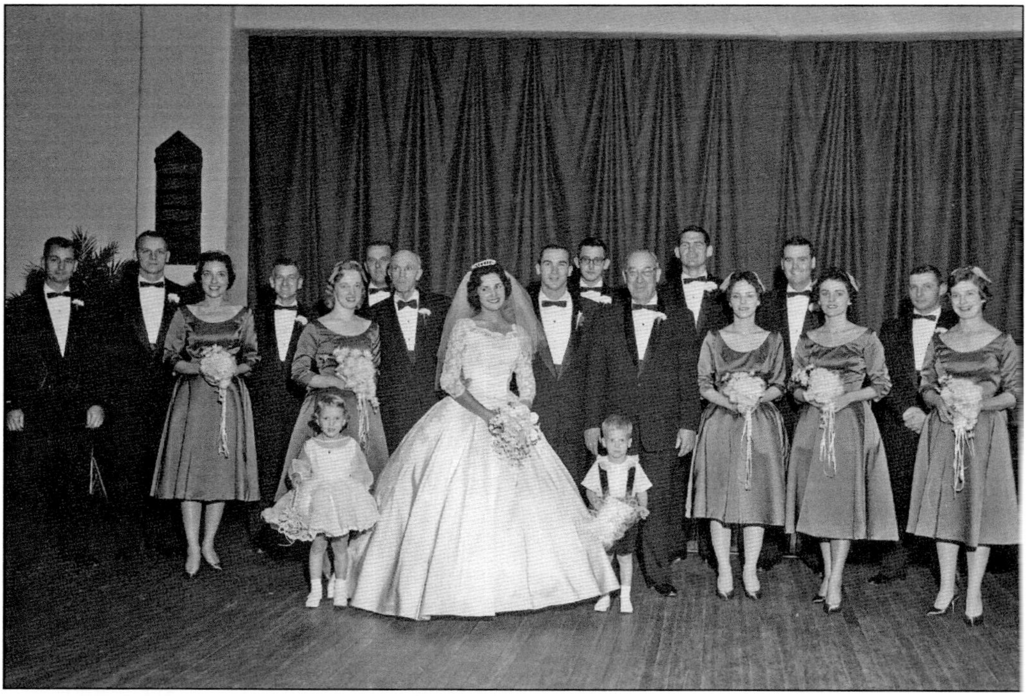

Shown above is John and Margaret Jordan's wedding party photograph. (Courtesy of Ben E. Jordan Jr.)

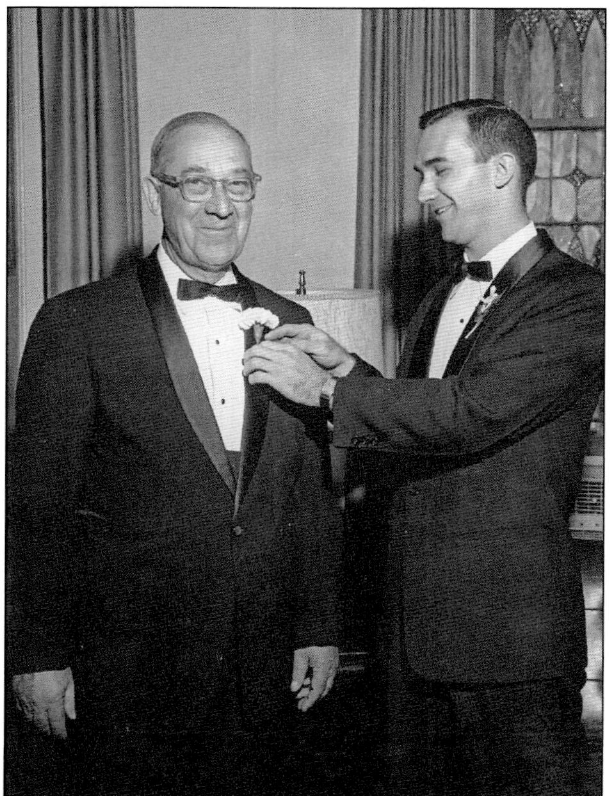

November 25, 1960, was John Jordan's wedding day. The senator was John's best man. John is pinning the boutonniere on his father's lapel. Having one's father as a best man was a normal tradition for the South but not normal for the North. When John Jordan's oldest daughter was married, the best man in the wedding was a college buddy of the groom. John and family were surprised it was not the groom's father as the best man. (Courtesy of Margaret Jordan.)

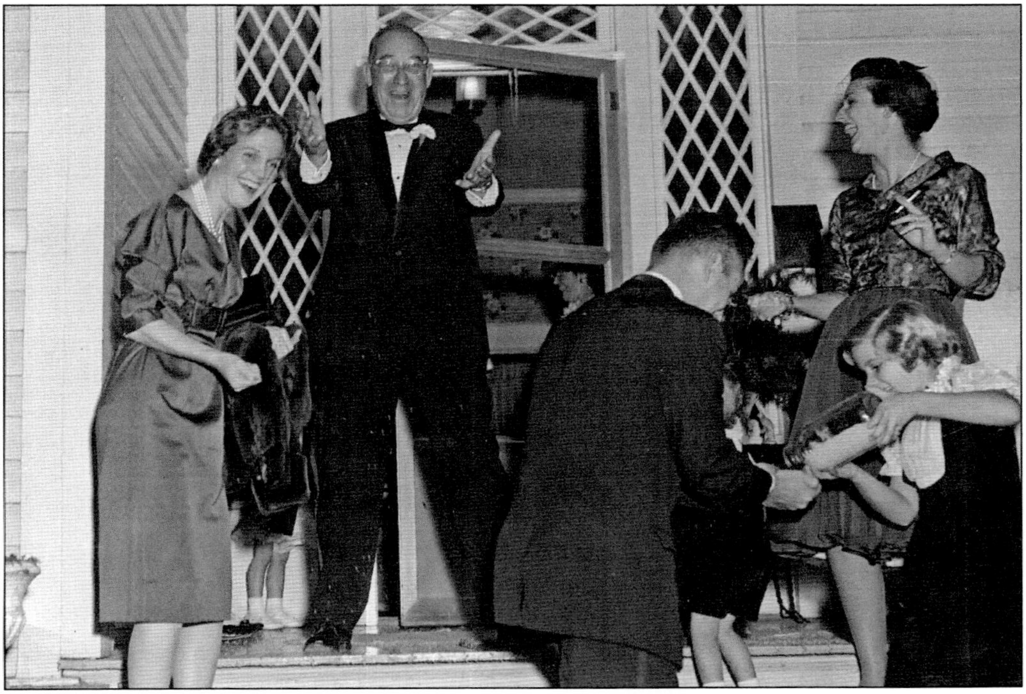

On John and Margaret Jordan's wedding day, Ben E. Jr. and Ellen Jordan's children are handing out rice that will be thrown as the bride and groom leave the home. Everyone laughed when someone pre-threw their rice at Senator Jordan as he came out of the home first. (Courtesy of Margaret Jordan.)

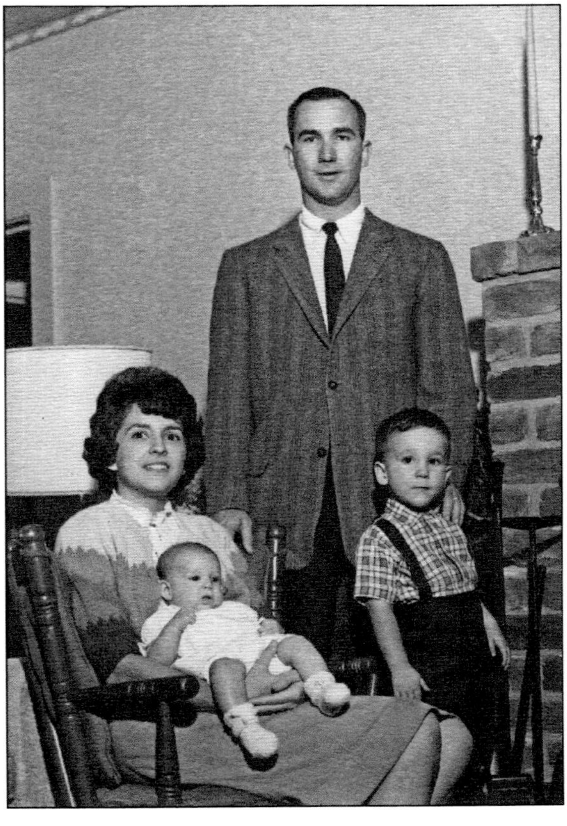

Margaret Jordan is holding her newborn daughter, Louise, and Mac Jordan is leaning up against his father. John told his son to never make noise while he watched the news. Mac ran right through the room anyway with a noise-making toy. John grabbed Mac and spanked him. Mac stood still, looked at his father very seriously, and said, "Why did you do that?" John replied, "Because I told you not to make noise during the news," to which Mac replied, "But it was during a commercial." John, who felt terrible for the unfair punishment he could not take back, told his son to spank his father in return. Mac laughed at his dad and trotted off to play. (Courtesy of John Jordan.)

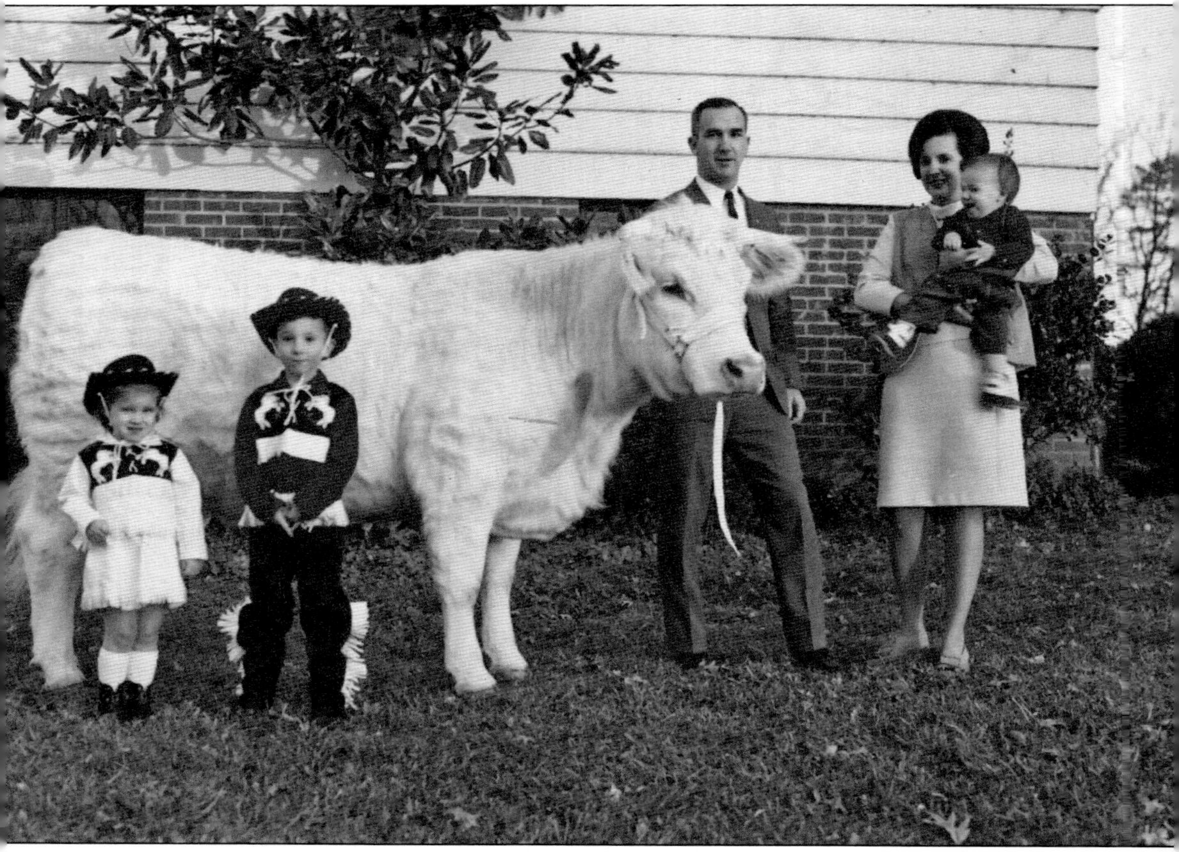

John M. Jordan previously raised cattle. He was the founder and president of the Carolina-Virginia Charolais and Chianina Associations. This cow, Azalea (pictured in 1965), was purchased from France and sat in quarantine in Canada for a month before being delivered to John. John eventually sold Azalea at an open auction for $65,000. She was the highest-grossing (non-pregnant) cow ever sold in the United States. The news of the sale made it all over the world and was read in the newspaper by his father, Senator Jordan, during a political trip to Peru. (Courtesy of Margaret Jordan.)

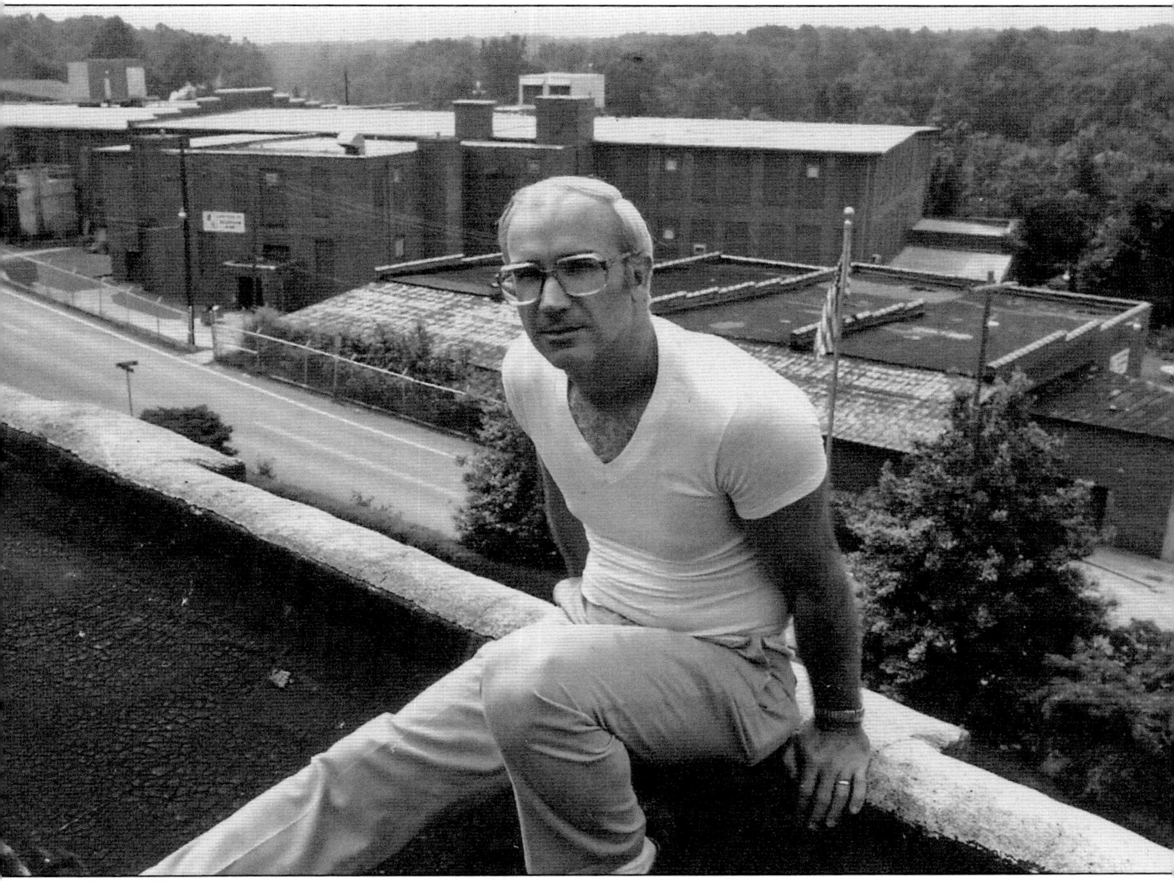

The T-shirt John Jordan is wearing in 1978 was made from the cotton produced at the Saxapahaw Cotton Mill. One day, John received a package from a customer sending back a T-shirt like the one John is wearing and declared the T-shirt a "defect." John put on the returned T-shirt, walked into the mill, and asked the workers to look at him because they were looking at a defect. The workers laughed and said, "We know we are looking at a defect" and went back to work. After a couple of times, John finally got through to them that the T-shirt was the defect and not him, but they all had a great time laughing about it. (Courtesy of John Jordan.)

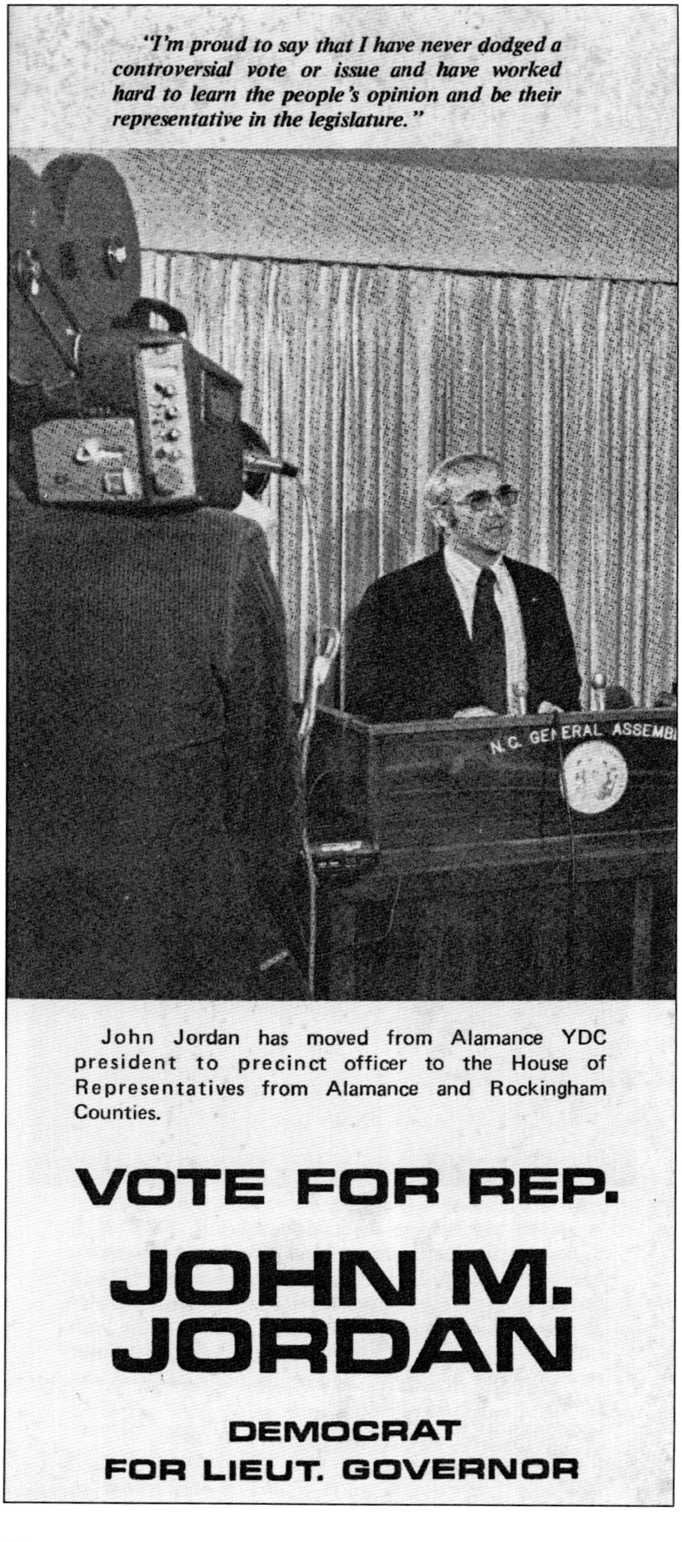


According to this brochure, John Jordan was a special deputy sheriff and a member of the North Carolina Sheriff's Association. He believed innocent citizens should have more rights, privileges, and protection than the criminal. In the General Assembly, John introduced new legislation to put prisoners on the roads to clean up and beautify the highways. The Alamance County sheriff, John Stockard, said he voted for John because he always supported law and order programs and the men who risked their lives to protect the people. John was also a youth teacher at the Saxapahaw Methodist Church for 10 years. The Reverend Jeff Davis believed in John because "he didn't just send his children to church, he always attended and walked with them." (Courtesy of Margaret Jordan.)

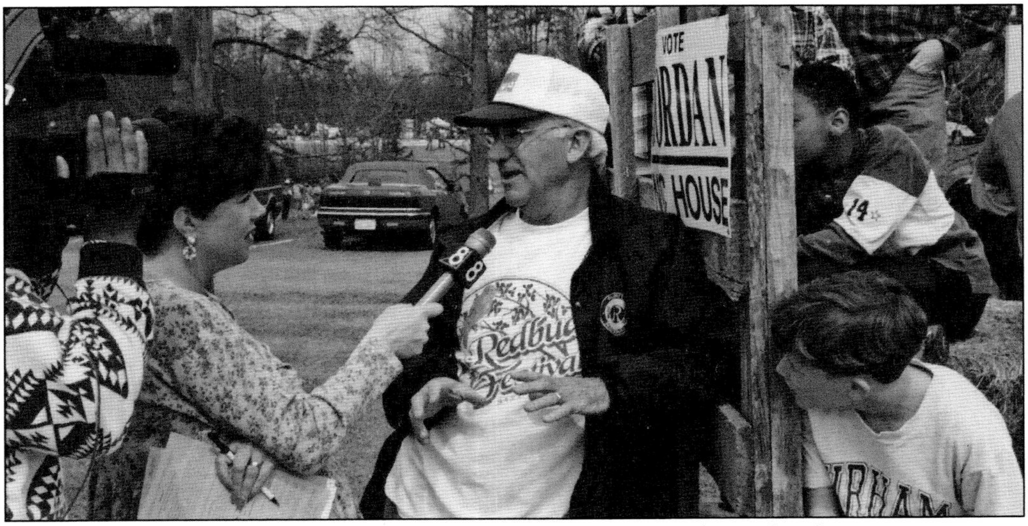


At the Redbud Festival in 1996, John Jordan is interviewed by Channel 8 about running again for state representative. The Redbud Festival continued for 13 years. It was a three-day bluegrass event held by the Saxapahaw Community Chest, of which John is chairman, to raise money for the Buddy Collins Community Center, Scout cabin, and ball fields. There were 100 acres provided for free camping. Events included hot air balloons, marathons, pig pickin', tractor rides, tractor sales, auctions, food, arts and crafts, bike races, karaoke, antique cars, and more. (Courtesy of John Jordan.)

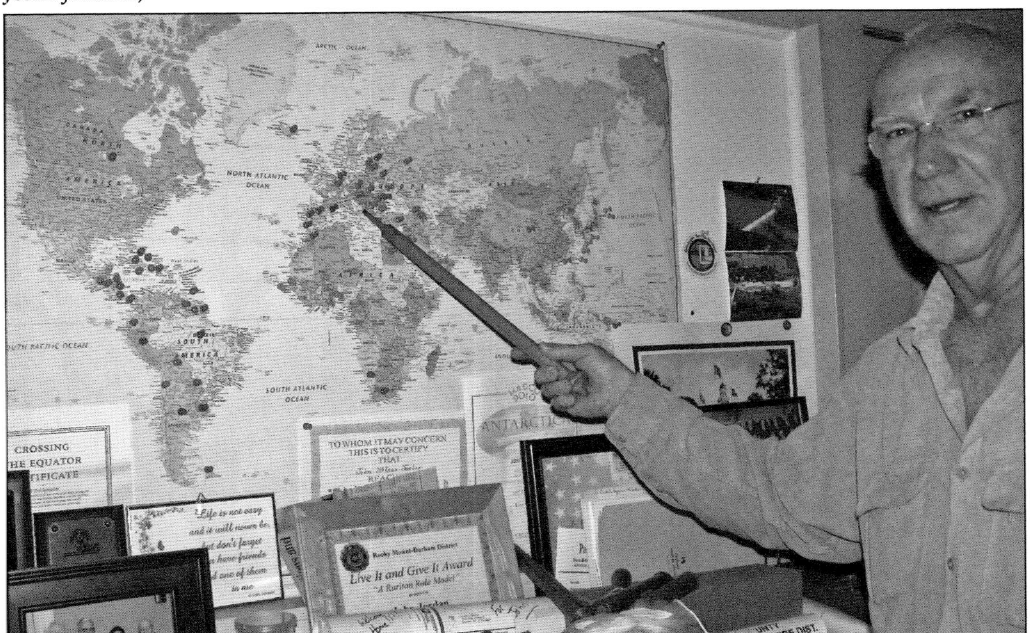


John Jordan is pointing to the 100th country that he visited in October 2008. John makes every vacation a personal endeavor to significantly learn about each country and their culture. John spends time in his mountain home retreat in front of a blazing fire writing the memoirs of his experiences after each vacation and has his wonderful administrative staff type them up. John is holding an original wooden spindle from the mill. (Photograph by the author.)

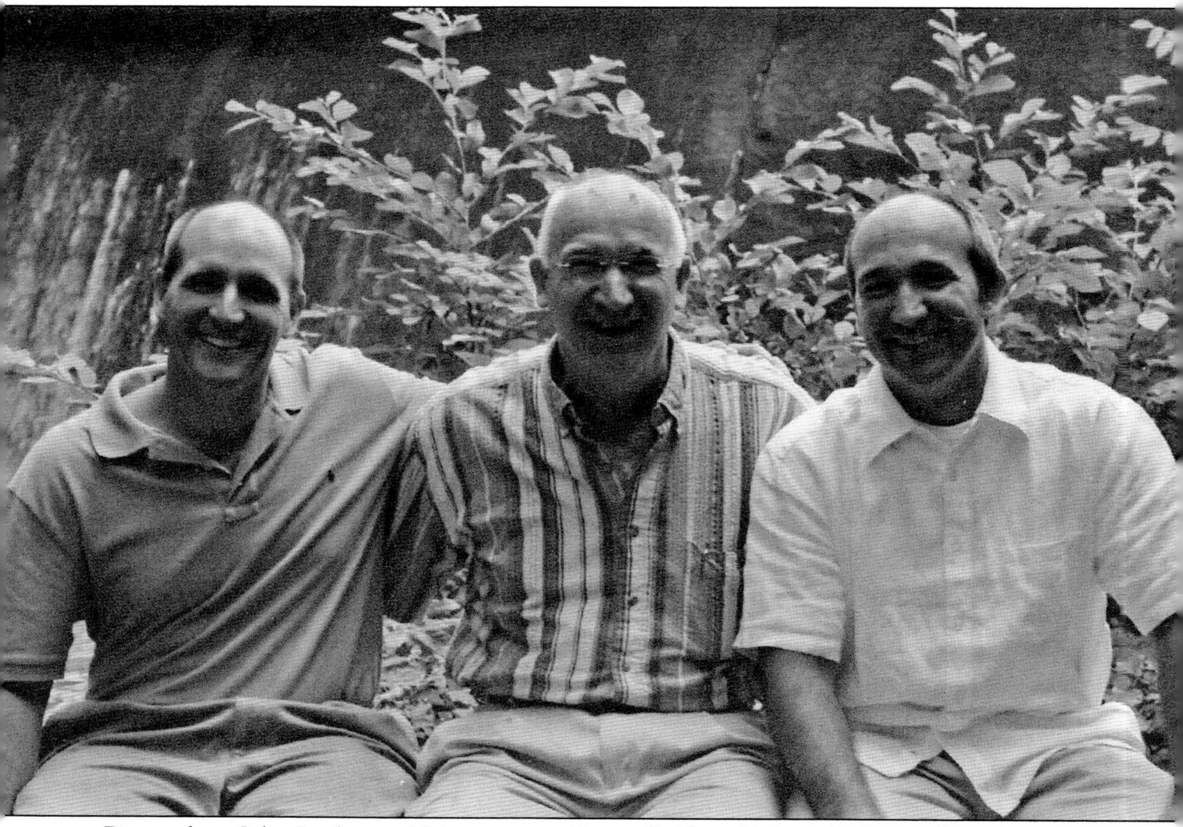

Pictured are John Jordan and his two sons, Carter (left) and Mac, which was short for McLean. Having studied downtown revitalization and public policy while at Duke, Mac believed the best way to save a community's future was to save its past. Mac pursued a masters degree in Architecture from North Carolina State University. His thesis topic was a plan to renovate the Saxapahaw Upper Mill. The Jordans bought back the mill property from Dixie Yarns, who closed it after it was damaged by a tornado in 1994. Mac, charged by his dad to "handle the mill project," called on his brother Carter for help. Carter, who lived in Jackson Hole, Wyoming, flipped a coin to decide his fate. The coin landed on heads, and Carter packed for home. The brothers immediately moved into the vacant spinning mill. Walking out into the empty mill at night to go to the bathroom and having their skin turn orange from the water flowing through the rusty pipes was just part of the job in Mac's mind. Carter recalls one night his dog started growling, his hair standing up at some straight light. Maybe the ghost of Papa Jordan was working late that night. Through the mill flood of Hurricane Fran in 1996 and the fire in 2005, the history of Saxapahaw and the Jordan family continues as Mac and Carter work to finish the revitalization of their grandfather's mill. Once done, a village will be complete, and a wood pile a little higher. (Courtesy of John Jordan.)

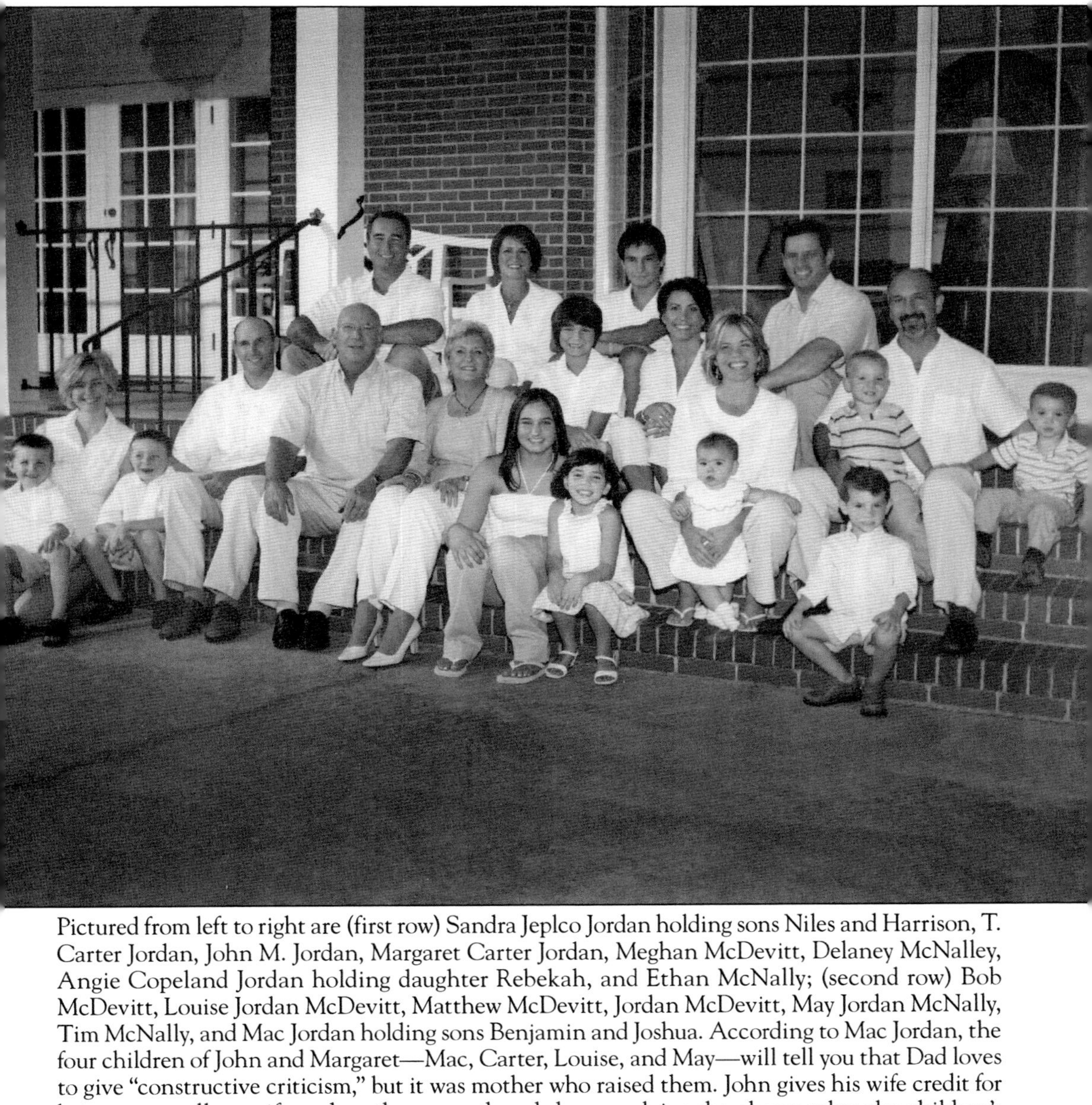

Pictured from left to right are (first row) Sandra Jeplco Jordan holding sons Niles and Harrison, T. Carter Jordan, John M. Jordan, Margaret Carter Jordan, Meghan McDevitt, Delaney McNalley, Angie Copeland Jordan holding daughter Rebekah, and Ethan McNally; (second row) Bob McDevitt, Louise Jordan McDevitt, Matthew McDevitt, Jordan McDevitt, May Jordan McNally, Tim McNally, and Mac Jordan holding sons Benjamin and Joshua. According to Mac Jordan, the four children of John and Margaret—Mac, Carter, Louise, and May—will tell you that Dad loves to give "constructive criticism," but it was mother who raised them. John gives his wife credit for being an excellent wife and mother even though he complains she always takes the children's side. The siblings roll their eyes when their dad argues they had it easy compared to him. John said his mother, an English teacher, would discipline him when he was not trying hard enough to read, and his father never told him he was proud. That may be true, but according to Uncle Ben and Aunt Rosie, their brother John always got whatever he wanted! A combination of John's work ethic and Margaret's selflessness and unwavering faith, Mac and Carter, along with their sisters, are extremely close.

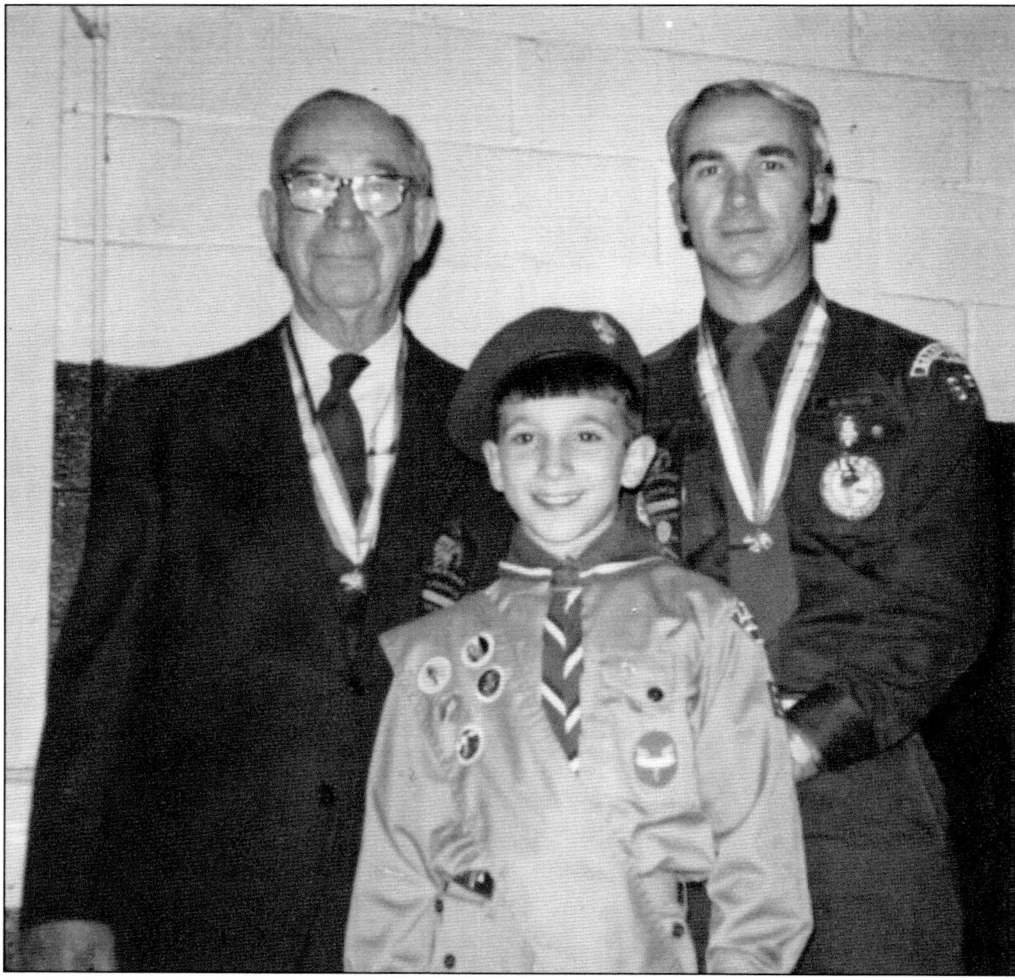

In this last known photograph of Senator Jordan (left), taken in 1973 before his illness and passing in 1974, are three generations of dedicated Scouting. John Jordan (right) and his father both received the Silver Beaver award, which is the highest award one can receive in a Boy Scout council. In the center is John Jordan's son Mac Jordan who, along with his brother, Carter, became an Eagle Scout. This is John Jordan's favorite photograph. He wishes his father was alive today to see what a wonderful job the whole family has done with Saxapahaw's progression and keeping his father's vision alive. (Courtesy of John Jordan.)

# *Four*

# THE SAXAPAHAW FLOOD, TORNADO, AND ICE STORM

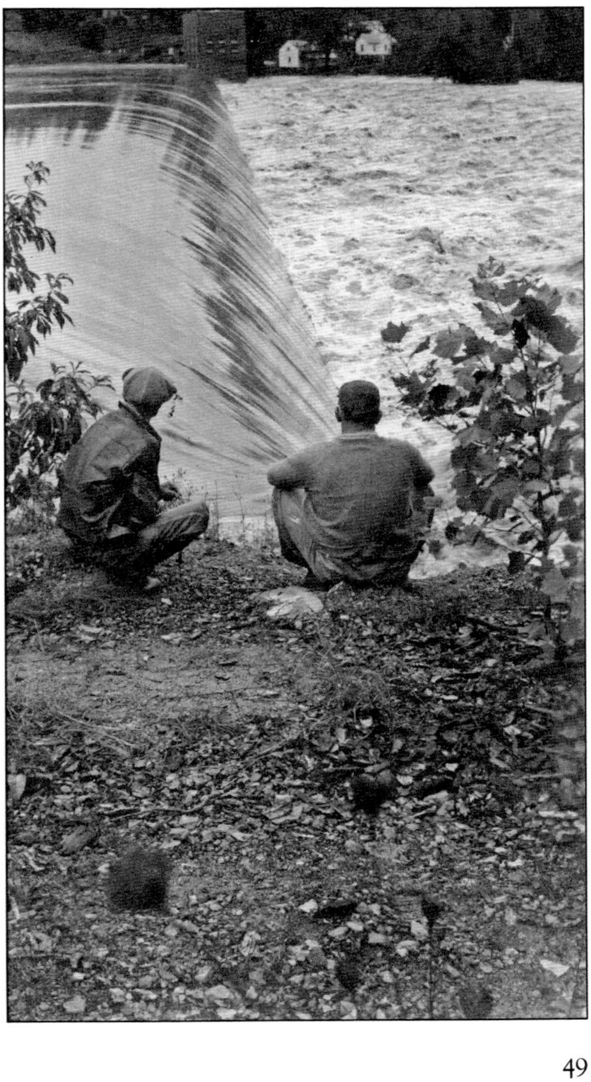

The "100-year flood" happened on September 18, 1945. June Hunter and Adrian "Speedy" Thacker sit on the banks of the Haw River to watch the Saxapahaw Dam overflow. The entire village stopped what they were doing to sit by the river and watch it swallow the island between the two bridges currently known as the Buddy Collins Bridges. Crayton Hardin proclaims that once people move to Saxapahaw and get the red mud between their toes, they never leave. It is believed everyone in the village that day got the red mud between their toes! (Courtesy of Crayton and Frances Hardin.)

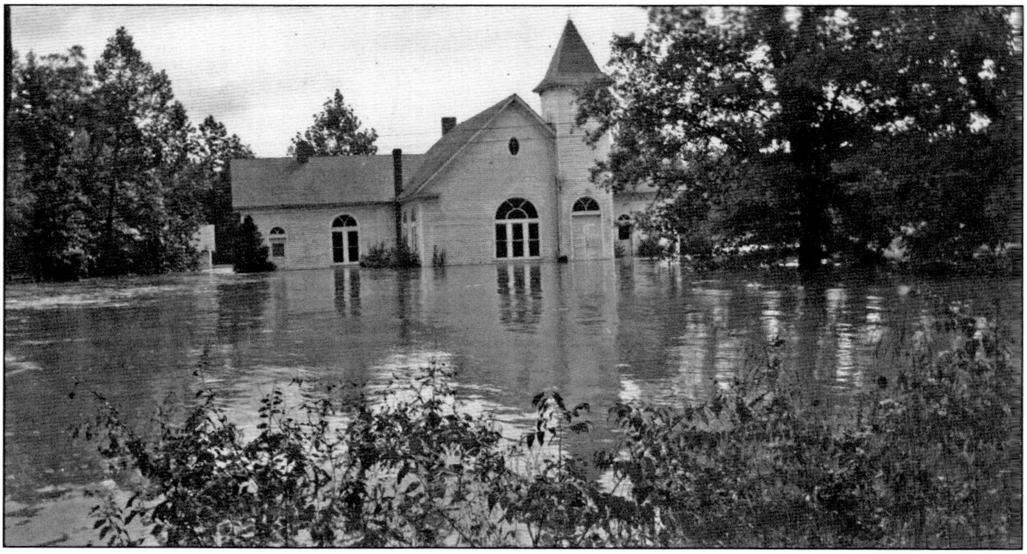

The Saxapahaw United Methodist Church was the main village church for many years. It is located next to Haw River and was significantly impacted by the flood on September 18, 1945. This church was also Sen. B. Everett Jordan's church. The water rose above the church steps and was 2 feet deep inside the church. Church members who worked at the cotton mill lifted the church piano and set it on top of the church pews so it would not sit in water. The water also destroyed the floors of the church. Senator Jordan paid for the floors to be replaced so his daughter (Rose Ann Jordan Gant) could be married in this church in 1949. The senator also paid to protect the church from future floods. (Both courtesy of Crayton and Frances Hardin.)

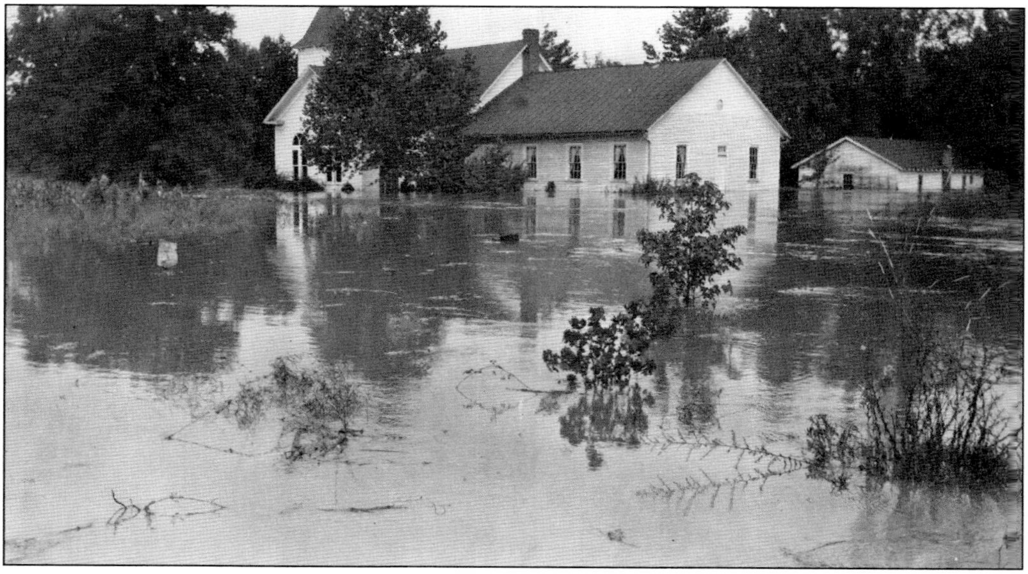

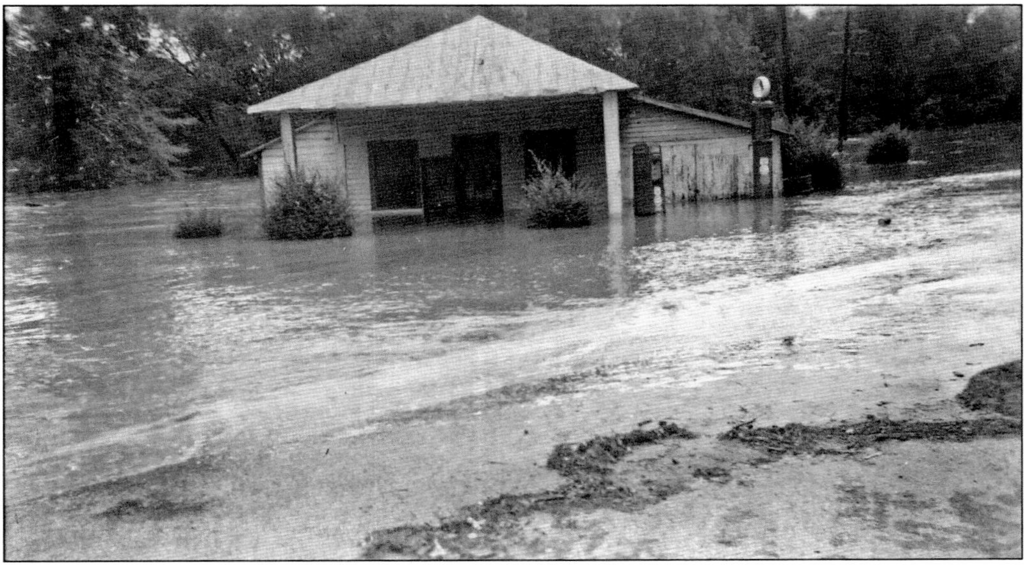

Additional effects of the September 1945 flood are shown here. Above is the filling station, which was never reopened. It was demolished and replaced by the community center, now known as the Buddy Collins Community Center. Below, the water level at the Saxapahaw Cotton Mill was several feet deep. The smallest building in the photograph, with the door open, was the fireproof structure that was built for cigarette-smoking employees. Only two employees were allowed in the smoking building at one time. John Jordan received a phone call from an angry female non-smoking employee that her husband and a smoking female employee were having an affair in the smoking house when they took their cigarette breaks. A coworker told the lady that perhaps she should consider taking up cigarette smoking. (Both courtesy of Crayton and Frances Hardin.)

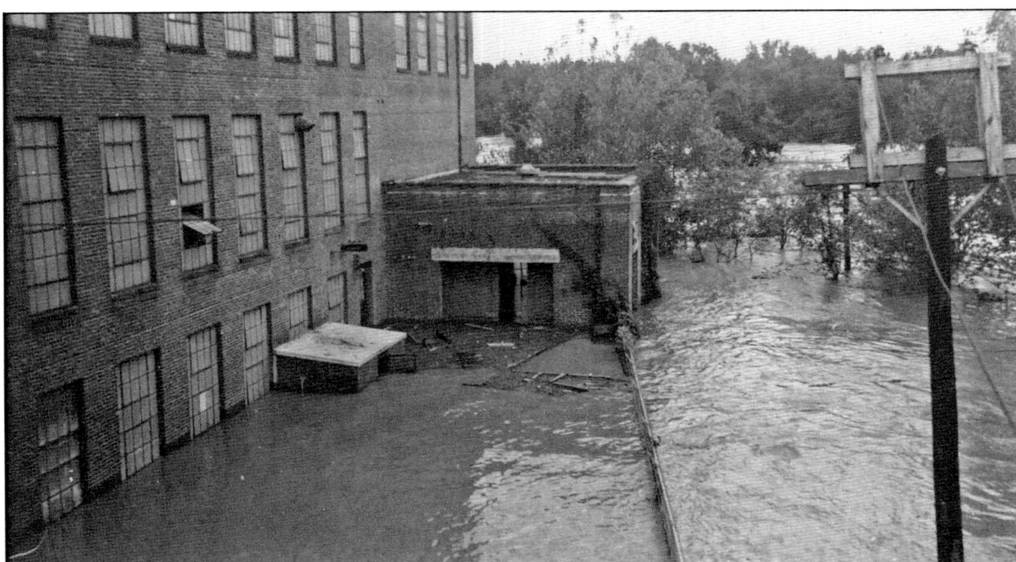

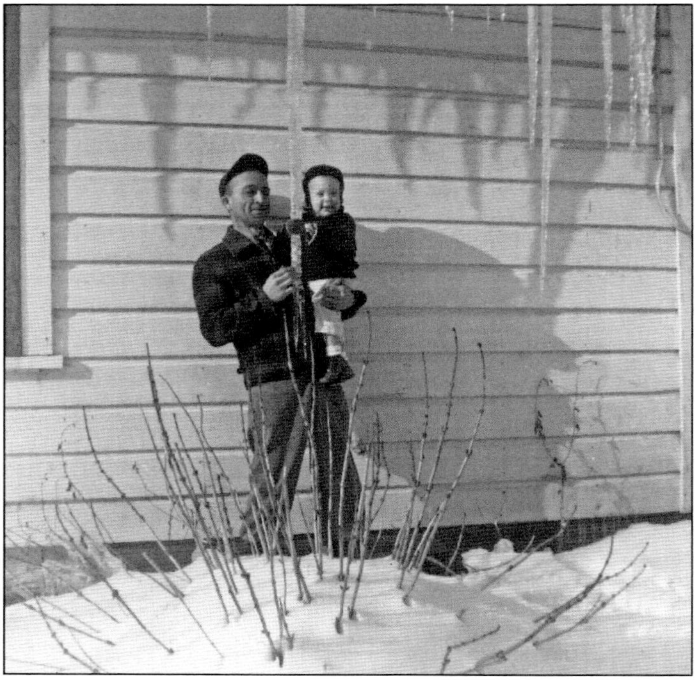

During the ice storm of 1960, D. L. Johnson and son Gary Johnson hold a very long icicle. For Saxapahaw, the average winter daytime temperatures are in the low 50s. Typically Saxapahaw receives only 1 inch of snow per year. The largest recorded single snowfall of Alamance County occurred in 2000 with 14 inches of snow. (Courtesy of Gary Johnson.)

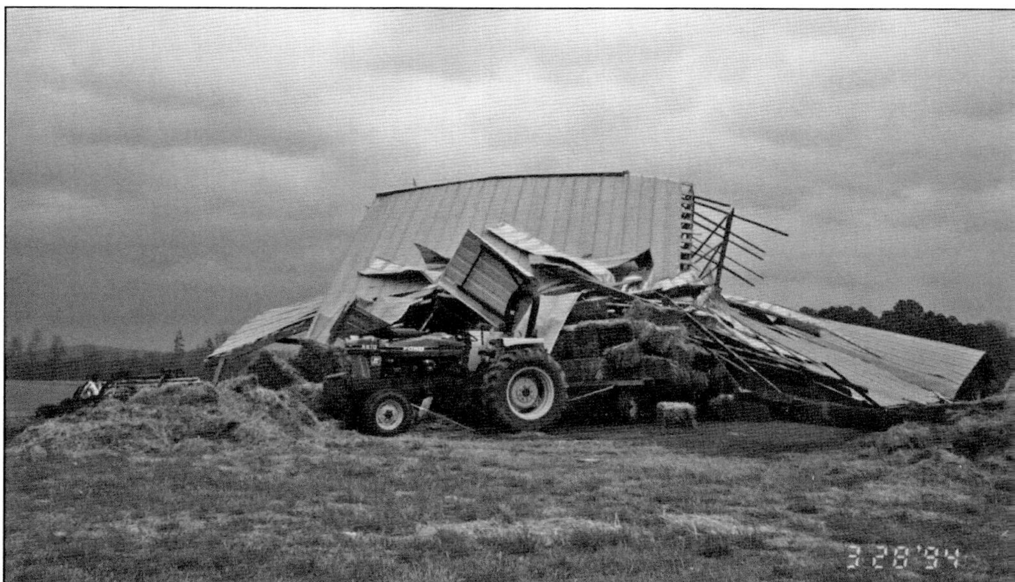


A series of storms dubbed the Palm Sunday Storms roared out of Alabama on March 27, 1994, spawning numerous tornadoes that headed into North Carolina across 40 counties. Forty-four people were killed. This Jordan family hay barn had already been rebuilt after a previous strong storm and another time after a fire was set by small children. This was the same storm that produced the tornado that tore through the Saxapahaw Cotton Mill and closed it down. The only Alamance County fatality resulting from a tornado was caused by F2 to F4 tornadoes from the 1936 Cordele-Greensboro tornado outbreak that affected the Southeastern United States. (Courtesy of John Jordan.)

# *Five*

# HISTORIC PLACES OF SAXAPAHAW

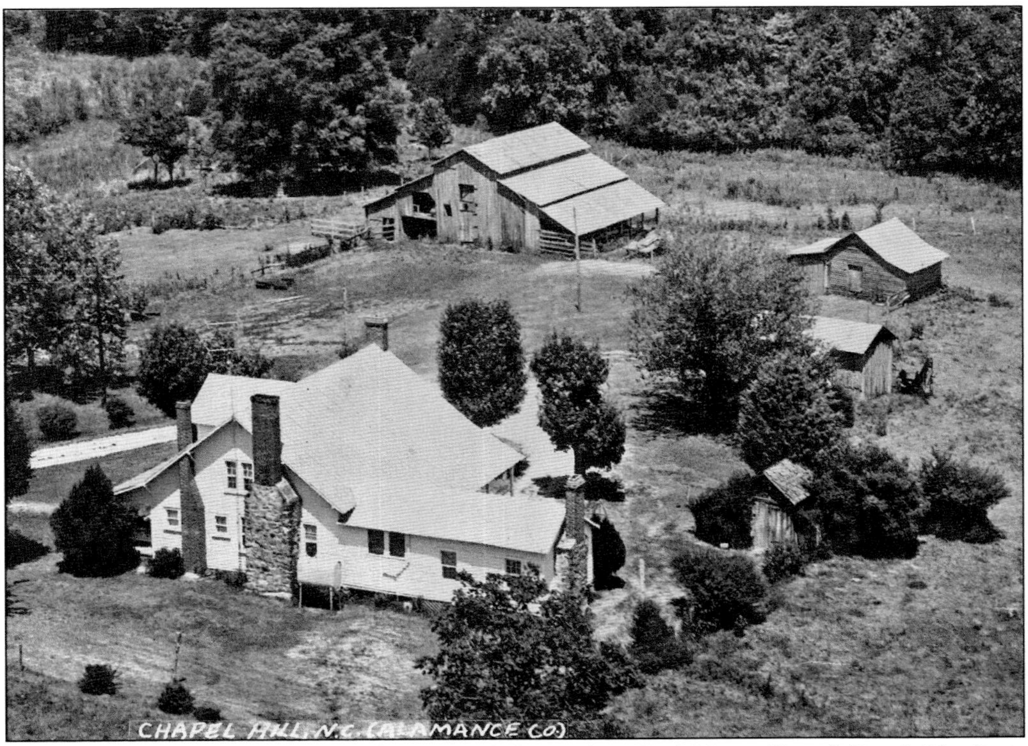


This is an aerial view of the Paris farm at 2147 Saxapahaw Bethlehem Church Road. The Paris Estate was granted the Century Farm Award by the State of North Carolina for having more than 100 years of continuous agricultural heritage within the same family. The farm has been celebrated at the North Carolina State Fair. Marie Paris Buckner still owns and runs the farmland. (Courtesy of Marie P. Buckner.)

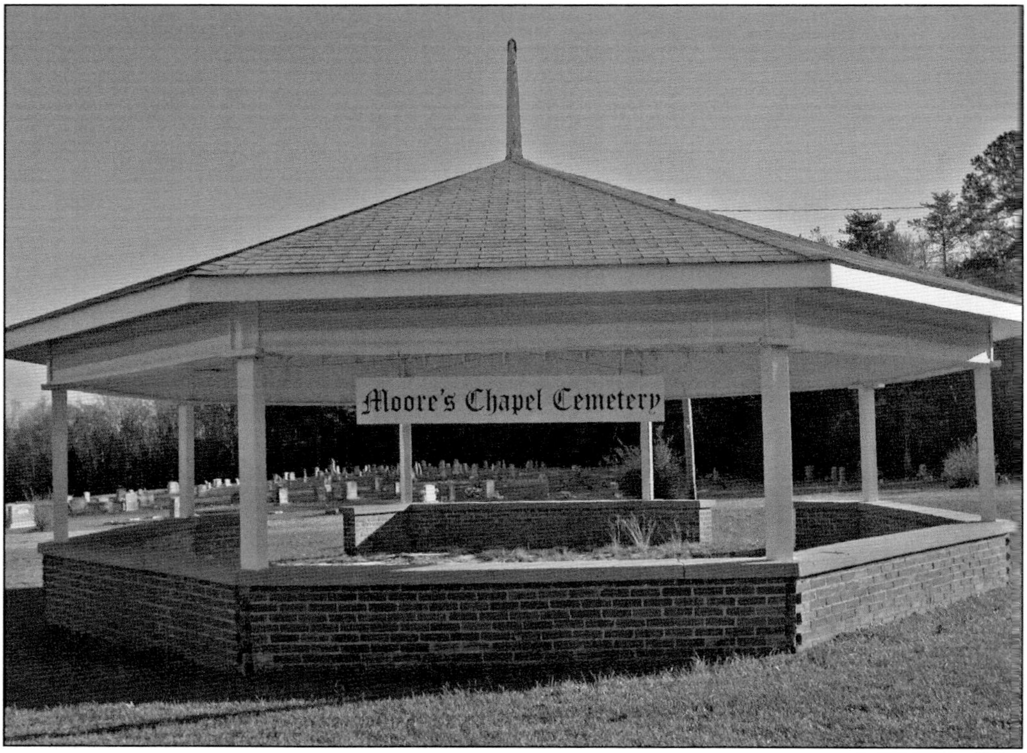


The Moore's Chapel Church Cemetery Pavilion is located on Highway 87 and Moore's Chapel Road. It is historic landmark No. 75. The church was organized in the 1870s. Salvageable oak timbers from the original church were purchased by the late Robert "Bud" Crutchfield and, with the help of Jess Smith, were used to construct the Crutchfield House east of Highway 54 on Mount Willing Road. (Photograph by the author.)

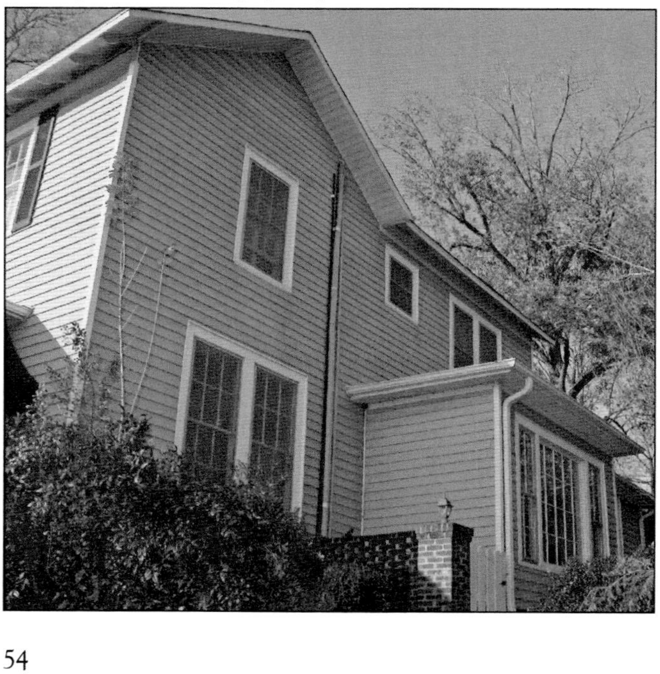

The B. Everett Jordan Home in Saxapahaw, historic landmark No. 57, was built around 1875 opposite the Saxapahaw Cotton Mill and next to the post office. A three-story clapboard home, the first floor of handmade brick, it housed the B. Everett Jordan family, beginning in 1927. The first floor contained the kitchen, from which food was taken up to the dining room on a dumbwaiter. The four rooms on the main (second) floor had brick-covered walls, making the home warmer in the winter and cooler in the summer. The home still belongs to the Jordan family. (Photograph by the author.)

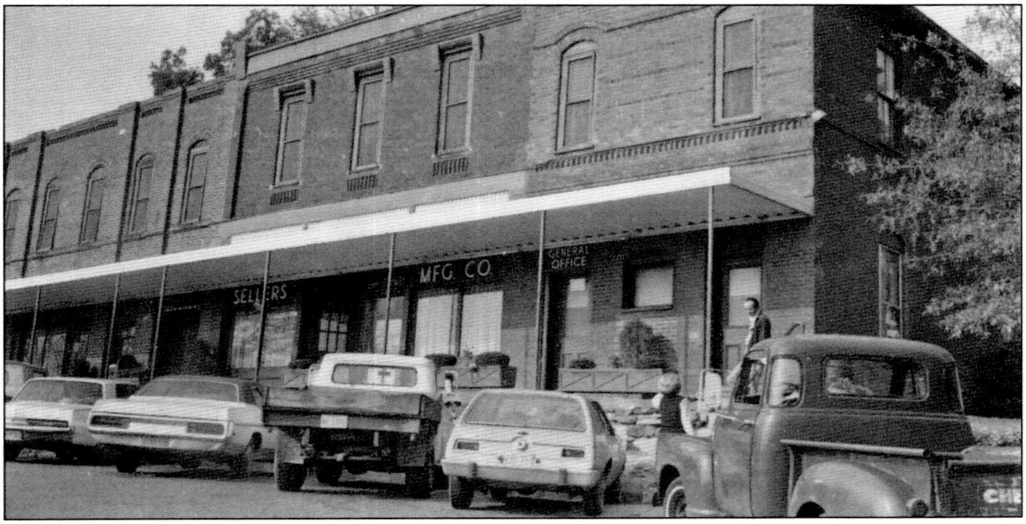


The original mill stores are opposite the Saxapahaw Mill at 1616 Jordan Drive. The original store buildings currently house Jordan Properties and the Saxapahaw Post Office. This is what the Saxapahaw Mill Company businesses (Alamance County Historic Code D-10-15) looked like when Sellers Manufacturing owned the Saxapahaw Cotton Mill and the associated 66 buildings. (Courtesy of Alamance County Planning Department, Chris Ong.)

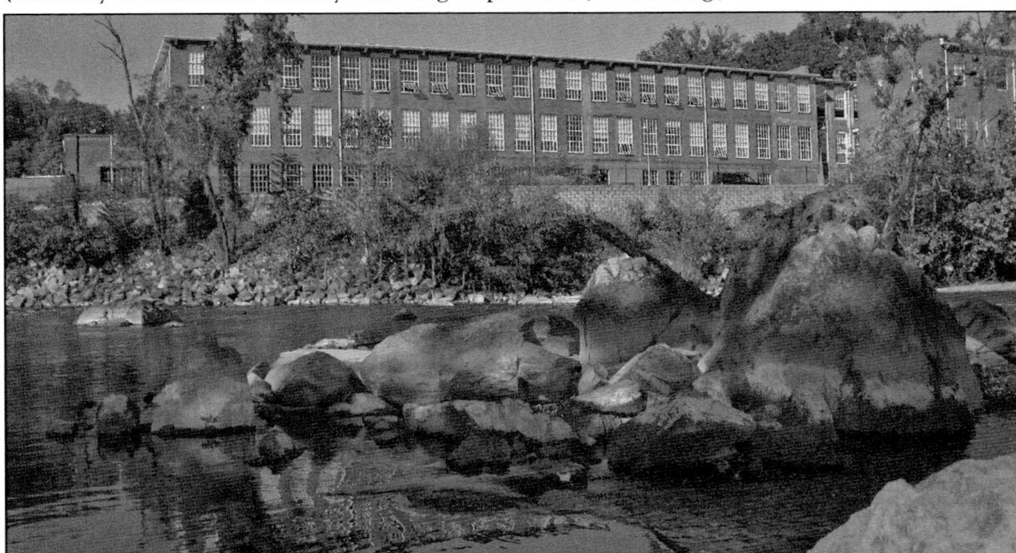

The former Saxapahaw Spinning Mill (added in 1998 to the National Register of Historic Places, No. 98000546) stood at 1647 Saxapahaw Bethlehem Church Road. The mill operated from 1844 to 1994. Starting out with fewer than 1,000 spindles, the company expanded in size until, at its peak, it employed 1,000 people and operated approximately 75,000 spindles. In 1930, the company began producing mercerized combed yarns and, in 1931–1932, established one of the South's first silk-throwing plants for making raw Japanese silk into thread for the hosiery industry. Jordan Spinning Company was created alongside the mill in 1941. By 1961, Sellers and Jordan Spinning produced a wide range of knitting and weaving yarns—combed, carded, nylon blends, dyed and natural, mercerized, and stretch. (Photograph by the author.)

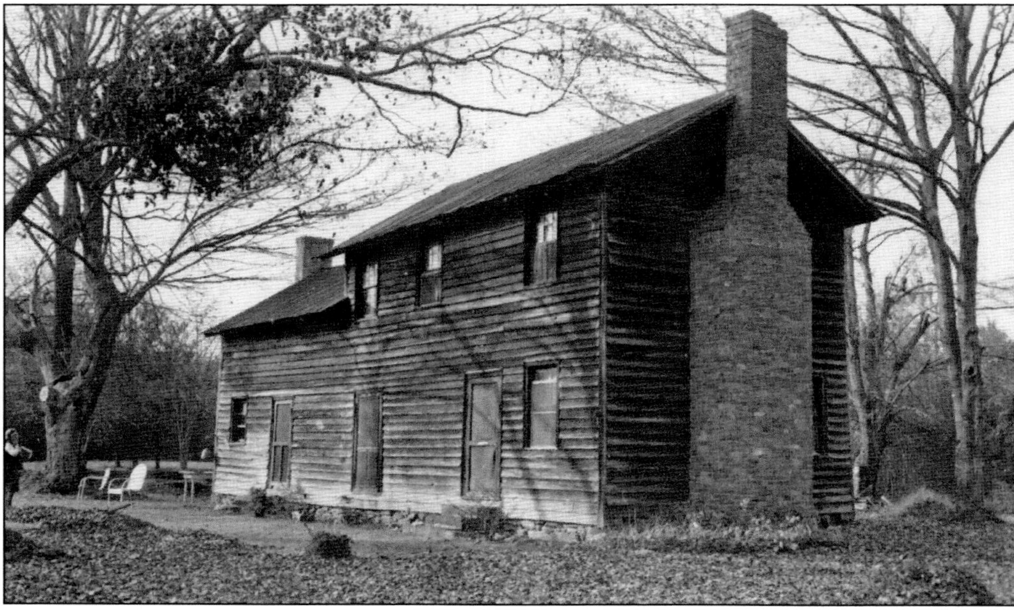

Shady Rest, the James Monroe Thompson House—historic landmark No. 82 (D-9-10)—stood at 5728 Swepsonville-Saxapahaw Road and entered the National Register of Historic Places in 1993. When Union soldiers invaded Saxapahaw during the Civil War, looting homes and businesses, the family hid their china in the outhouse. The home is currently the summer residence for James Monroe's granddaughter, the lovely Dorothy Jobe Crawford, who grew up at Shady Rest with her brother, Adrian; her mother, Maggie Thompson Jobe; and her grandmother, Rebecca "Becky" Patton Thompson. The home was originally a centerpiece to 123 acres of land and now sits on 2.4 acres of land. In 1872, when James Monroe married Rebecca, he built a two-story log addition next to the original *c.* 1850 log home. (Courtesy of the Alamance County Planning Department, Chris Ong.)

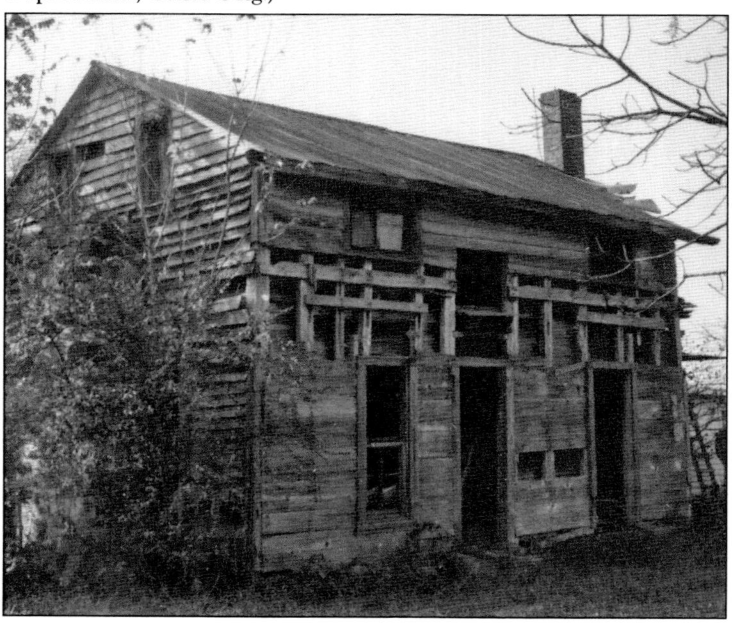

Part of the Nathanial Woody Home, or "Natty Home"—Alamance County Historic Code D-10-12—is shown here. John Woody received a land grant from England in 1759 when he came to America. Nathanial Woody was the son of John, Samuel Woody was the son of Nathanial, and Frank Woody (Olive Cashwell's father) was the son of Samuel. The new Woody home was built in 1885. (Courtesy of the Alamance County Planning Department, Chris Ong.)

# *Six*

# Events Big and Small

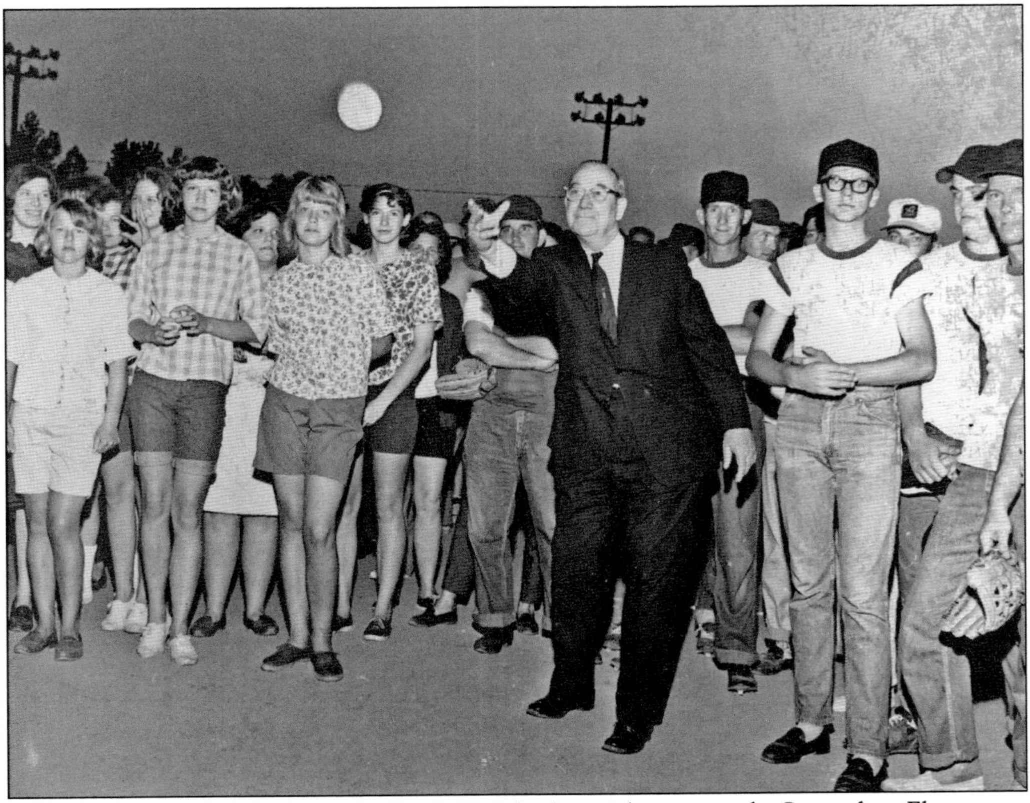

Sen. B. Everett Jordan threw out the first ball of the first night game at the Saxapahaw Elementary ball field. The Saxapahaw ball team is on the right with the spectators on the left. The main people who can be seen in this photograph include Judy Crutchfield (second from left), retired police captain Vickie Neal (third from left), Vivian Crutchfield (fourth from left), Dennis Curtis (third from right), Wayne Crisson (second from right), Harold Knighton (far right). (Courtesy of Edgar Cashwell.)

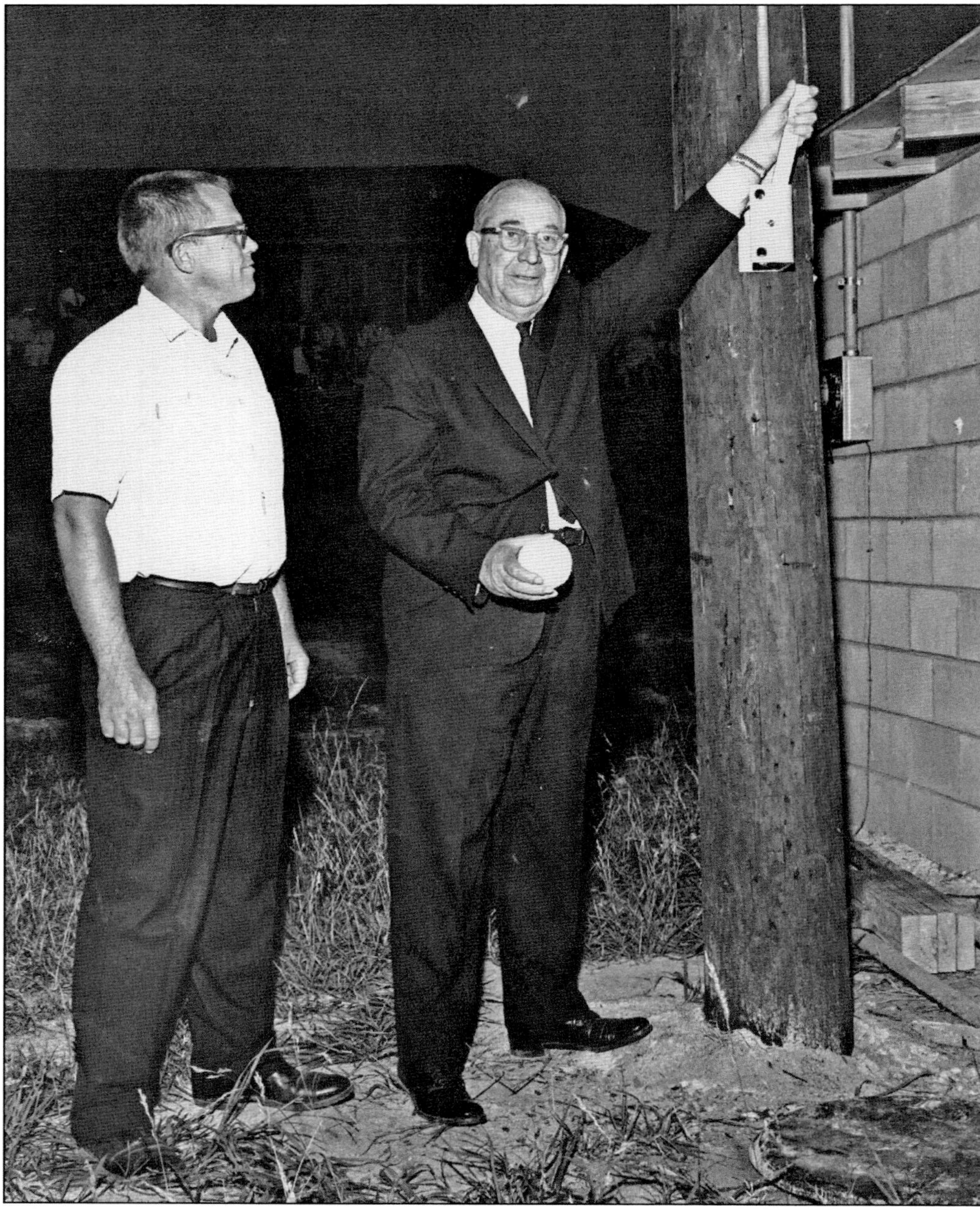

Edgar Cashwell (left) and Senator Jordan are at the Saxapahaw School ball field (now known as B. Everett Jordan Elementary). They are posing for a picture as Senator Jordan gets ready to flip the switch to turn on the new ball field lights for the first night game. When Senator Jordan was approached by Edgar Cashwell, the head of the community center, to donate money for the addition of the lights, he told Edgar he would match the total amount of money that everyone else would donate. Money was raised by having suppers and square dances. The senator kept his word and matched the amount of money donated dollar for dollar. (Courtesy of Edgar Cashwell.)

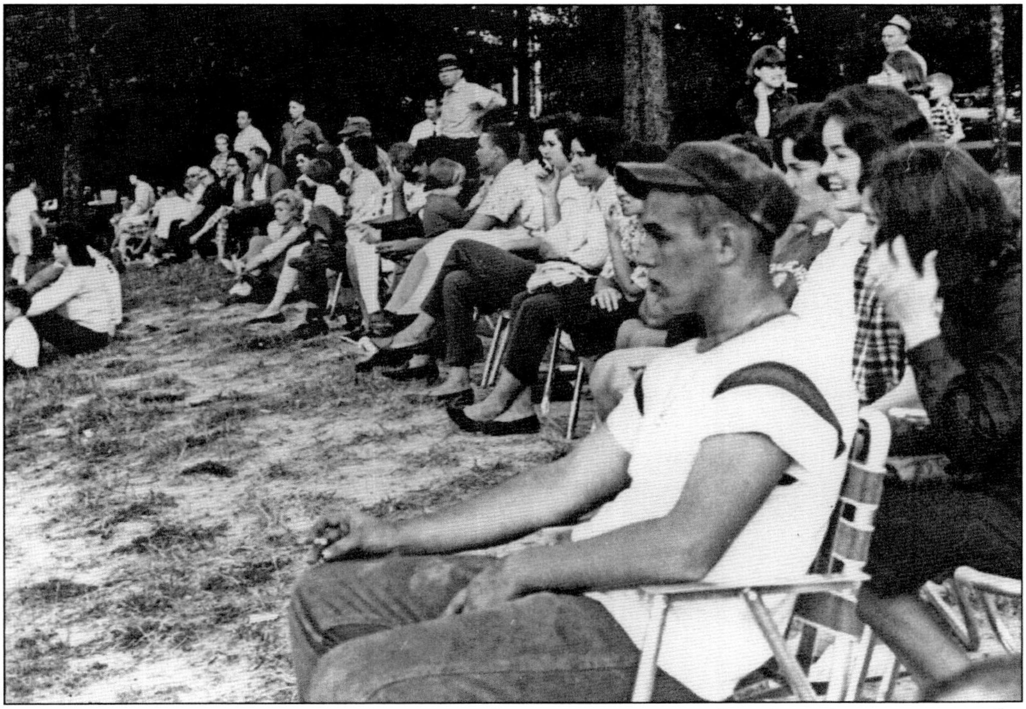

Baseball has been part of Saxapahaw since the 1800s. Many trophies have been given to the Saxapahaw Ball Club. The trophies are kept on display in the Buddy Collins Community Center. The locals are sitting at the back of the ball field waiting for the first-ever night game to begin. Ronald Davis is pictured front and center. (Courtesy of Edgar Cashwell.)

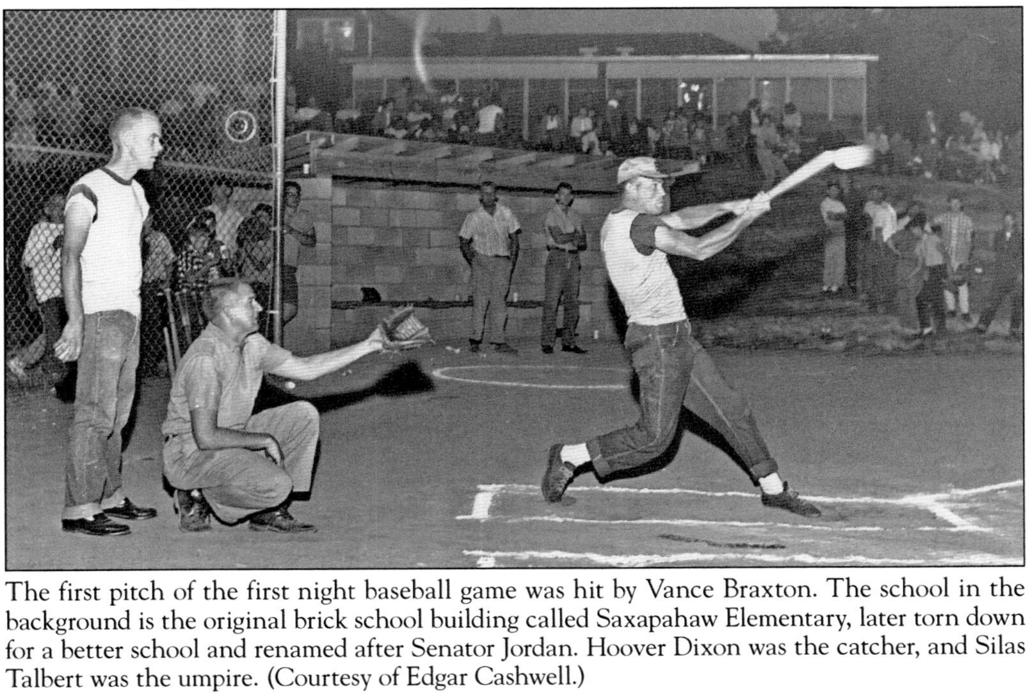

The first pitch of the first night baseball game was hit by Vance Braxton. The school in the background is the original brick school building called Saxapahaw Elementary, later torn down for a better school and renamed after Senator Jordan. Hoover Dixon was the catcher, and Silas Talbert was the umpire. (Courtesy of Edgar Cashwell.)

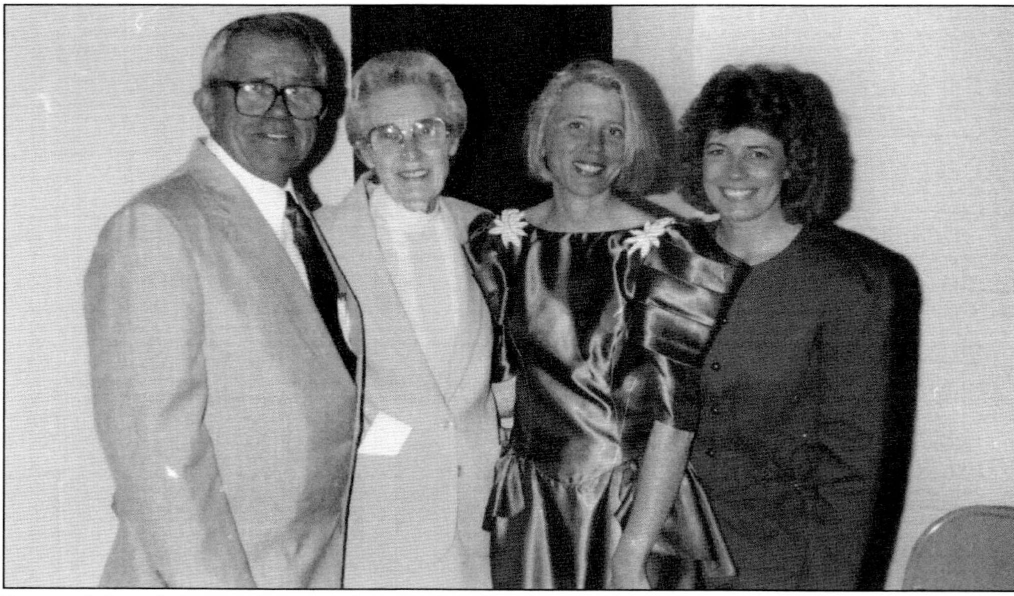

Pictured from left to right are Edgar Cashwell, Olive Cashwell, Ellen Marie Cashwell Caldwell, and Linda Carol Cashwell Franklin. Ellen and Linda became schoolteachers, and Ellen's daughter Grace also wants to be a schoolteacher—all just like Olive! (Courtesy of Edgar Cashwell.)

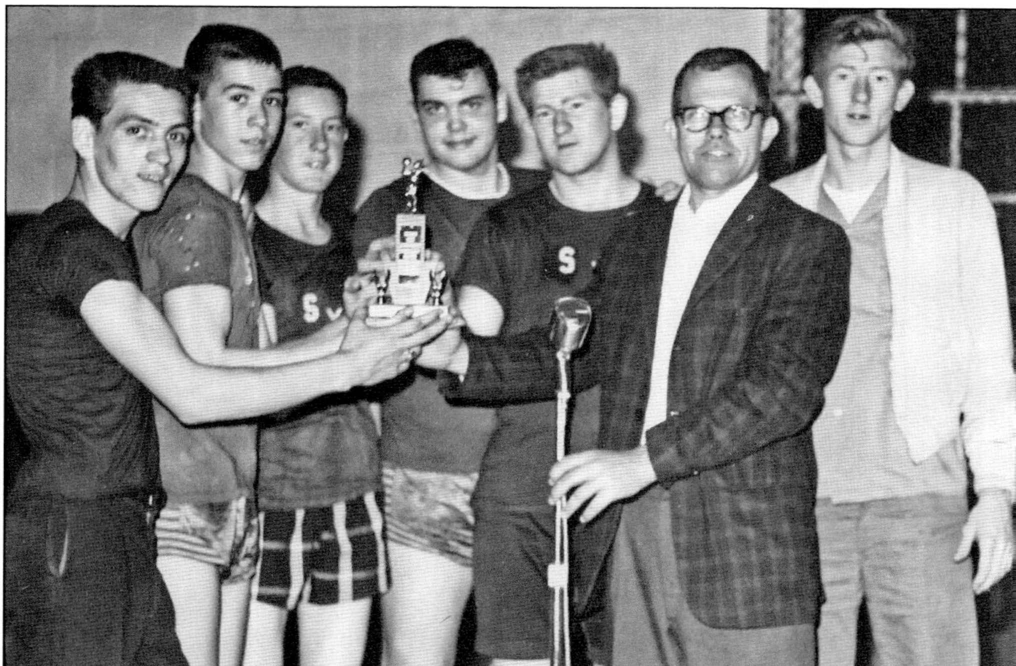

This 1955 photograph was taken after yet another tournament win. Pictured from left to right are Jackie Grumble, of Petty family descent; Steve Madden, Leon Madden's son; Gene Barrett; Wayne Crisson; Billy Gene Knighten; Edgar Cashwell; and Leveritte Knighten, who was part of the bluegrass band the Ramblers. Edgar Cashwell was the head of the community center in which most of the games were played. (Courtesy of Edgar Cashwell and John Petty.)

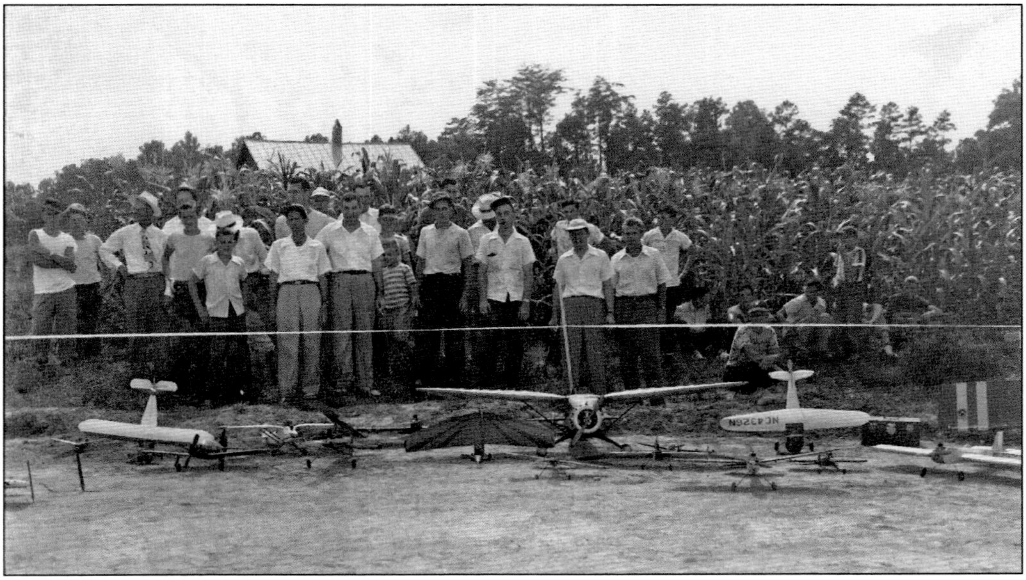

The men and boys of Saxapahaw formed a model airplane club. They would show and circle the planes. The big prize was bragging rights until the next get-together. The Cessna model (No. NC4326N) was first shown to the public in May 1947. This photograph was taken shortly after. Nobody knew Thomas C. Boone (standing second from the right in the cap) was sworn to secrecy during World War II as a cryptographer who broke enemy codes. (Courtesy of Edgar Cashwell.)

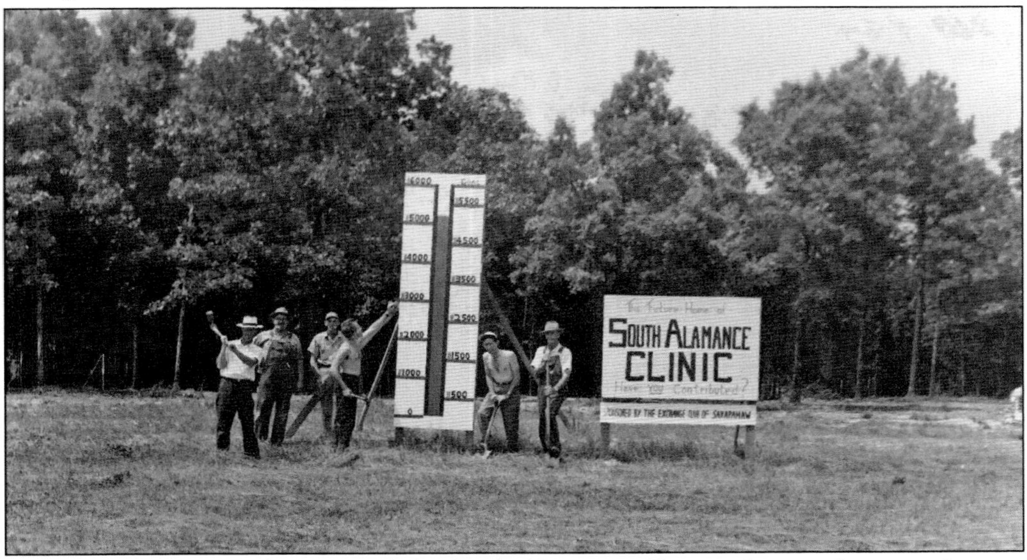


The residents of Saxapahaw wanted the South Alamance Clinic to bring a doctor to the area and held a drive in 1958. The building was later turned into a nursery. From left to right are Bob Roberson, Luther Grumbles, Brooks Corney, Edgar Cashwell, Jake Miller, and Ken Bailey. Luther Grumbles was one of the main carpenters for Saxapahaw. He helped build the Saxapahaw dam. Luther built a building out of cement, sand, and sawdust, which he stamped to make it look like it had boards on it. The home is located on Moores Chapel Cemetary Road. In 1956, Luther fell off the roof of a home onto a bucket of tar and died. Also pictured are Edgar Cashwell, Brooks Covney, Jake Miller, and Ken Bailey. (Courtesy of Edgar Cashwell and John Petty.)

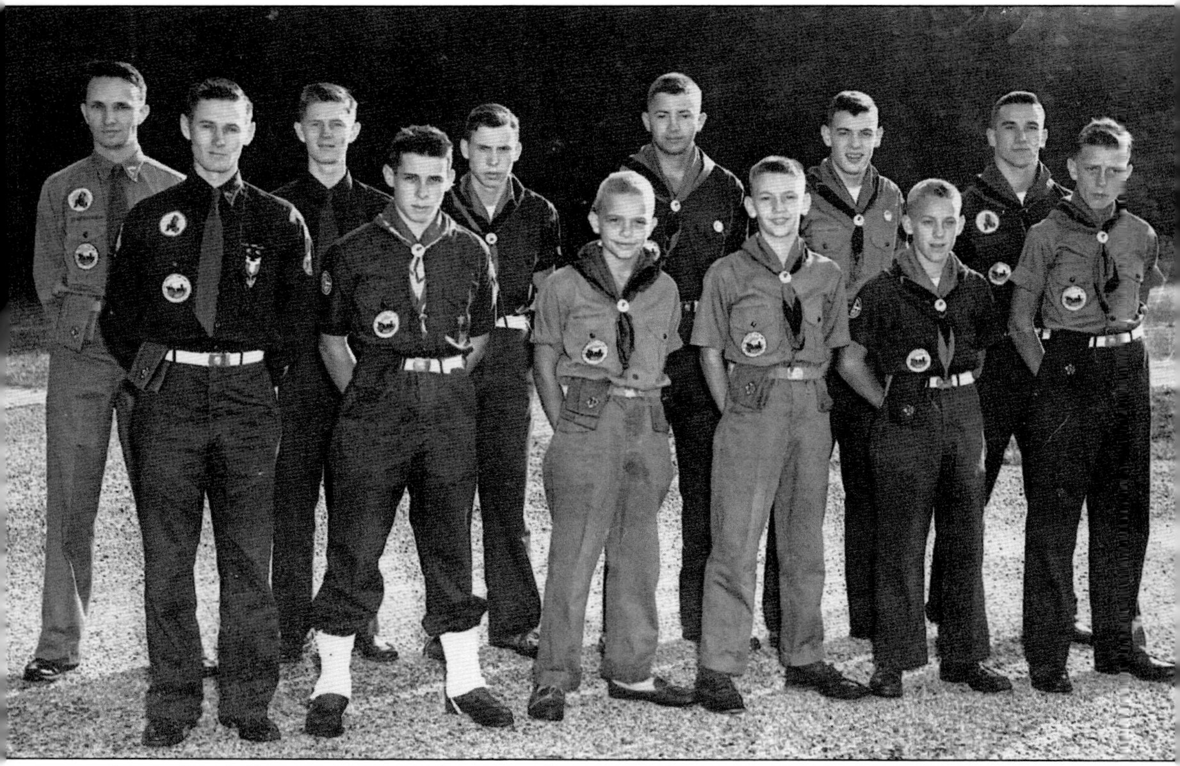

Saxapahaw's Scouting Troop 65 went to the National Scouting Jamboree in 1953 in Santa Ana, California. Gerry Wicker (first row, center) was very poor. The other children raised money so he could have shoes for the trip. He now owns a successful K&B Bootery in Burlington, North Carolina. John Jordan still visits Gerry every year to patronize his shoe store and keep in touch. Also in the photograph are Ben F. Bulla (left, as leader) Jackie Thompson (placement unknown), who was able to put his hands in scalding water without complaint, so the boys always made him do the dishes. Also pictured, in no particular order, are Carson Lloyd, Johny Lloyd, Bill Oberman, James Johnson, Delmer Crisson, Melvin Phillips, John Jordan, and Billy Riley. (Courtesy of John Jordan.)

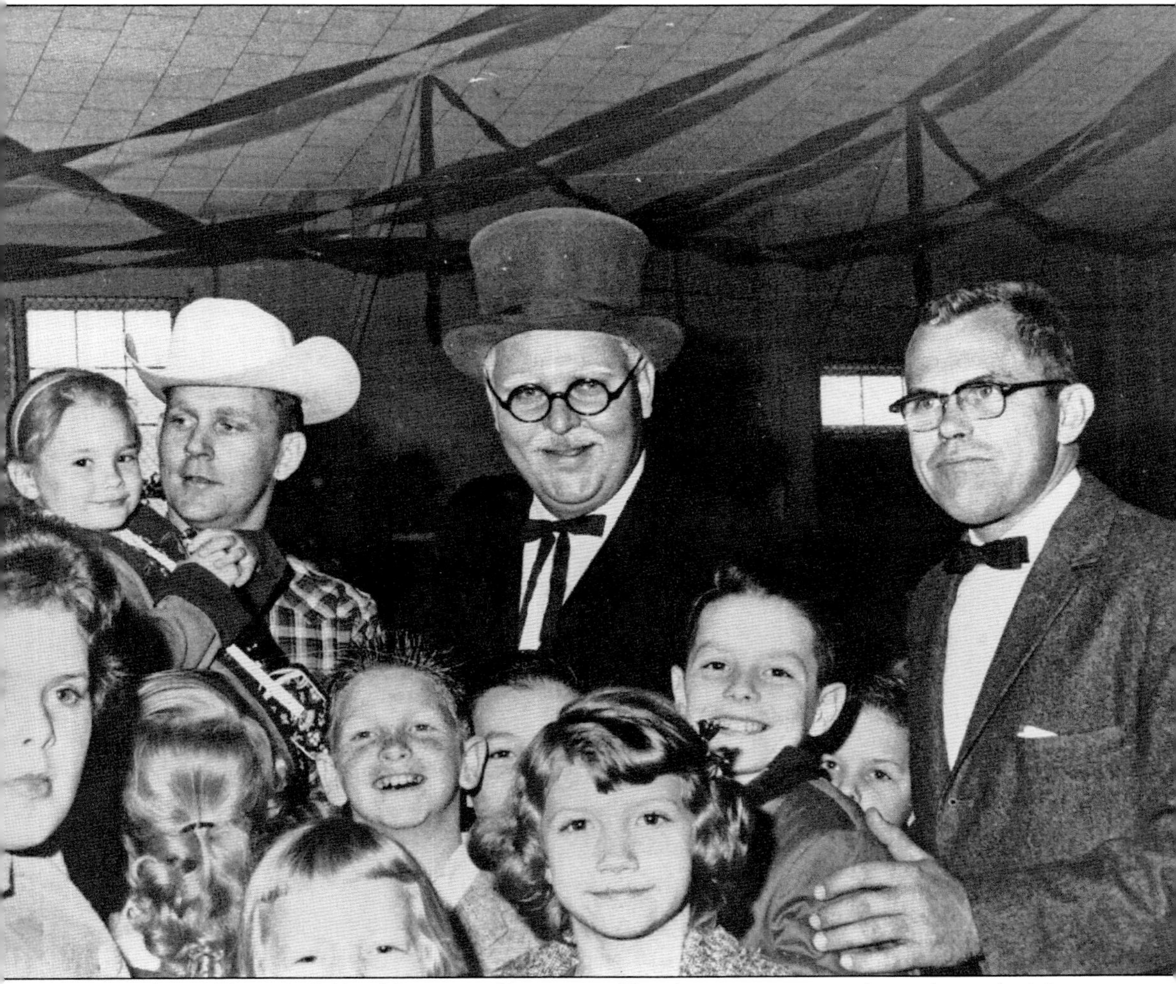

During the 1950s and 1960s, Alamance County could only receive one to three clear television stations (with rabbit ears), but the stars of the hit television series *The Old Rebel and Pecos Pete Show* came to Saxapahaw to visit with local children at the community center. The show aired right after *Captain Kangaroo*. The theme song went, "Some of us are rebels, and some are buckaroos, and we are very helpful, from our helmets to our shoes, and when we're asked to lend a hand, we never do refuse, 'cause some of us are rebels, and some are buckaroos." Miss Stanford can be seen on the far left. Judy Crutchfield is front and center, and the boy to her left is Wayne Crutchfield. Edgar Cashwell is on the far right with his hand on E. A. Bundren's shoulder. (Courtesy of Edgar Cashwell.)

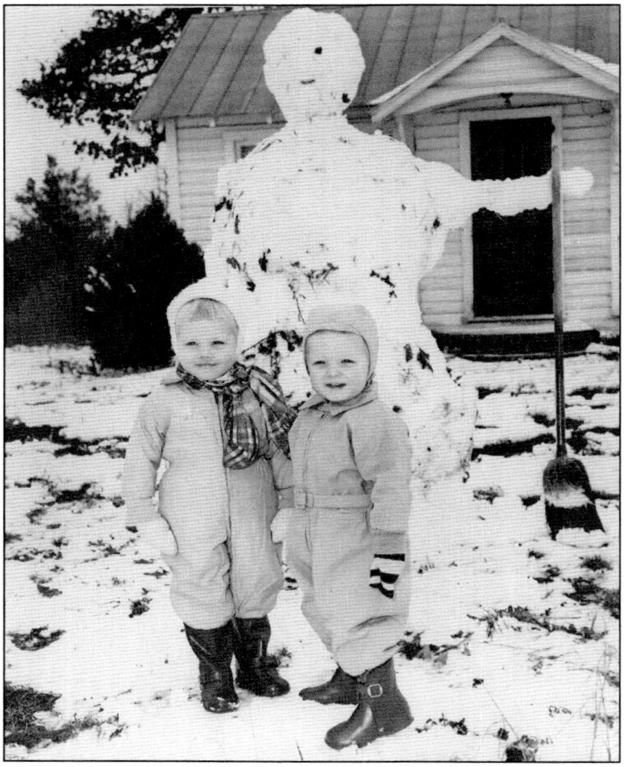

Edgar and Olive Cashwell's daughter Linda and her cousin Rusty play here in a rare snowfall in Saxapahaw. (Courtesy of Edgar and Linda Cashwell.)

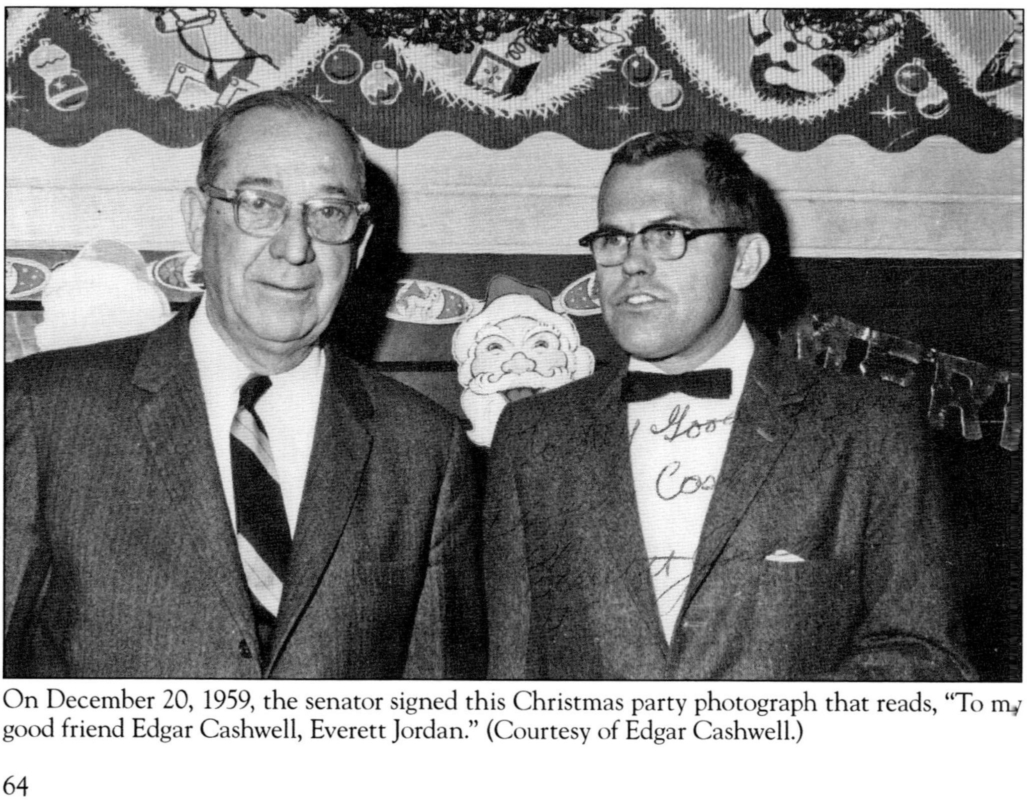

On December 20, 1959, the senator signed this Christmas party photograph that reads, "To my good friend Edgar Cashwell, Everett Jordan." (Courtesy of Edgar Cashwell.)

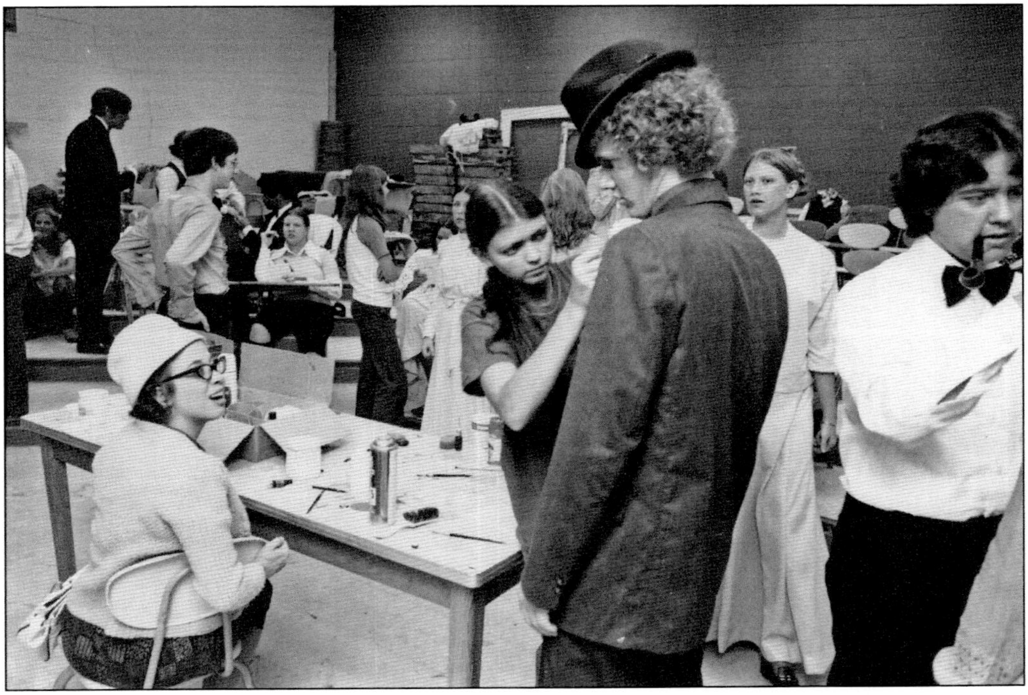

The high school for Saxapahaw students was Southern Alamance High School. In 1975, classmates put on the musical *Mame*. Cast included, from left to right, Brenda Richardson (seated with hat); Lisa McPherson (pinning); Jimmy Teague (with hat); and Gary Johnson (with the pipe in his mouth). (Courtesy of Gary Johnson.)

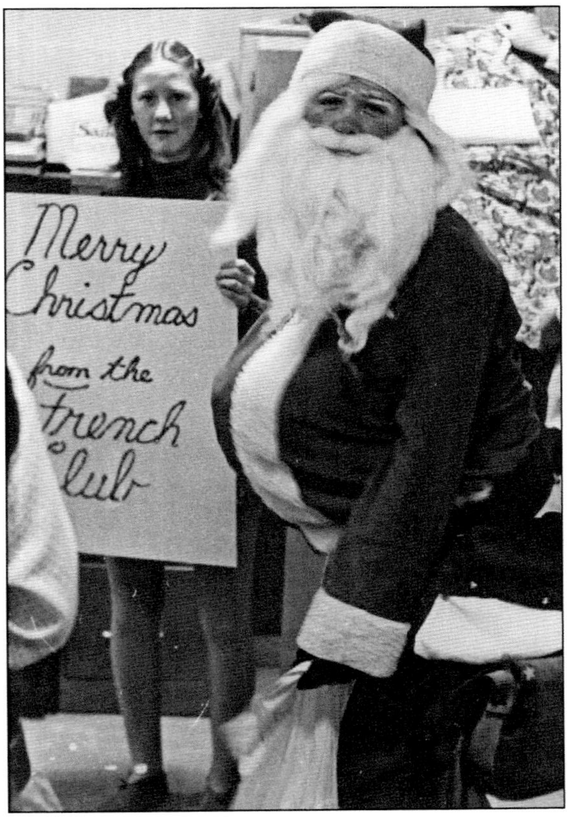


The French Club held a Christmas party in 1974. Debbie Bumgardner, holding the sign, graduated in 1976. The person dressed as Santa Claus is unidentified. Notable Southern Alamance High School graduates include Chris Conklin, a tight end with the Carolina Panthers. Alan Dinh Lam, U.S. Marine Corps lance corporal, a 2001 graduate of Southern Alamance, died in Iraq in 2003. (Courtesy of Gary Johnson.)

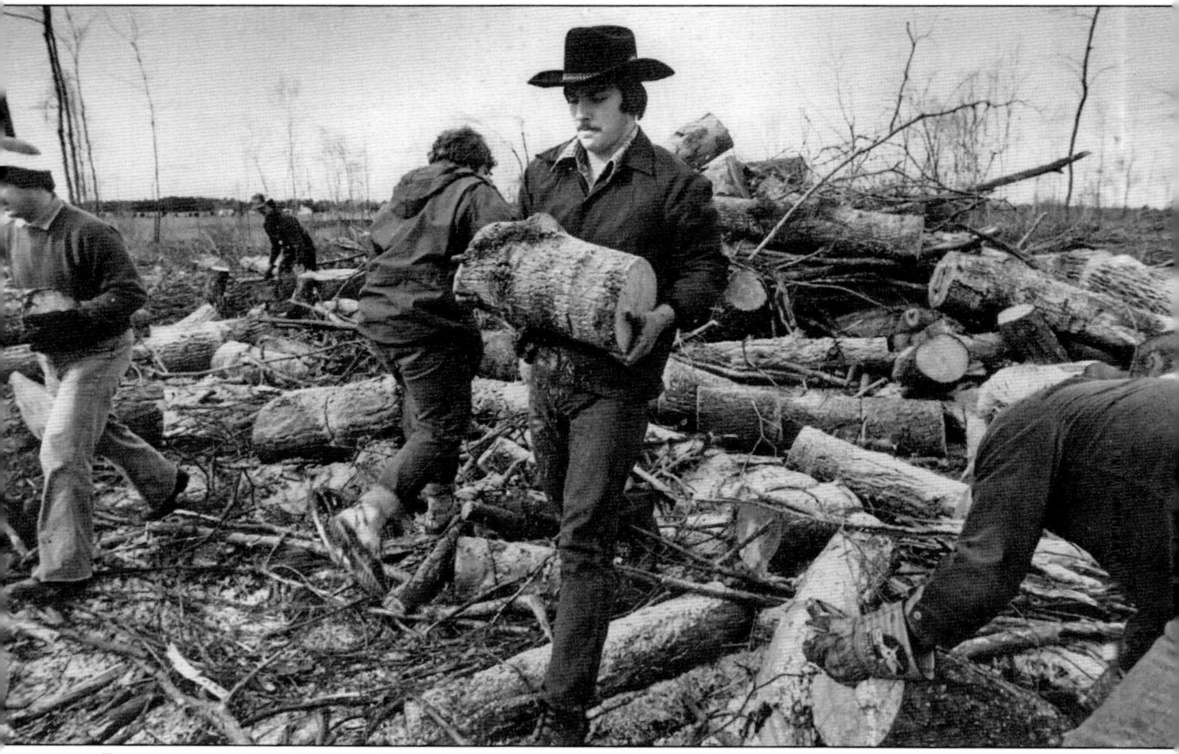

During an 18-week period in 1979, some 14 members of Explorer Troop 65 of Saxapahaw cut, hauled, split, and loaded firewood from a 100-acre tract of land donated by the Jordan family. They gave the wood away for "free" and earned $750 in donations to help finance the troop's scuba diving trip to Florida. Although folks were plenty charitable with their donations, Bill Thompson (with hat) was in excruciating pain when he pulled a hernia by helping a man who wanted a 100-pound chunk of wood hauled. The man drove off without giving a hand or saying a word. The troop also carried a load of wood 30 minutes to Burlington to a woman on welfare who could not afford to pay for the wood to heat her home. This land was later filled with 26,000 white pine trees paid for by John M. Jordan to create a natural barrier for the new Energy Star home development called Haw Village. (Courtesy of John Jordan.)

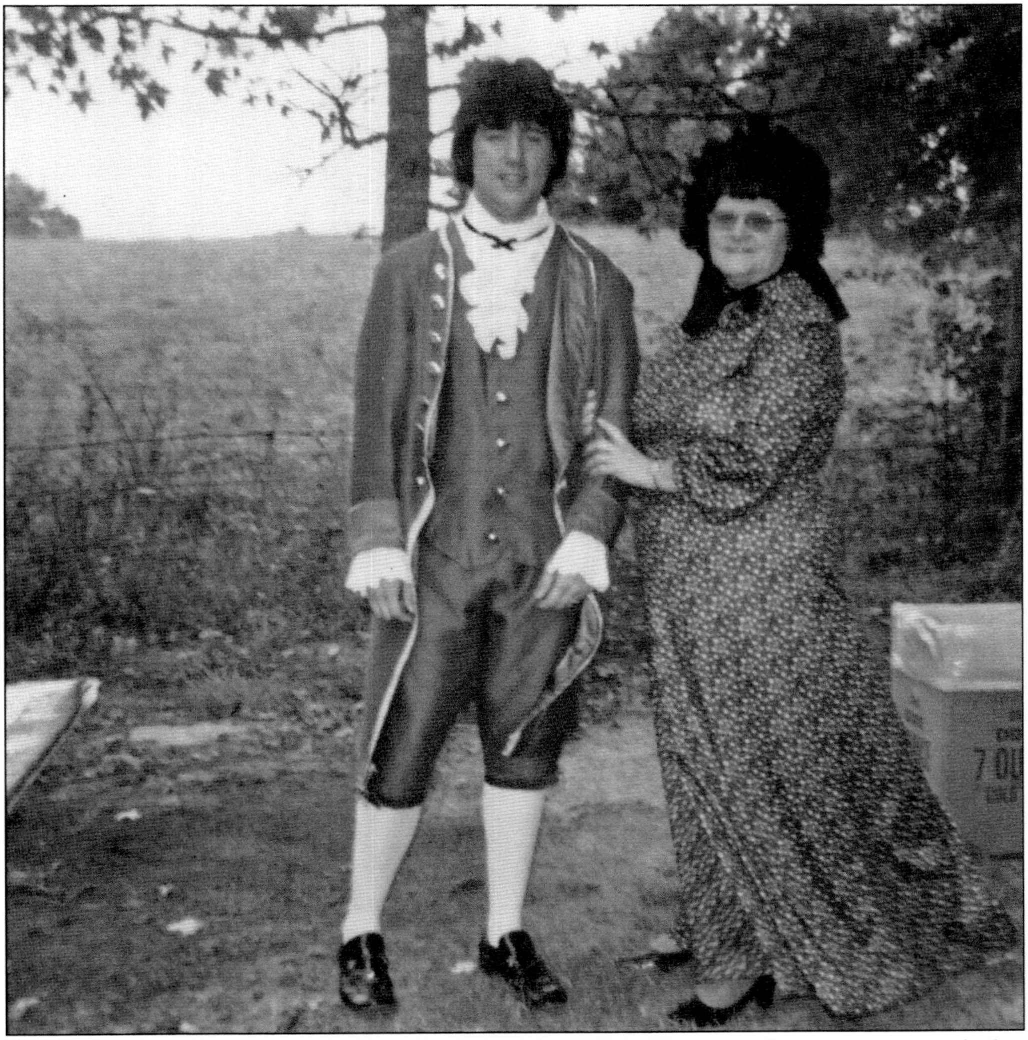

Gary Johnson and Margaret Johnson are pictured in 1976. Alamance County was named after the Great Alamance Creek (11 miles long), site of the Battle of Alamance (May 16, 1771), a pre–Revolutionary War battle in which militia under the command of Gov. William Tryon crushed the Regulator movement. According to legend, the Great Alamance Creek and, in turn, the Little Alamance Creek, were named after a local Native American word of the Sissipahaw Indians to describe the blue mud found at the bottom of the creeks. (Courtesy of Gary Johnson.)

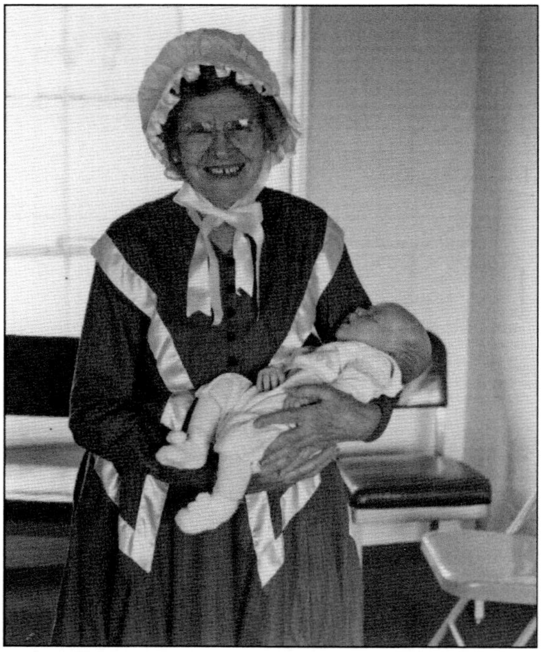

Bessie Woody Nall celebrates Founder's Day in 1989. Bessie married Rev. Luther Nall of the Calvary Baptist Church. The baby could have been any one of her honorary grandchildren. Jerrie Nall of Nall Printing remembers Bessie as always being involved within the church and community. (Courtesy of Gary Johnson.)

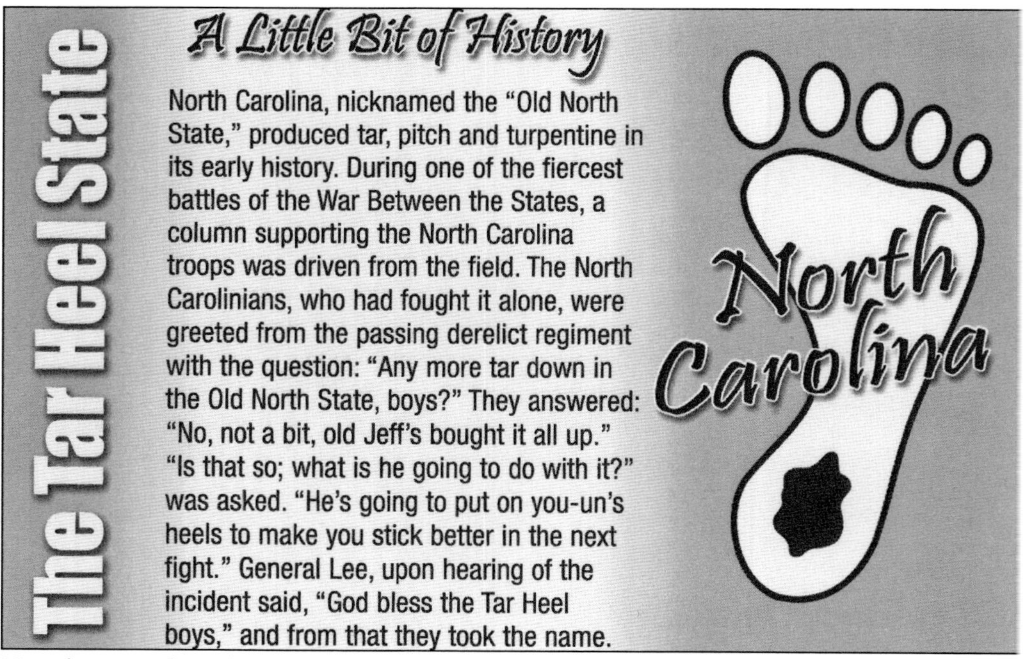


How the state of North Carolina and its people started being referred to as "tar heels" is a common local discussion. The exact origin of the nickname is truly unknown, but most experts believe its roots come from the fact that tar, pitch, and turpentine created from the vast pine tree forests were some of North Carolina's most important exports early in the state's history. Some experts believe tar heel was a nickname given during the U.S. Civil War because of the state's importance on the Confederate side and the fact that the troops "stuck to their ranks like they had tar on their heels." (Courtesy of the author.)

Howard Coble (left) and Edgar Cashwell are shown at one of the Redbud Festival fund-raisers in Saxapahaw. Congressman Howard Coble received his doctor of law degree from the University of North Carolina School of Law in Chapel Hill. He has been serving the Sixth District of North Carolina since 1985. He was also commanding officer of the U.S. Coast Guard Reserve Unit, Wilmington, North Carolina. Edgar is wearing his official appointed ham radio call sign on his T-shirt and hat. (Courtesy of Edgar Cashwell.)

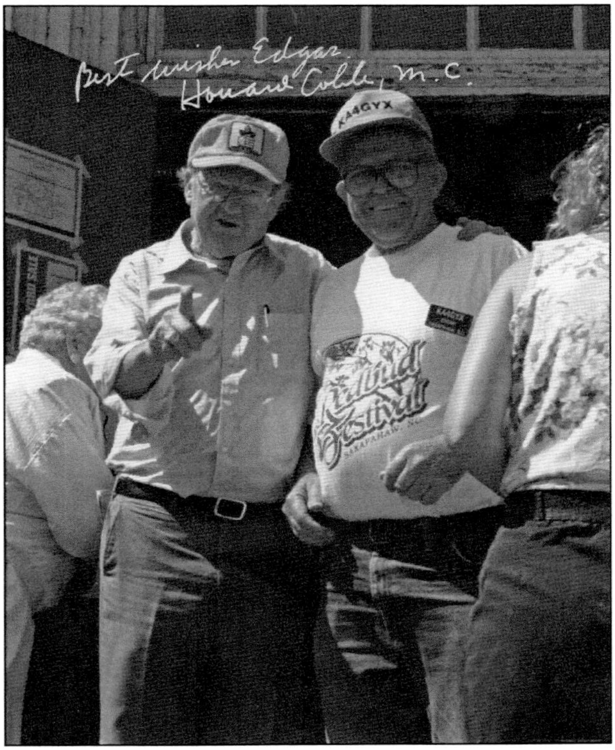


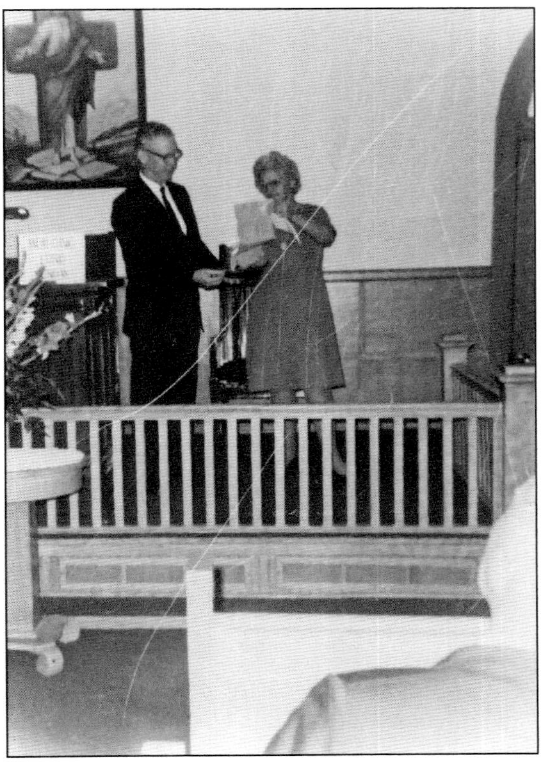

Myrtle Mann and Rev. Gaither B. Reich of Saxapahaw Friend's Church are shown here at the burning of the mortgage in the 1970s. Afterward, they realized they accidentally burned the deed. (Courtesy of Gary Johnson.)

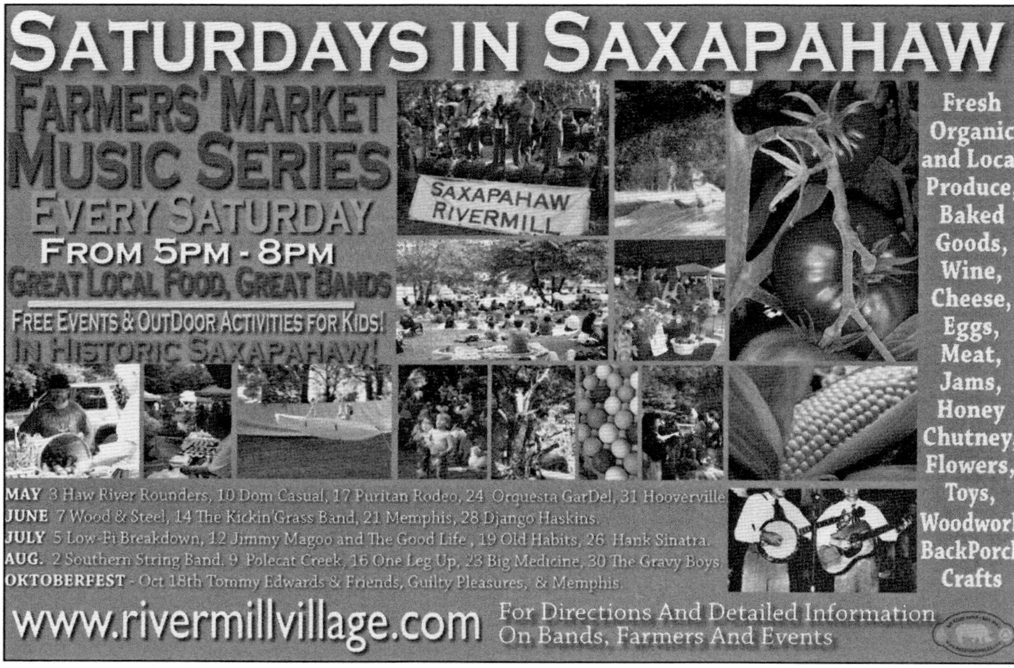


Tom LaGarde, former UNC, Olympic, and NBA basketball player, runs the sound at the Haywagon Stage for Saturdays in Saxapahaw events and oversees the series with his wife, Heather LaGarde. They are the co-owners of Barn Star Vintage wood salvage company and have two young children. "We moved to Saxapahaw after over a decade in New York City," said Tom LaGarde. "We've been amazed by the community, old-timers and people from around the world coming together. It is a welcoming place." (Courtesy of the author.)

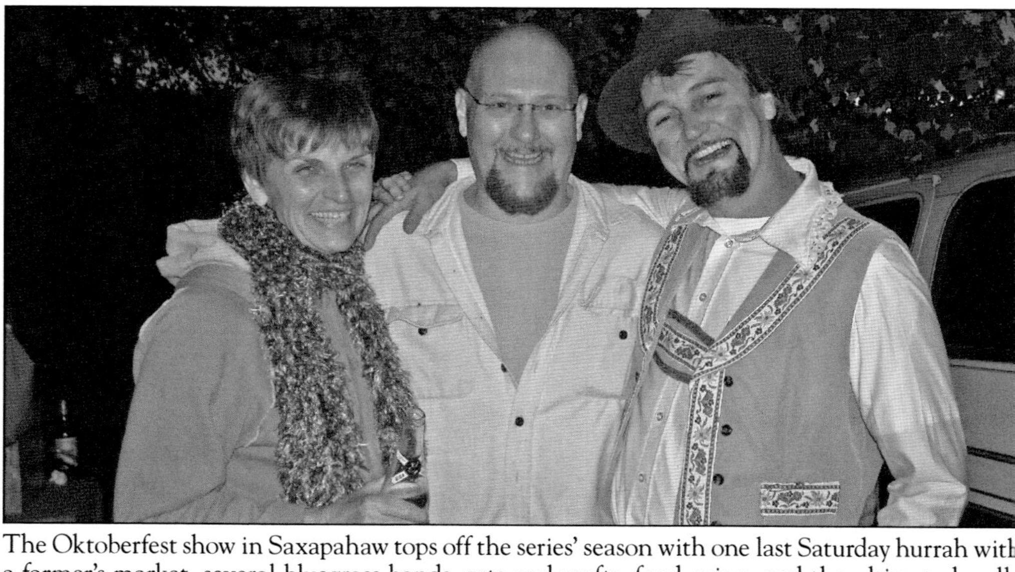

The Oktoberfest show in Saxapahaw tops off the series' season with one last Saturday hurrah with a farmer's market, several bluegrass bands, arts and crafts, food, wine, and the ultimate locally microbrewed beer. A few of the very popular locals include, from left to right, Suzanne Connors (textile artist), Nick Murray (head chef and metal sculptor), and Frankie Hayes (hairdresser, musician, and socialite extraordinaire). (Photograph by the author.)

# *Seven*

# Sustainable Saxapahaw Businesses

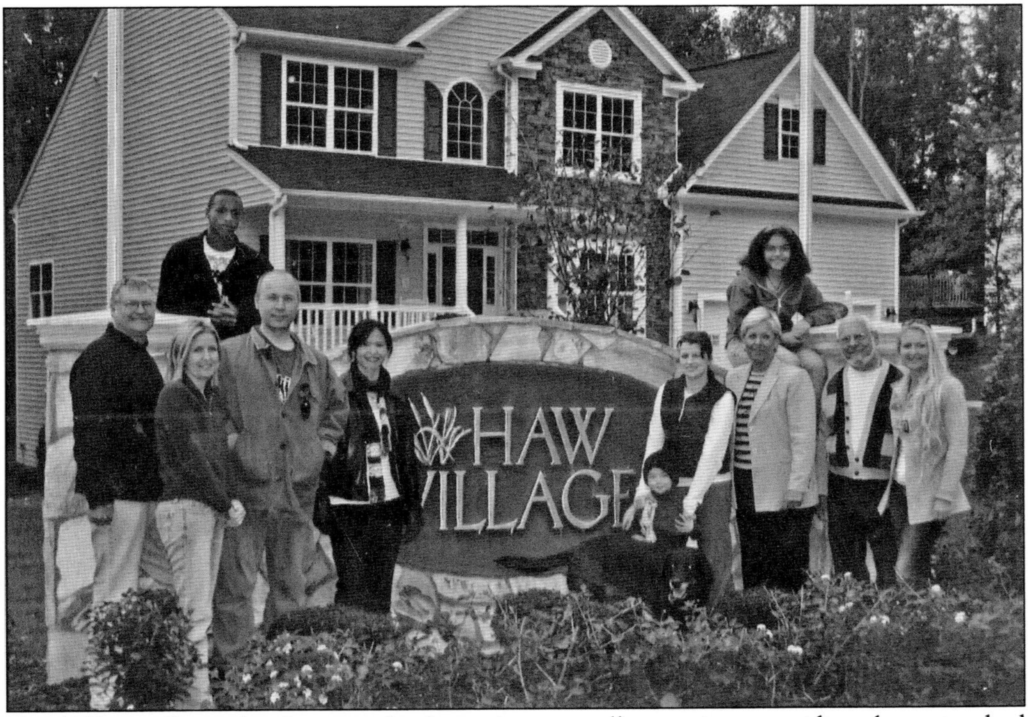

Haw Village is Saxapahaw's answer for the environmentally conscious, providing above-standard Energy Star–certified, single homes. The community offers lots approximately an acre or more in size (unlike bigger cities that have postage stamp–size lots), and all are within walking distance to the heart of Saxapahaw and the Haw River. Haw Village is the area's best-kept secret and the ideal community for those who love to work and play in Chapel Hill but desire natural tranquility without the noise and hustle and bustle. Pictured from left to right are John Treworgy, Deanna McClay, Tony ? (above), Mike Harwood, Mindy Mong Harwood, Jersey (the dog), Michael Mues Jr., Reaba Mues, Randi ?, Tyese Williams (above), Kenny Marsters, and Heather Wallace. (Photograph by the author.)

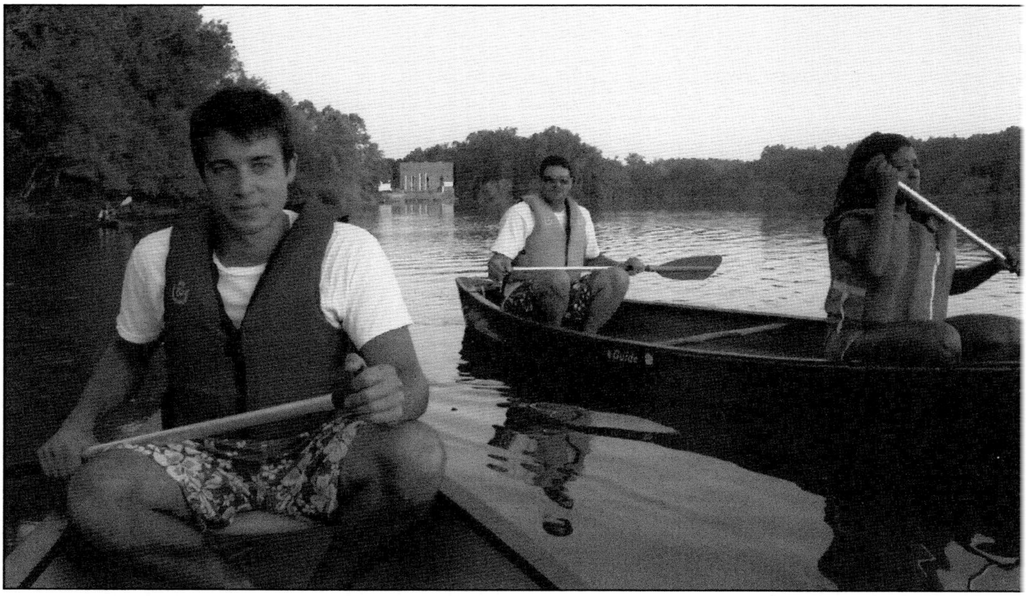

Harvest Moon Weekend in Saxapahaw combines a full-moon paddle trip with the Haw River Canoe and Kayak Company of Saxapahaw, grape harvesting the following morning at Benjamin Vineyards, and lunch and music at the River Landing Inn. La Tanya Gentile, a professional singer from Philadelphia (above right), came to Saxapahaw to enjoy Harvest Moon Weekend and her first canoe trip. She sang for everyone for 2.5 hours as they paddled down the Haw River and around Saxapahaw Lake in the light of the full moon. The Saxapahaw dam creates a 300-acre lake just for Saxapahaw. Canoe trips are led by river naturalists whose knowledge and concern for the environment is matched with a sense of adventure and discovery. Monique de Latour often leads canoe trips. In the photograph above, the mill power generator can be seen in the background. Nicholas Macaulay is on left, and John Horner is in the background. Below is a real-photo postcard of the Saxapahaw Lake sold in stores by Saxapahaw's own Monique de Latour. (Both courtesy of Monique de Latour.)

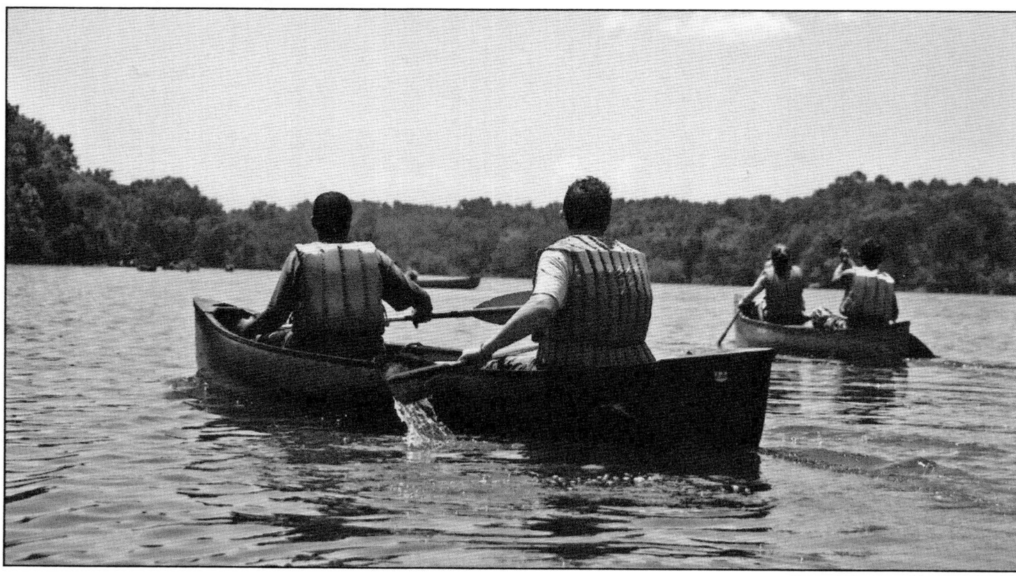

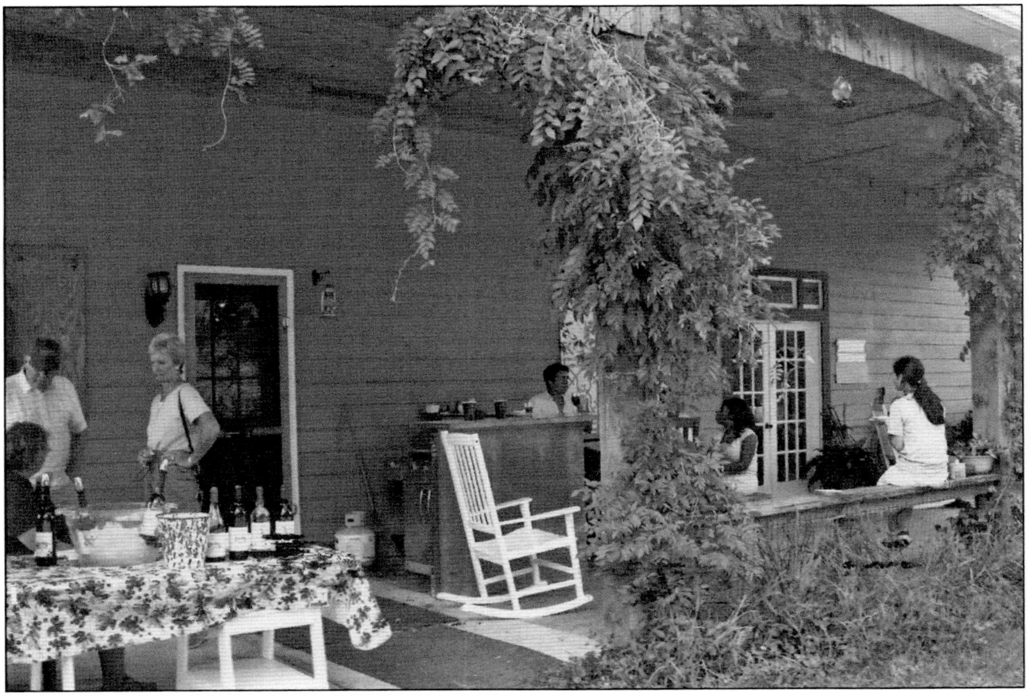

The River Landing Inn (5942 Whitney Road, Saxapahaw) sits on more than 20 acres of rolling pastures and hardwood forest along the banks of the Haw River. The private four-room bed-and-breakfast is within 20 minutes of Chapel Hill and was made from a horse farm. Owner Matt Diehl ensured the external structure of the farm was kept intact. A delicious breakfast is cooked to order as part of the stay at River Landing Inn, and Benjamin Vineyards is within walking distance. Locals and guests come to grab a handmade walking stick and go for long walks with their dogs along the marked trail overlooking the Haw River. Above is lunchtime during Harvest Moon Weekend on the deck of the River Landing Inn. Below, chef and manager Dave Wilson (far right) is seen with locals from Haw Village who came to walk their dogs. From left to right are Mike Harwood, Mindy Mong Harwood, Jersey (the dog), Nicholas Macaulay, and Dave Wilson. (Photographs by the author.)

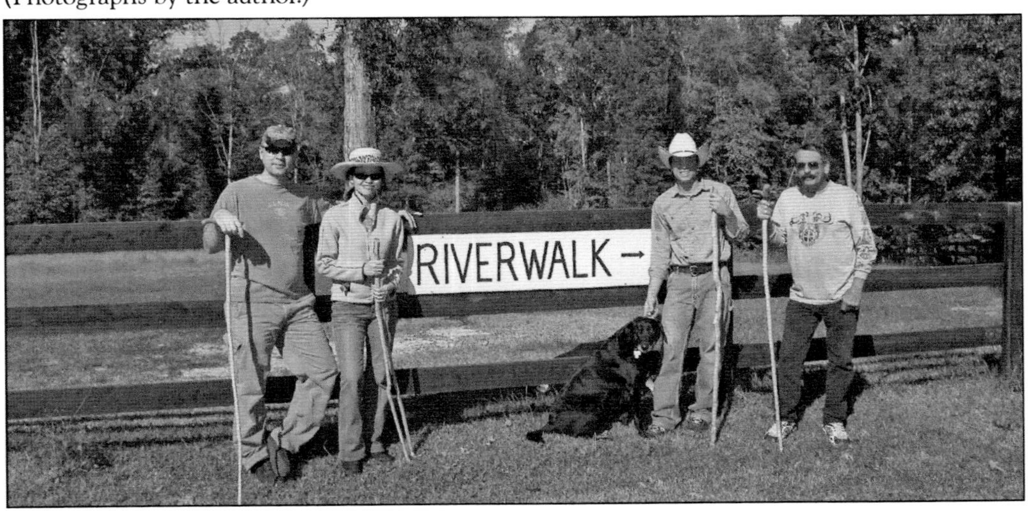

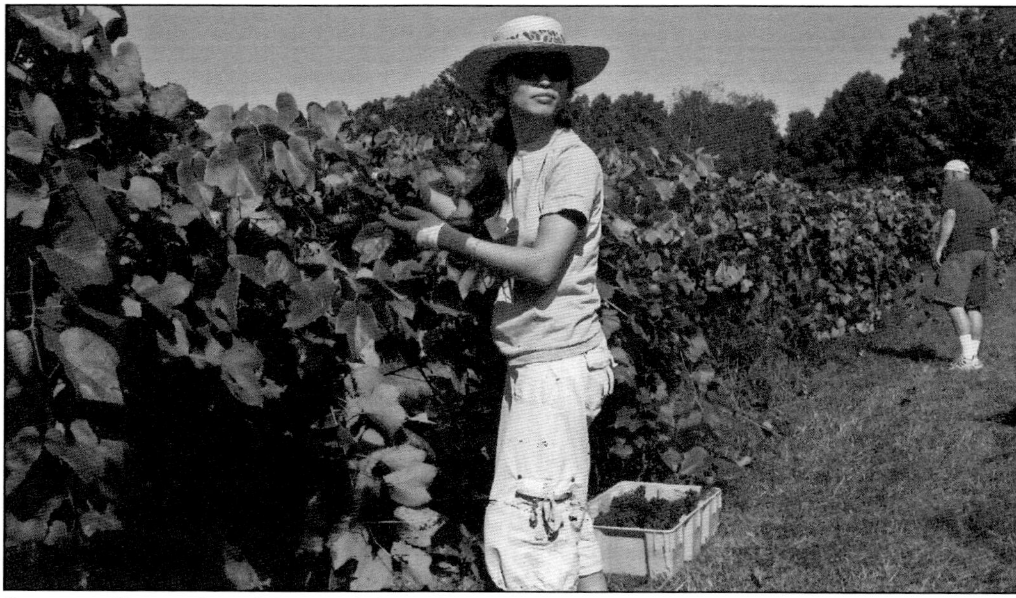

Benjamin Vineyards and Winery (6516 Whitney Road) is 5 acres and includes 16 different varieties of grapes. The soil on the east side of the Haw River in Saxapahaw is red clay, while the soil on the west side of Saxapahaw is sandy loam soil ideal for growing Muscadine grapes—including Scuppernong, the nation's first cultivated wine grape—as well as French and French-American hybrid viniferas. Their 2007 Sauvignon Blanc is a full-bodied premium white wine and a Gold Medal winner at the Mid-Atlantic Wine Competition. Tour the vineyards, pick some grapes for sampling (seasonally to buy by the pound), enjoy lunch at the picnic tables, and browse the gift shop to enjoy paintings for sale by local artists. Mindy Mong Harwood (above) is learning how to harvest grapes during Harvest Moon Weekend with Andy Zeman, who co-owns the vineyard with his wife, Nancy. Below, Mindy Mong Harwood (left), Jersey (the dog), and Heather Wallace enjoy the sun after a nice picnic on the Benjamin Vineyards porch. (Photographs by the author.)

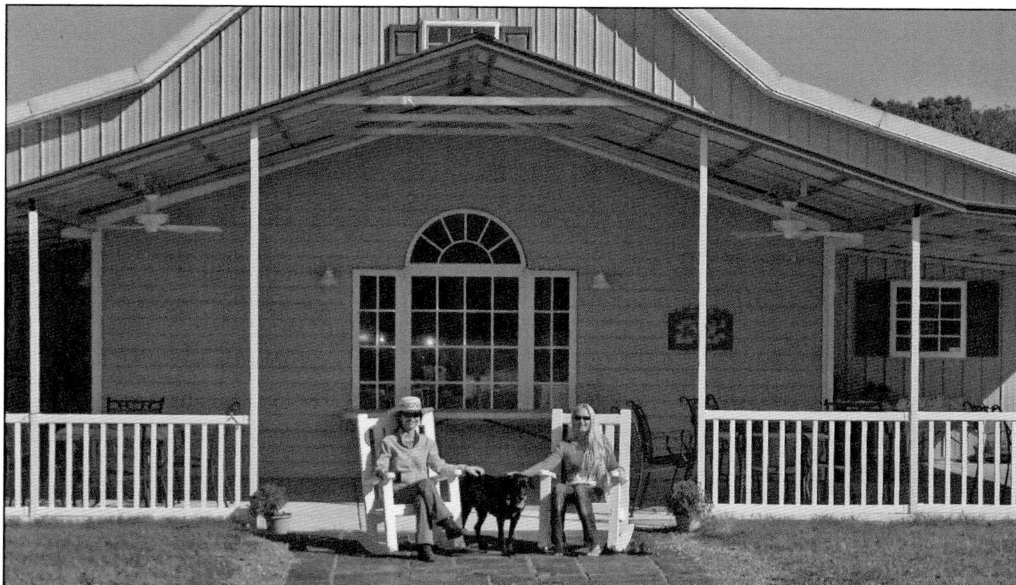

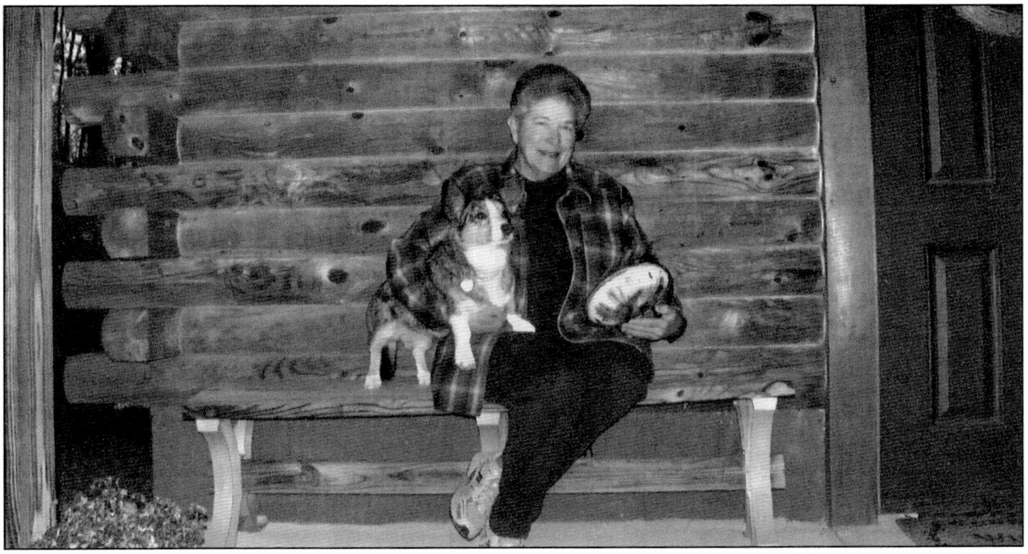

"When I work with clay," says Jane Holloman of Little Dog Pottery, "I am reminded of my connection to the earth. I take pleasure in thinking of my finished pieces being held in human hands, used and enjoyed, perhaps even long after I have left this earth." Maggie May, the blue merle Cardigan Welsh Corgi sitting with Jan, gave Little Dog Pottery its name. About 1200 B. C., the Celts brought a small working dog to the country of Wales, now part of Great Britain. It is believed that the name for this dog, Corgi, came from the Welsh language and meant "wee dog" or "little dog."

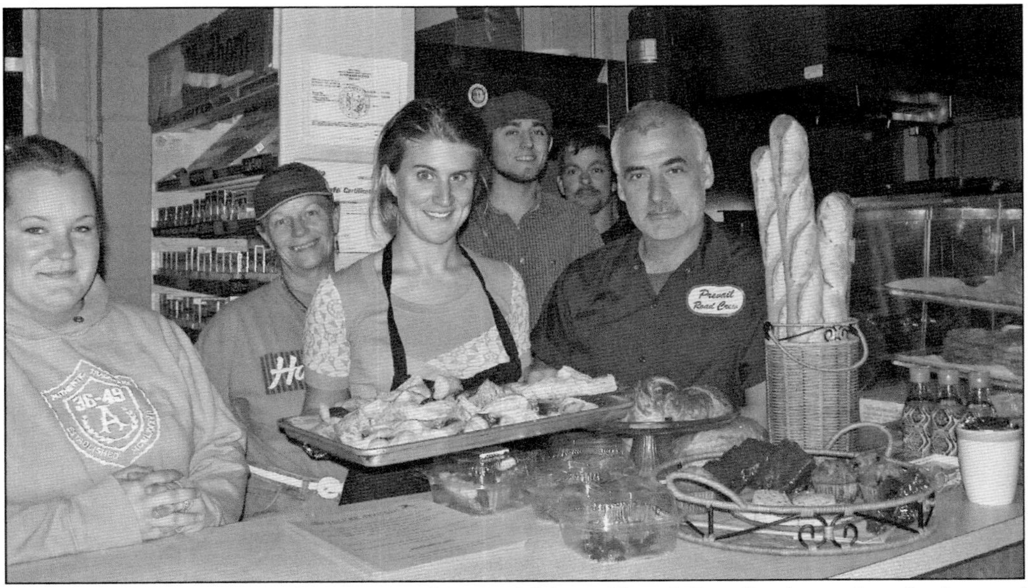

Saxapahaw General Store (1735 Saxapahaw Bethlehem Church Road) is located in the heart of Saxapahaw. Chef Jeff Barney and Cameron Ratliff, the geniuses behind the new design, promise wholesome, local cheeses; produce; wines; deli meats; coffee; freshly baked pastries; and prepared foods for brunches, lunches, breakfast, and dinner, as well as their greatest love, the "anytime you're hungry" almighty sandwich. Pictured from left to right are Megan Andrews, Sherry Livingston, Cameron Ratliff, Casey Foster, Jeff Brooks, and Jeff Barney. (Photographs by the author.)

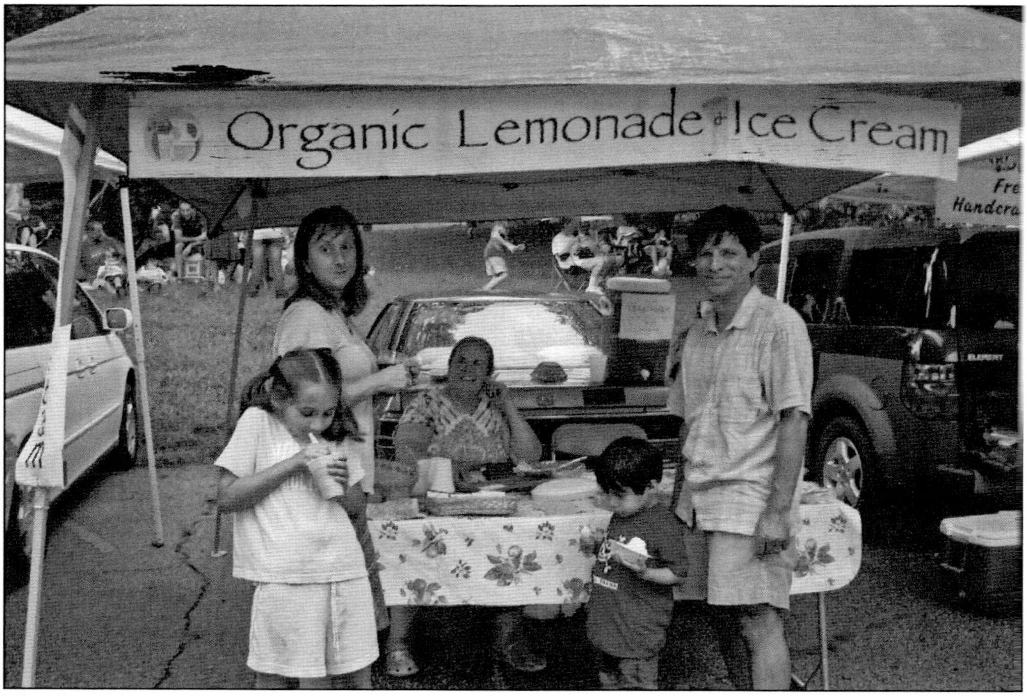


The Saturdays in Saxapahaw event brings a couple thousand people to the village every weekend. Some come just for the organic produce, and some stay and listen to the area's best bluegrass band music. Folks bring their picnic necessities and stake out their favorite spot on the hillside during the four-hour event. Above, locals visit the well-known organic lemonade stand to cool off during the hot summer. Below, Jerry "Poppy" Clyburn has been making cedar furniture by hand his whole life. He often sells out before the show is over, leaving him with nothing to sit on. (Photographs by the author.)

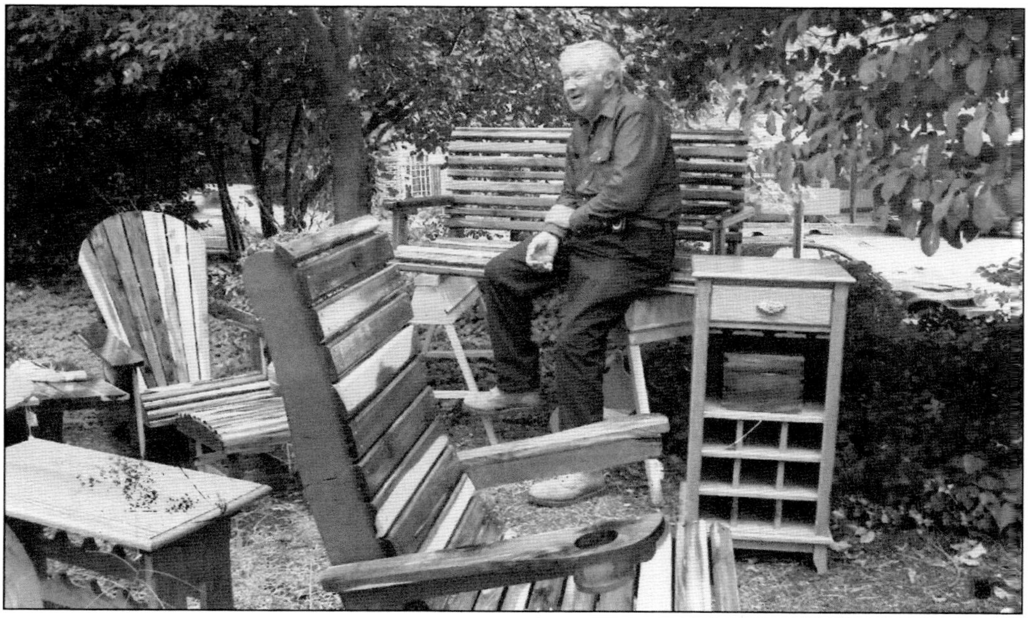

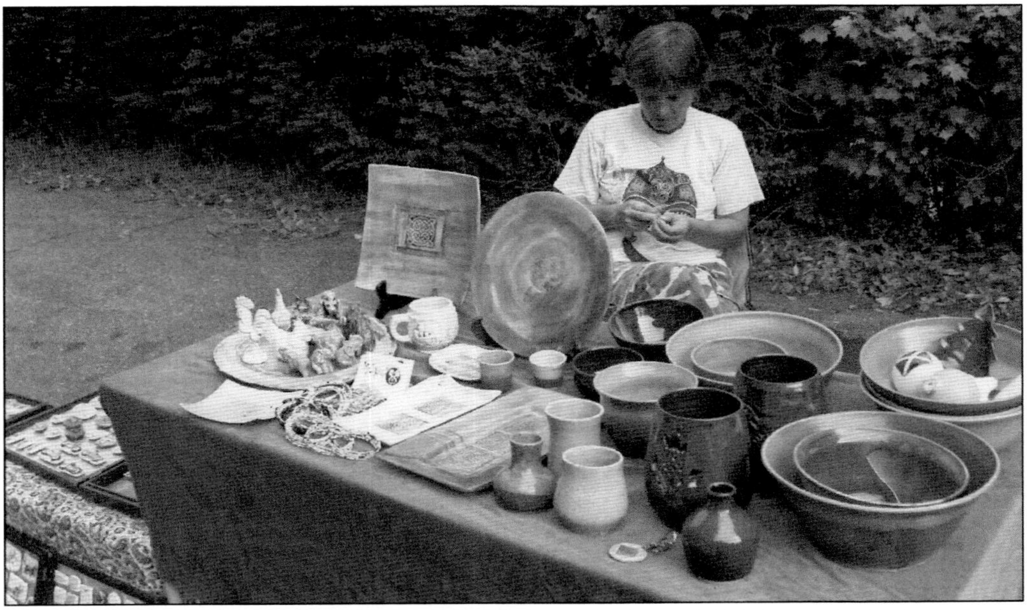

Above, Mary Glasgow of Kelpie Pottery displays her Irish- and Celtic-inspired pieces at the Saxapahaw Music Festival. She uses 100-percent rich organic red clay from mother earth within Saxapahaw to make her pottery, primarily in porcelain and clay. She learned pottery from the well-known Japanese instructor Hiroshi Sueyoshi, who received the North Carolina Living Treasure Award in 2006. Below, the Hillsborough Cheese Company is another regular vendor at the Saturday Swell in Saxapahaw. Cindy and Dorian West are the Hillsborough Cheese Company. The Wests are fond of quoting Monty Python: "Blessed are the Cheese-makers." They work with several local dairy farms, developing long-term relationships and trying to help each other out with cheese-making advice. Dorian visits the farms often and is committed to using only sustainably produced milk. Helping this Hillsborough customer is Lea Calderon-Guthe. (Photographs by the author.)

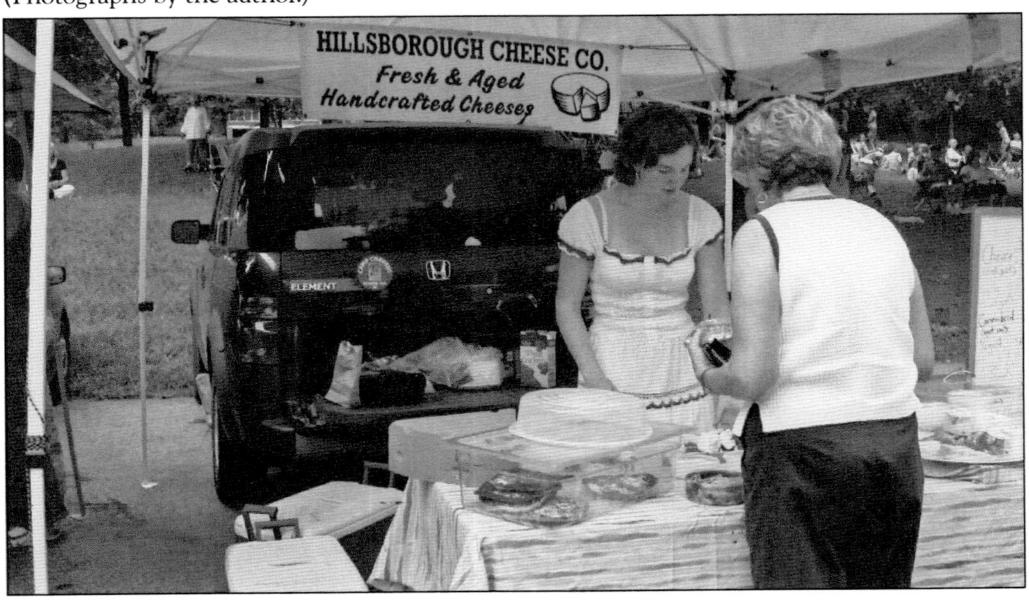

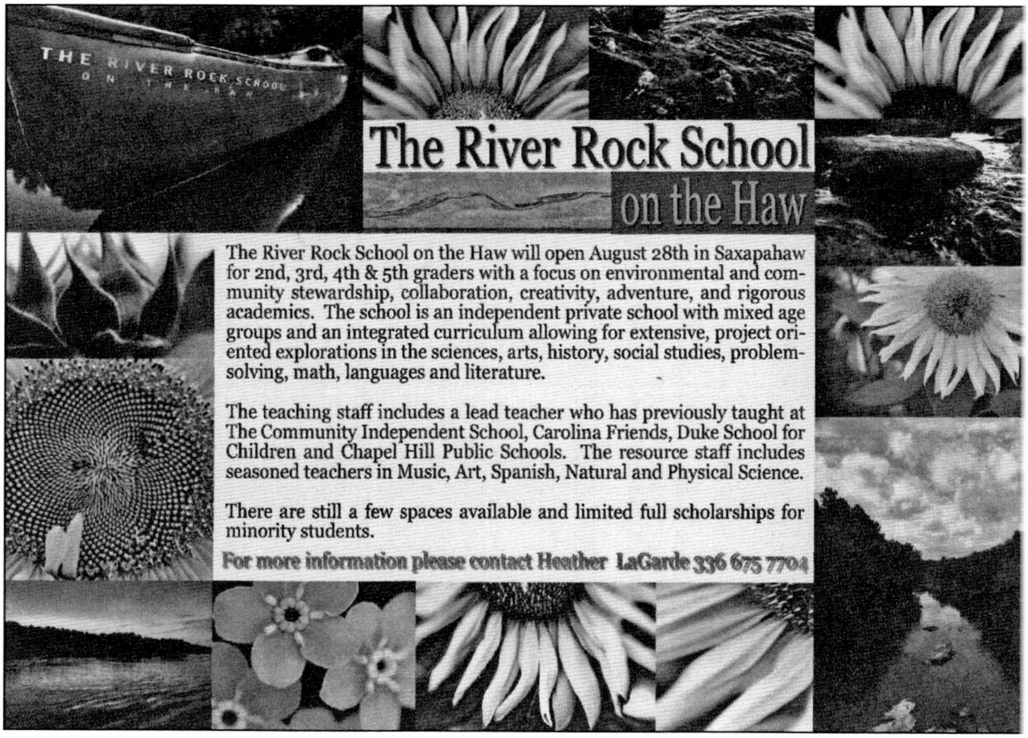


Saxapahaw now has a public charter environmental high school (Hawbridge School) and a private environmental elementary school (the River Rock School). The River Rock School is set in the beautifully restored historic Saxapahaw Cotton Mill on the banks of the Haw River. The school's proximity to the Haw River and the 300-acre Saxapahaw Lake make it possible to offer canoeing and kayaking as part of physical education. (Courtesy of Heather LaGarde.)

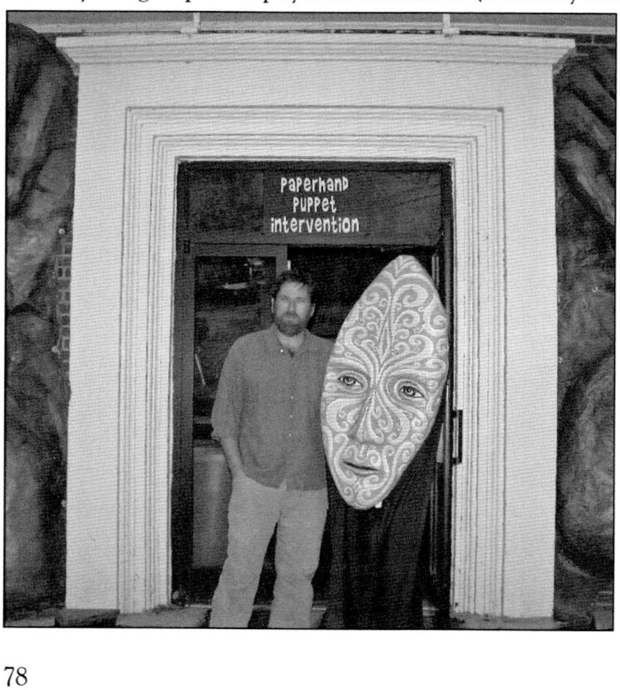


Donovan Zimmerman is pictured in front of Paperhand Puppet Intervention, which he cofounded with friend Jan Burger. According to Paperhand's Web site, their mission is "to make work that inspires people, promotes social change, and is deeply satisfying for everyone involved. The puppet shows we create are a synthesis of many art forms including (but not limited to): sculpting, painting, music, dance, improvisation, costume/set design, and theater. We are celebrants. We are activists. We are puppeteers. Our will is set on undermining and eventually eradicating the institutions of greed, hate, and fear that plague the world in myriad forms." (Photograph by the author.)

# *Eight*

# The People of Saxapahaw

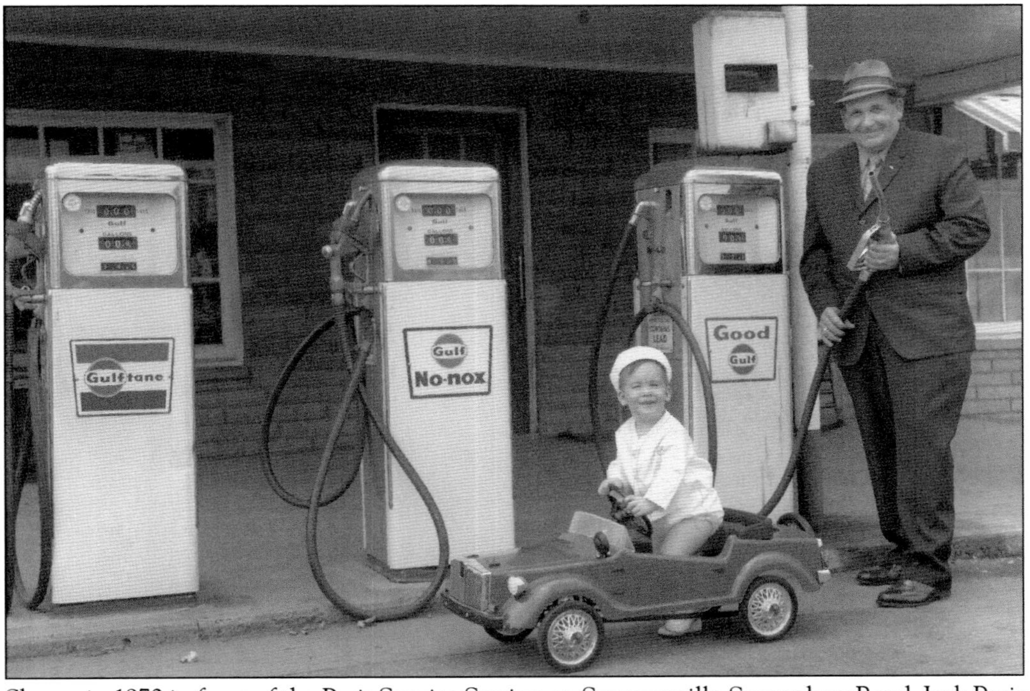


Shown in 1970 in front of the Paris Service Station on Swepsonville-Saxapahaw Road, Jack Paris (owner) is pretending to pump gas into his grandson Keller Paris "Toddy" Smith's classic pedal car. The prices per gallon on the pumps, from left to right, read 34¢, 41¢, and 37¢. Jack was county commissioner for 12 years and never voted to raise taxes. The experience that touched him the most while in public office was delivering a fish dinner to an elderly African American gentleman on Christmas. The man, who had nothing to eat but cold corn bread and warm water said, "Jack, Santa Claus has surely come." Jack served on the carrier USS *Ranger* during his tenure with the marine corps. He married Essie Leach and had three children: George "Buddy" Paris, who served two tours in Vietnam; Bennie Louise (Paris) Smith, who had daughter Caroline Keller (Smith) Chandler; and Nelson Rex Paris, who married Rachel Paris and had daughter Natalie Ann (Paris) Maness. Natalie Anne had daughters Hannah Ruth-Ann and Lindsey Lee-Ann. (Courtesy of Nelson and Rachel Paris.)

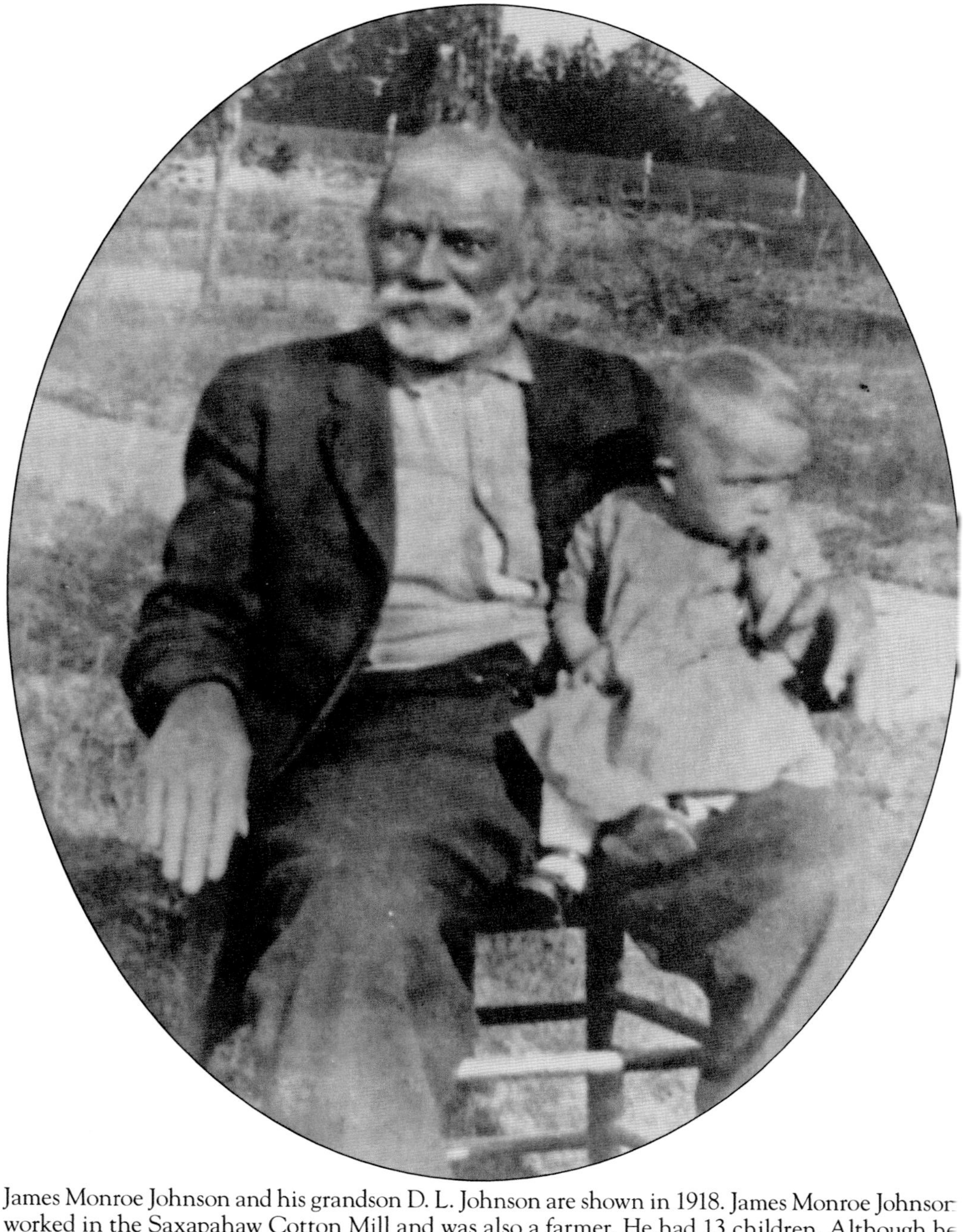

James Monroe Johnson and his grandson D. L. Johnson are shown in 1918. James Monroe Johnson worked in the Saxapahaw Cotton Mill and was also a farmer. He had 13 children. Although he drank too much and worked very hard, he still lived well into his 80s. He is buried in Moore's Chapel Cemetery. There has been great speculation from the townspeople about whether or not James Monroe Johnson was of Cherokee Indian decent. (Courtesy of Gary Johnson.)

Thomas Woody (born 1805) and his wife, Mary Woody (born 1803), are pictured in 1870. The Woodys had 11 children between 1828 and 1847. Thomas Woody was so large that he could not fit in the front of the same buggy with his wife. Mary Woody's brother, Nathanial Woody, would save money to buy slaves just to set them free. Thomas Woody's father, Hugh Woody, had a stop at his home for the Underground Railroad. The family supported manumission and were considered abolitionists. Manumission by American slaveholders was restricted by laws in many states. Thomas's brothers refused to serve in the Civil War and were arrested and paid a fine for their release. (Courtesy of Gary Johnson.)

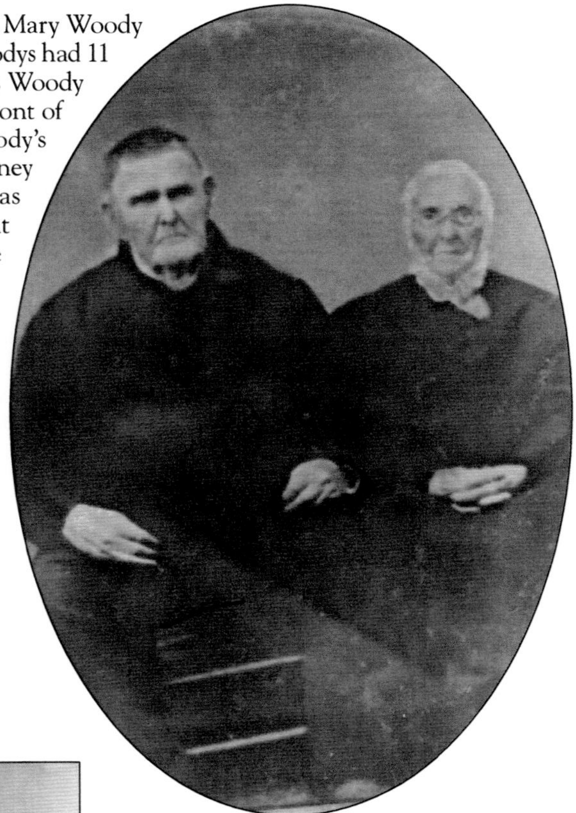

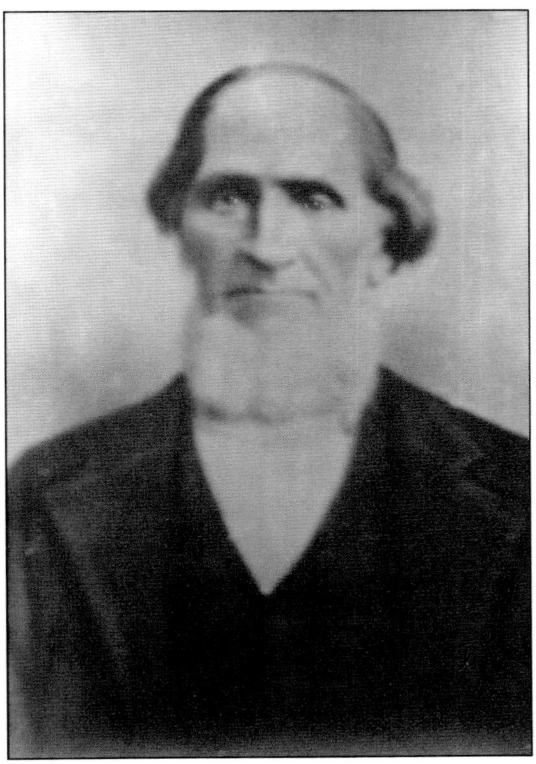

Wesley Green Cheek, pictured in 1869, was born in 1828 and died in 1909. Cheek was the third born of 10 children and fought in the Civil War. He also started the Mount Olive Baptist Church. He married Emeline Johnson in 1851 and later married Elizabeth Buckner in 1861. His father, Eli Cheek, was born in 1790, and his grandfather, Mastin Cheek, was born in 1760. (Courtesy of Gary Johnson.)

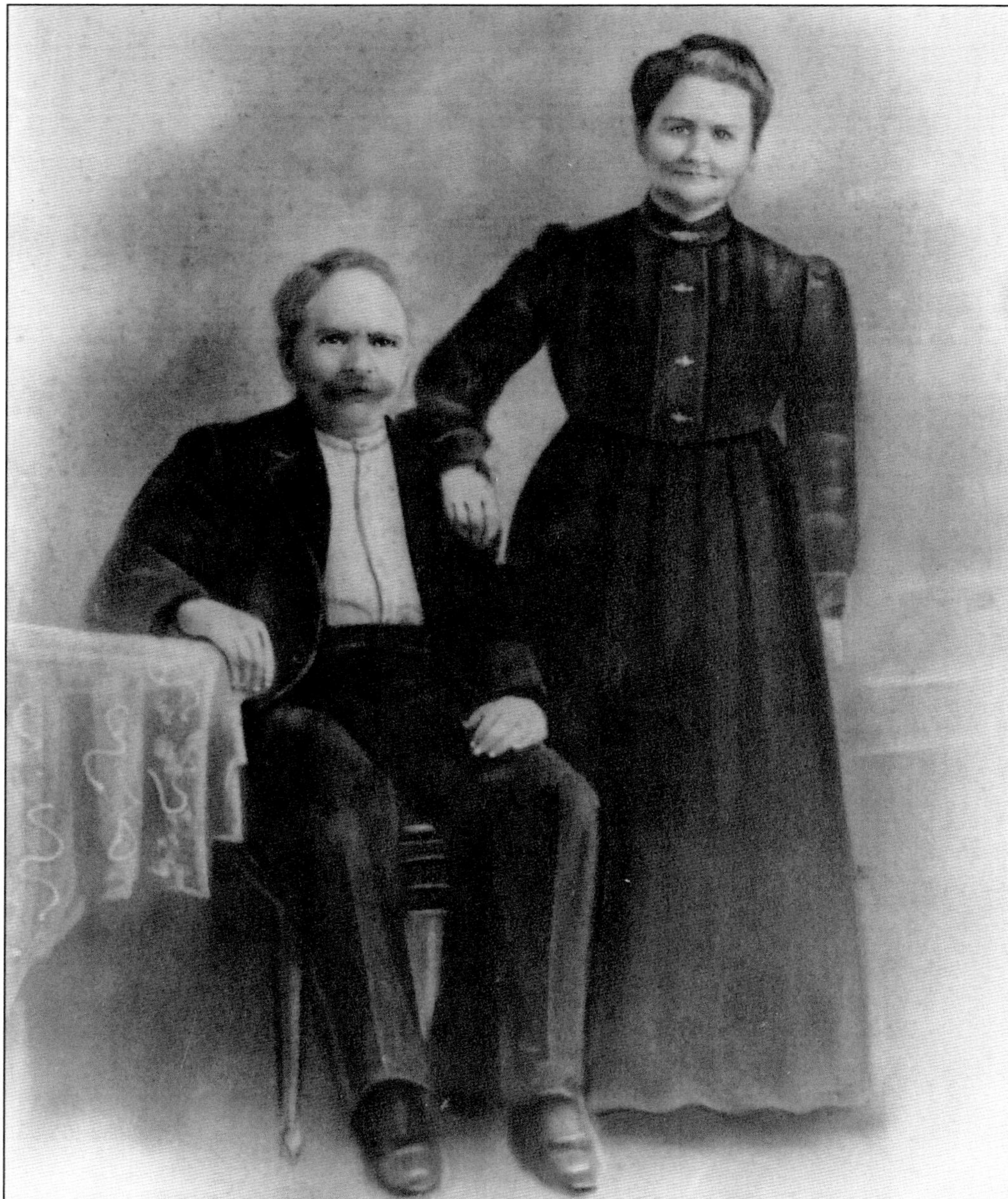

This early painted portrait of James Monroe Johnson and his wife, Virginia Thacker Johnson, was captured in ceramic (most likely porcelain), embedded in cement, and used for their headstone, seen today in Moore's Chapel Cemetery. The Johnsons had 13 children. They moved to Saxapahaw in the late 1800s from Danville, Virginia. Their daughter, Hattie Johnson Petty (born 1883), married Ollie Petty (died 1943). Hattie and Ollie retired from the Saxapahaw Cotton Mill (Sellers Manufacturing Company), and Hattie died at the age of 90 in 1973. Hattie had 20 grandchildren and 25 great-grandchildren. Saxapahaw local family residents included her daughters, Caroleen Ursery (died 1996) and Ollie Petty Bowers (died 2003); her son Floyd Petty (survivor of World War II who died in 1994); her brother Boley Johnson (died in 1975); and her sisters, Ann Johnson Petty (died, date unknown) and Earlie Johnson (died 1981). (Courtesy of Gary Johnson.)

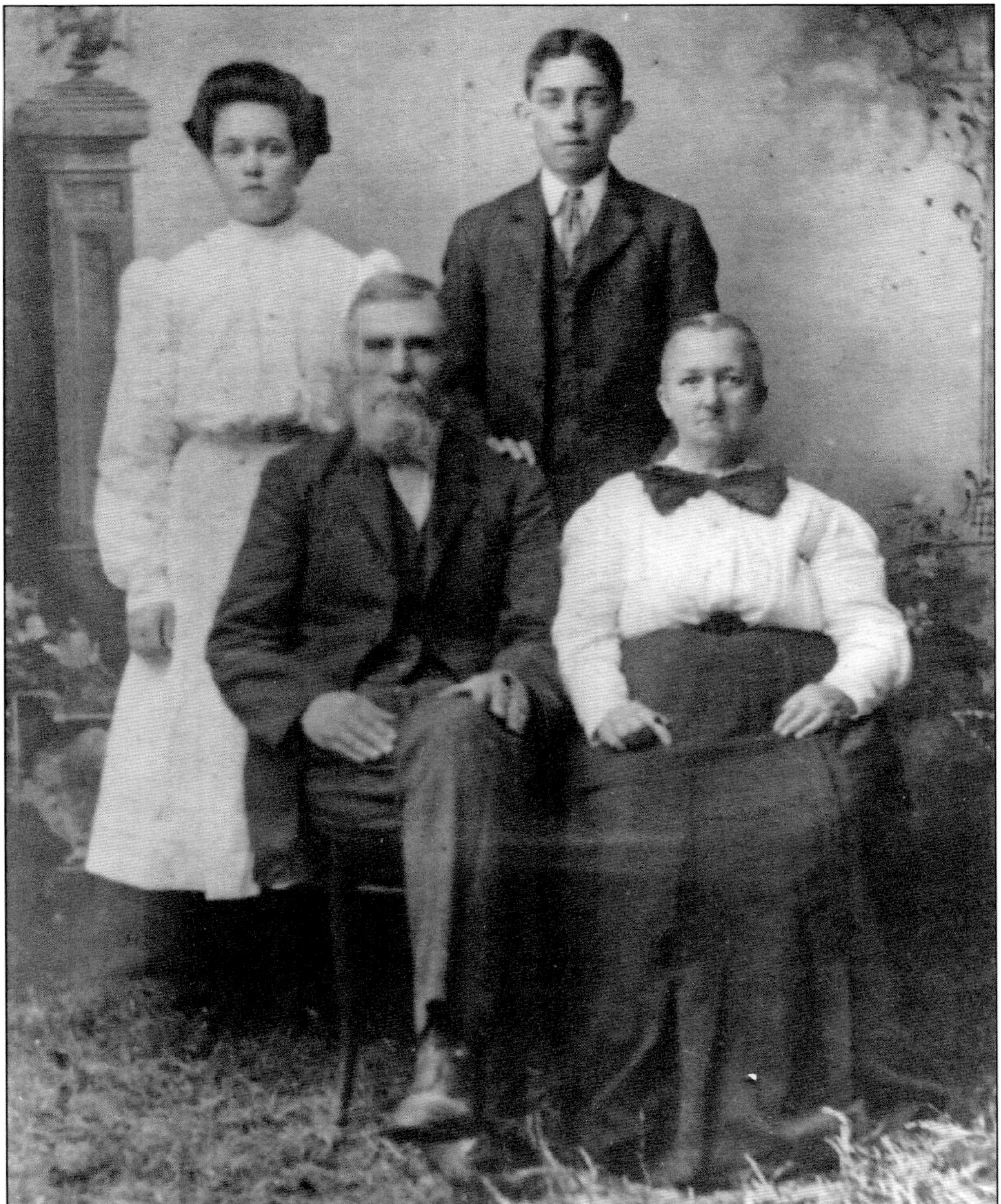

There are no photographs of the David Johnson family prior to this 1905 photograph. At the time, the family was comprised of Primitive Baptists who, back then, did not condone the taking of photographs. The Primitive Baptist faith is still alive but with very few numbers. They believe the 1611 King James Version is the superior English translation of the scriptures. There was not much difference between Baptist denominations in the 1800s, but if Primitive Baptists were compared today, there would be a vast difference. Included from left to right are (first row) Mr. Crutchfield and Frances Jones Johnson Crutchfield; (second row) Ida Johnson (Hinshaw), born August 2, 1892, and died March 20, 1967; (second row) David Johnson. Ida was married to Thomas Franklin Hinshaw (born 1898 and died 1970). (Courtesy of Gary Johnson.)

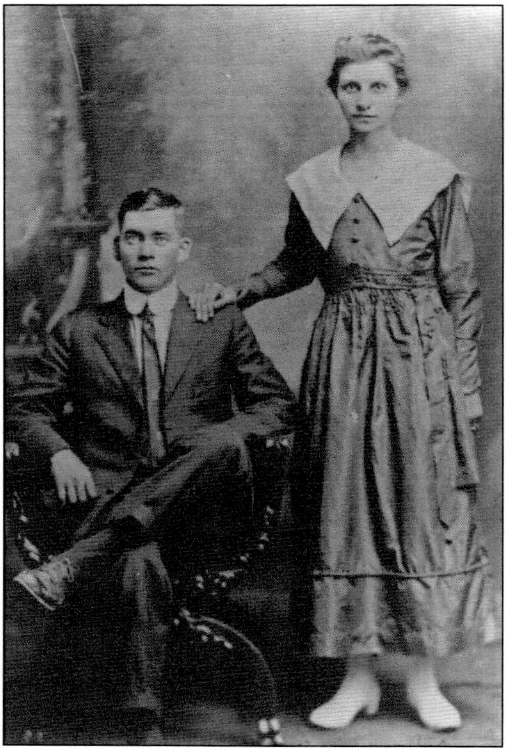

Jesse James Johnson and his wife, Earlene "Earlie" Johnson, are pictured in 1915. Earlie Johnson was born July 27, 1899, and died November 9, 1981. She was one of 13 siblings. Her parents were Monroe and Virginia Thacker Johnson. Jesse James was born February 2, 1892, and died January 30, 1967. Jesse worked at the Saxapahaw Cotton Mill and was also known by the name "Bogger." Jesse James Johnson was born 10 years after the famous outlaw Jesse James died. (Courtesy of Gary Johnson.)

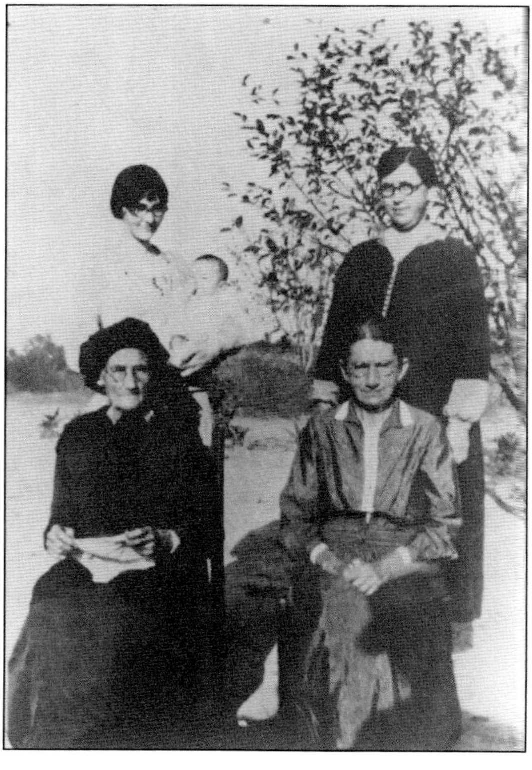

This *c.* 1927 family photograph celebrates five generations coming together. In the 1800s, the average number of children per family was seven. It was not uncommon for mothers and their daughters to have children at the same time. By 1933, the average family size had declined to 2.3 children. Pictured from left to right are (first row) great-great-grandmother Mary Louise Hassleton Woody and the baby's great-grandmother, whose name is unknown; (second row) mother Yula Woody Braxton holding baby Doris Brackston Frye (still living) and grandmother Lona Ann Cheek Woody (who married John Woody). (Courtesy of Gary Johnson.)

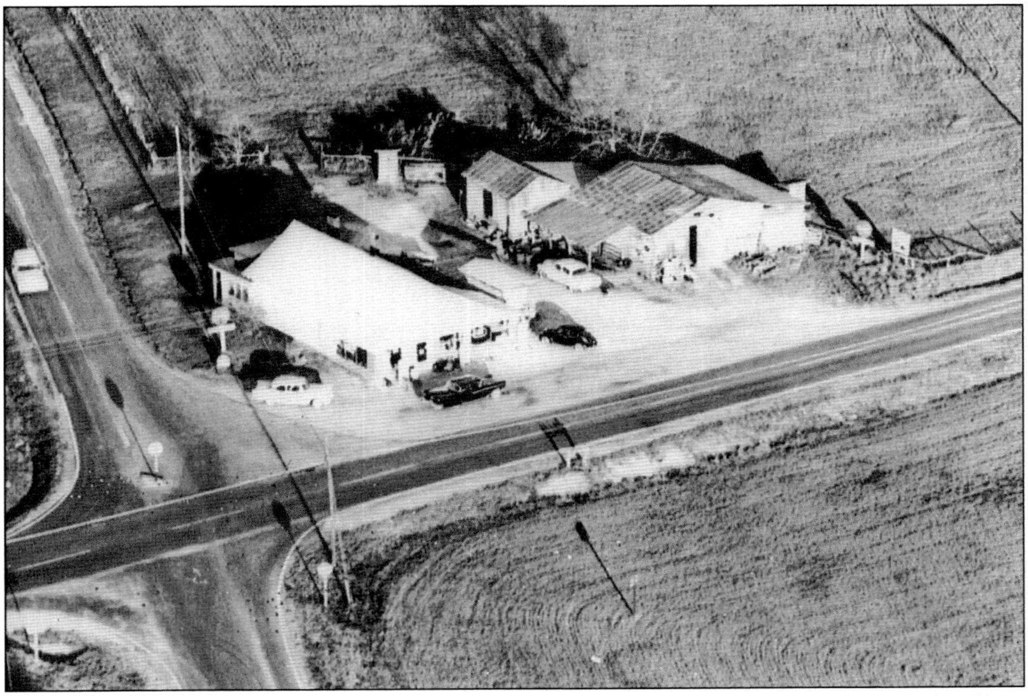

Above is an aerial view of the Johnson General Store on the corner of Highway 87 and Rolling Rock Road, now known as Moore's Chapel Road. Most of the structures have since been demolished. Below, D. L. Johnson (left) is shown with his son David Johnson. The Johnsons owned the grocery store through three generations. They used their surrey (pictured here) to deliver grocery packages to neighbors who could not get to the store because of illness or the lack of transportation. David Johnson's grandson, Gary Johnson, still owns artifacts from the store. D. L. Johnson died in 1969. Two thousand families signed the guest list at his funeral. The Johnson family stayed at the grave until 11:30 waiting for the last guest to go through. (Both courtesy of Gary Johnson.)

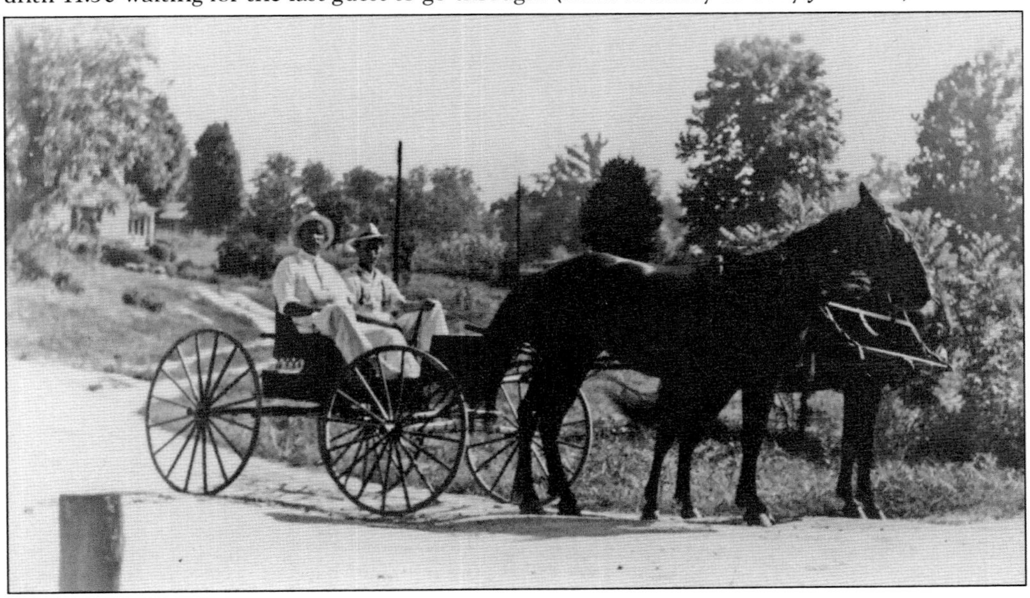

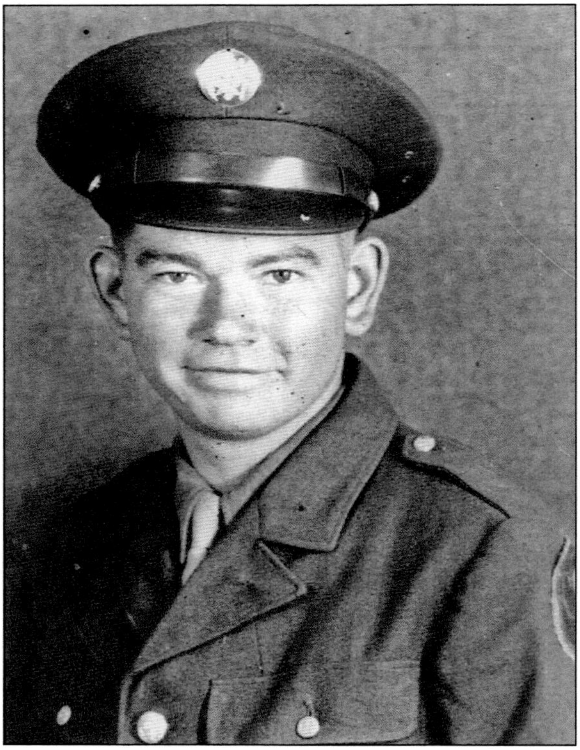

Calvin Johnson is pictured in his uniform during World War II. There was suspicion during the war about men entering the military and lying about their age just so they could fight for their country. Others volunteered for the war before they could be drafted so they would not be sent to the front lines. Calvin is one of the sons of Jesse and Earlie Johnson. (Both courtesy of Gary Johnson.)

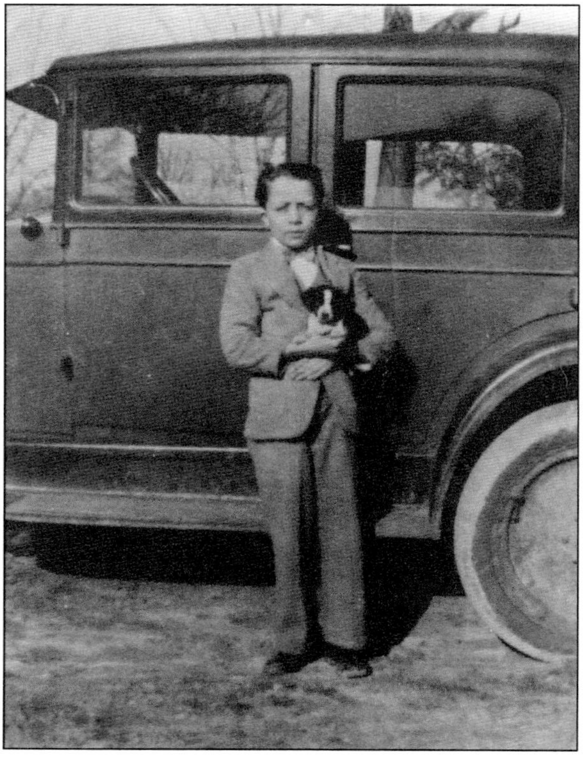

D. L. Johnson and his puppy pose in front of the family car in 1925. The letters of D. L.'s first name are the first initials of his mother and father, David and Lula Johnson. He is the father of Gary Johnson. D. L. Johnson was born December 23, 1917, and died April 19, 1969. He is buried in Moore's Chapel Cemetery. (Courtesy of Gary Johnson.)

David and Lula Johnson pose with their children, D. L. and Christine, in front of the family car they used to drive into Lumberton, North Carolina, to pick up watermelons and peaches, which they would bring back to Saxapahaw to sell in their store and deliver to those who could not travel. The drive today is about two and a half hours, but back then, in 1929, the round-trip would take them all day. (Courtesy of Gary Johnson.)

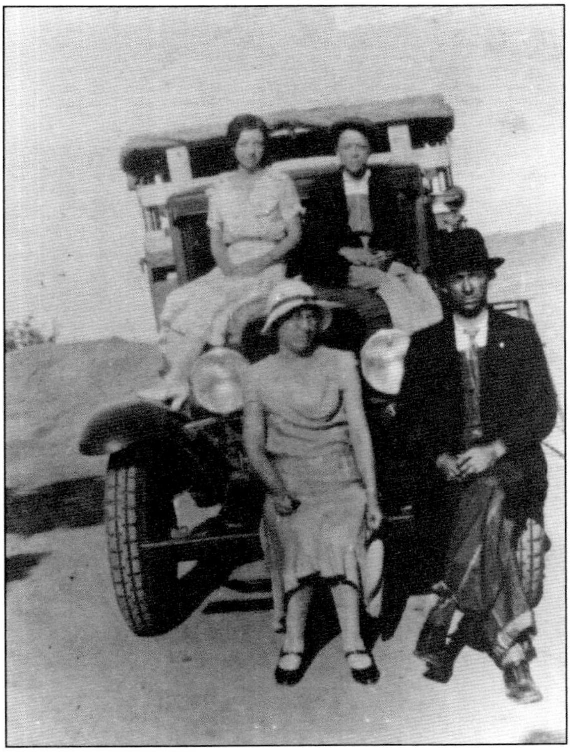

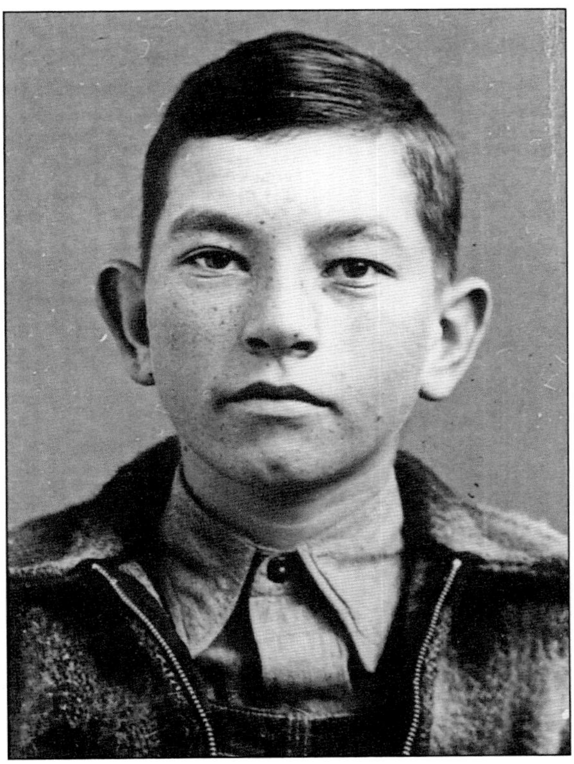

Henry Johnson is pictured just prior to entering World War II. He is the brother of Calvin Johnson and son of Earlene and Jesse James Johnson. He was stationed in Greenland. He married Virginia Dare in 1956. Henry worked at the Saxapahaw Mill for many years in the dye house and cotton mill. (Courtesy of Gary Johnson.)

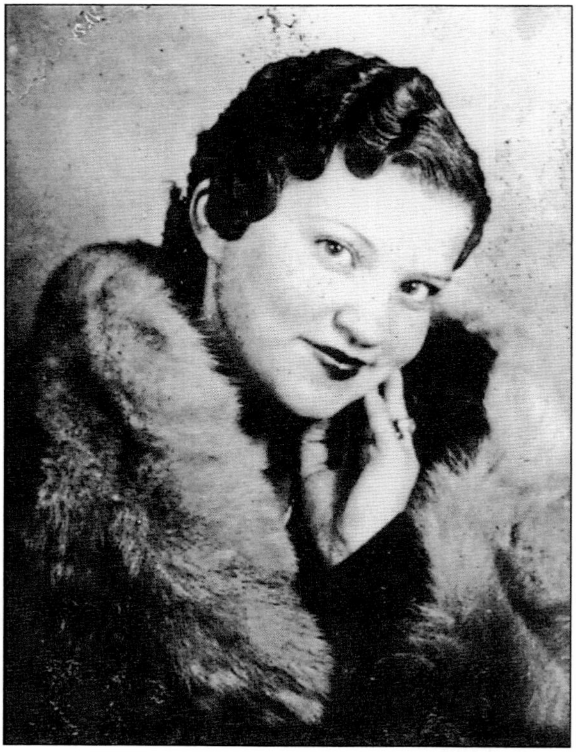

Obera Johnson Jones is remembered as being quite the looker in these parts. She chose to marry J. Thomas Jones (August 27, 1912–April 4, 1977). She and her husband are remembered as being very fun-loving with everyone they met. Obera lived to be almost 100. (Courtesy of Gary Johnson and John Petty.)

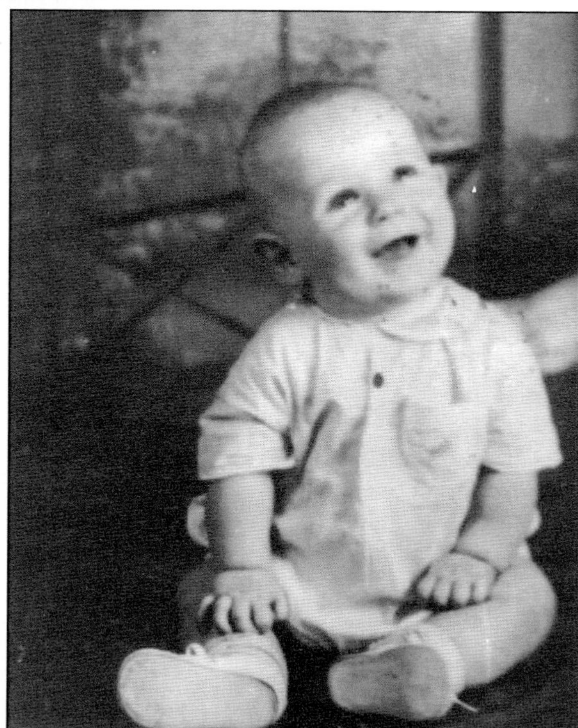

This baby photograph of David Johnson was taken in 1942. He was the son of D. L. Johnson and grandson of David Johnson, who all managed the Johnson store together. (Courtesy of Gary Johnson.)

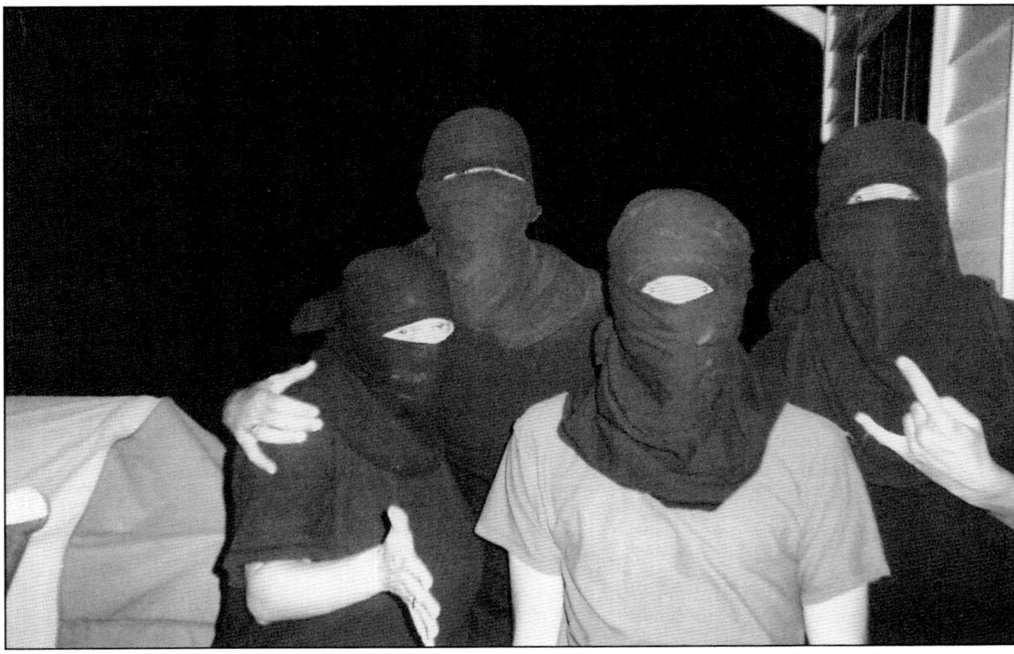

Shown here are the Environmental Ninjas. Today, still wanted by Green Peace, they survive as soldiers of fortune. If you have an environmental problem, if no one else can help, and if you can find them, maybe you can hire . . . the E-team. Pictured from left to right are Kim, Paul, Keith, and Nick. (Courtesy of the Neubauers.)

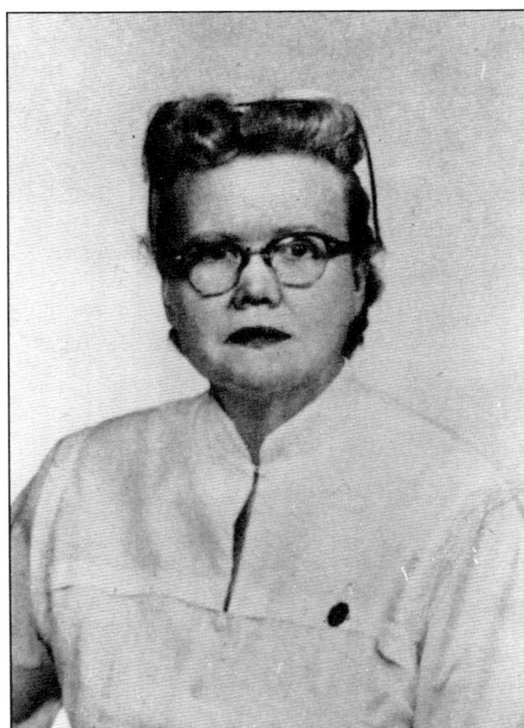

Lala Lee Paris was a registered nurse in 1930. During Senator Jordan's ailing health in 1974, he had nurses by his side around the clock. Lala Paris was the nurse with Senator Jordan when he died at his Saxapahaw home. Lala was born December 11, 1901, and died May 9, 1978. (Courtesy of Marie P. Buckner.)

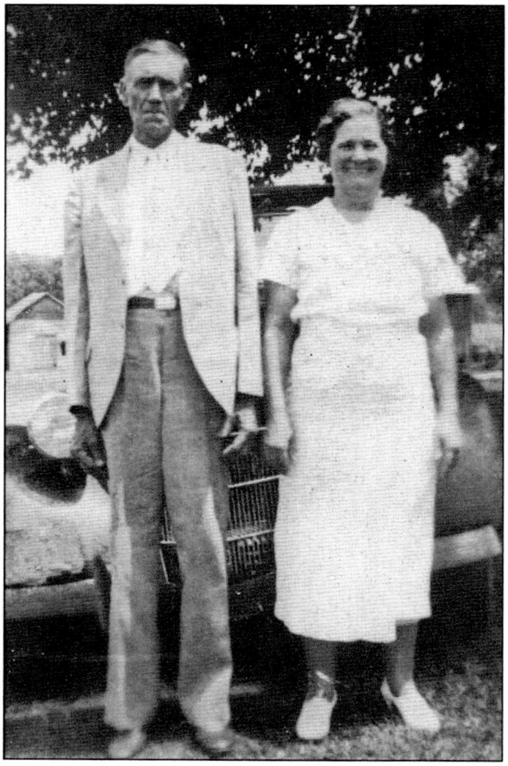

Henry G. Paris and Roxie Patterson Paris (parents of Marie Paris Buckner) pose in 1935 in front of the historic Paris farm. Henry Paris purchased the farm in 1898. (Courtesy of Marie P. Buckner.)

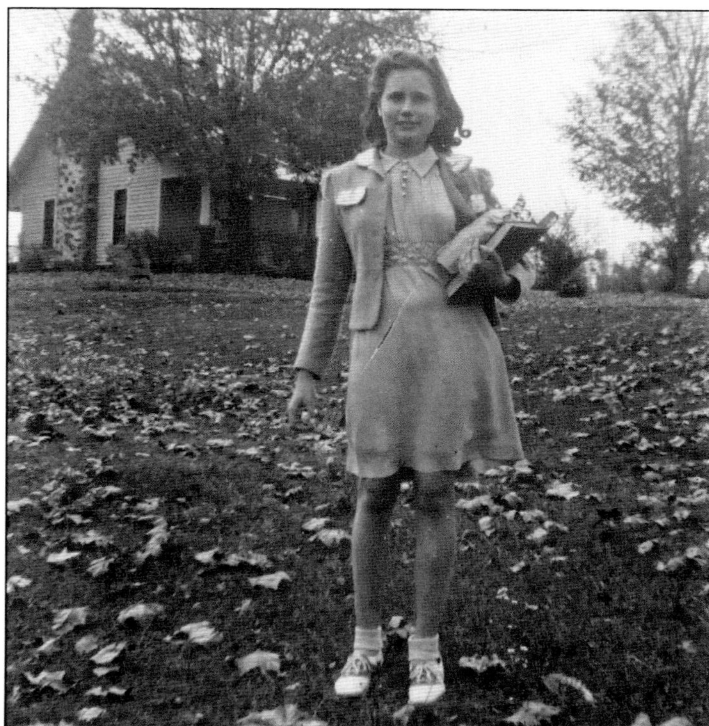

Marie Paris Buckner, pictured in 1940, attended business school and then worked at the Saxapahaw Cotton Mill for 35 years. Marie's husband, Henry "Clyde" Buckner, was courting her in 1945. When the flood occurred in August, the roads were flooded so badly that Clyde had to literally drive around the entire county just to be with her. He married her three months later in December in her home. The day they were married, a rare snowstorm occurred, preventing the preacher from leaving them. Marie and Clyde knew nothing could keep them apart. (Courtesy Marie P. Buckner.)

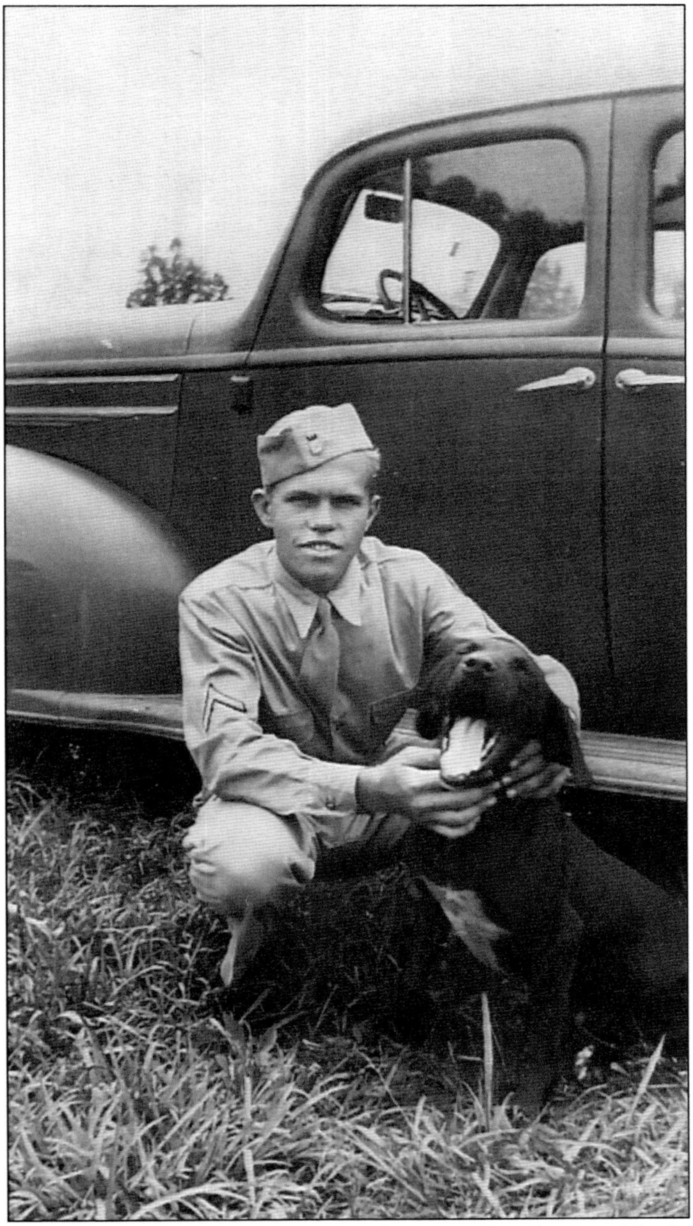

In 1939, Paul Woody had a female English setter that mated with a neighbor's hound and had some pups. Woody was a bird hunter and decided to euthanize the pups because he only wanted pure-bred dogs. Unknown to Woody, the setter had taken one of the pups and hidden it down by the Haw River. When the dog slipped off to feed her pup, Woody's nieces—Olive, Iris, Marilla, and Ruth-Marie— followed her and discovered the pup. The girls' grandmother, Elzina McBane Woody, decided the pup should appropriately be named Moses. When Paul Woody found out about Moses, he decided to euthanize him as well. The nieces persuaded Woody to give the pup to a friend in the Saxapahaw Mill village who was working on a learner's wage of 20¢ per hour. The friend was Edgar Allen Cashwell. Edgar kept the dog, signed up for the military, and later married one of the nieces, Olive Woody. (Courtesy of Edgar and Olive Cashwell.)

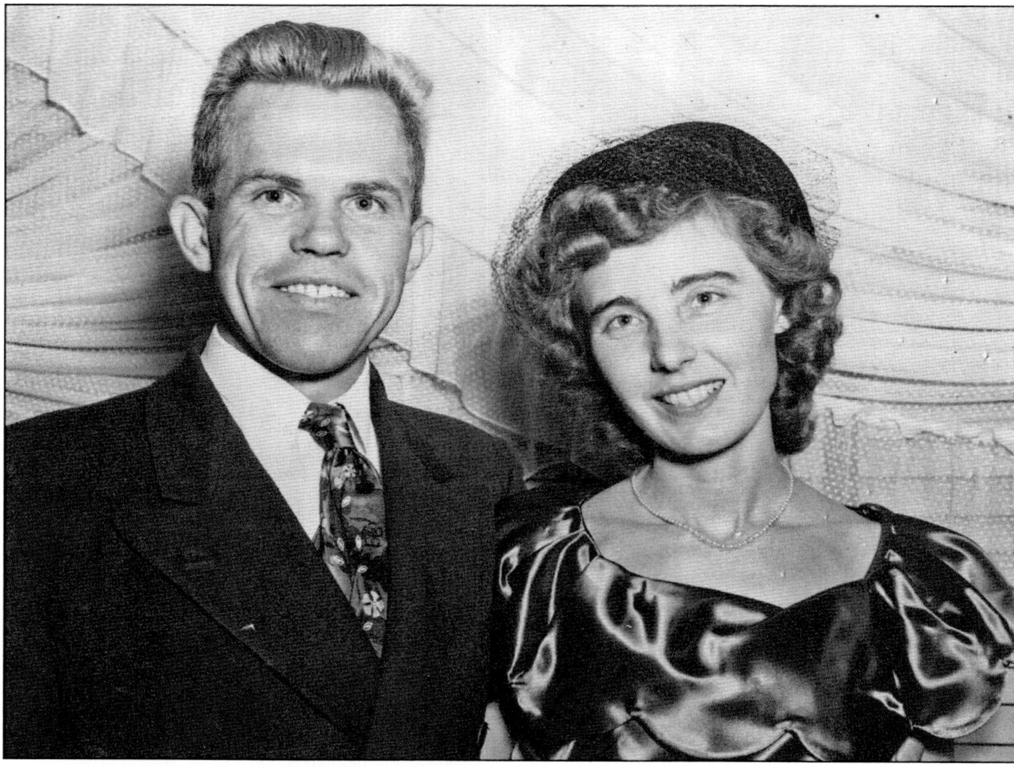

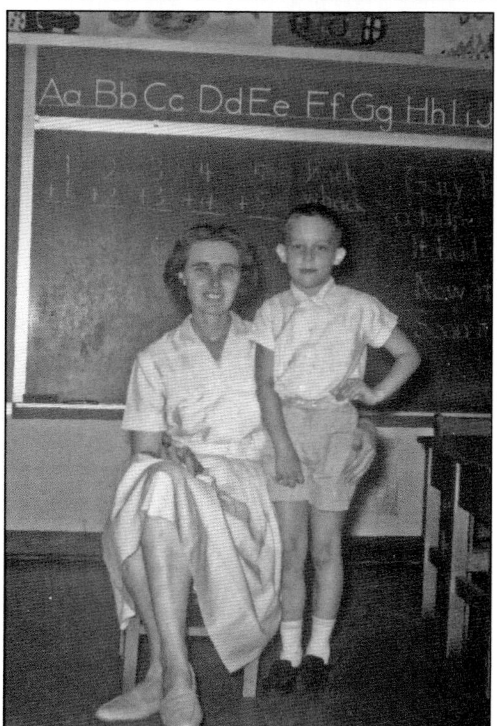


This is Edgar and Olive Cashwell's wedding night photograph from August 17, 1950. Olive Cashwell was a well-known first-grade teacher in Saxapahaw. After Edgar completed the service, he worked at the Saxapahaw Cotton Mill for 40¢ an hour. In 1953, Edgar was appointed recreation director at the newly built Saxapahaw Community Center, later renamed the Buddy Collins Community Center. In 1968, Edgar became the Saxapahaw postmaster. Edgar was awarded a special citation by the North Carolina Recreation and Parks Society in 1973, for he, "more than any other single individual, was instrumental in the creation of the one of the first County Recreation programs in NC into what is known today as the Alamance County Recreation and Parks Department." Edgar continued his devotion to the Recreation and Parks Society during his time as postmaster and later retired in 1983. (Edgar Cashwell.)

In May 1965, Olive Cashwell, first-grade teacher at Saxapahaw Elementary, poses with student Gary Johnson. (Courtesy of Gary Johnson.)

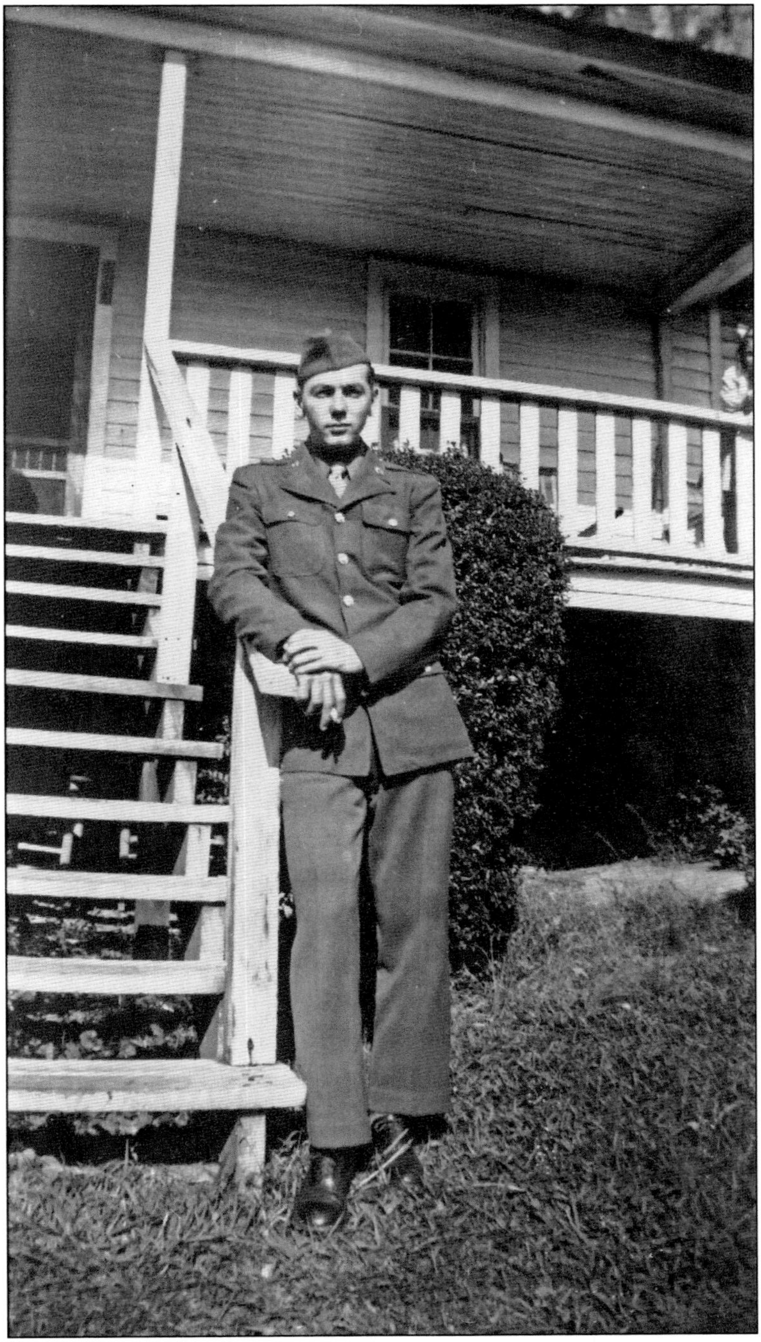

Crayton Hardin was in General Patton's Third Army. He was a field telephone line operator. According to Crayton, "the Army did not want any grass to grow under [his] feet," so they sent him to Scotland, England, France, Germany, Czechoslovakia, and Belgium. Crayton smoked until 1972, when he quit cold turkey. Both Crayton and his wife, Frances, worked in the Saxapahaw Cotton Mill and were devoted to B. Everett Jordan. Crayton was a tender twister, and Frances was a payroll clerk. (Courtesy of Frances and Crayton Hardin.)

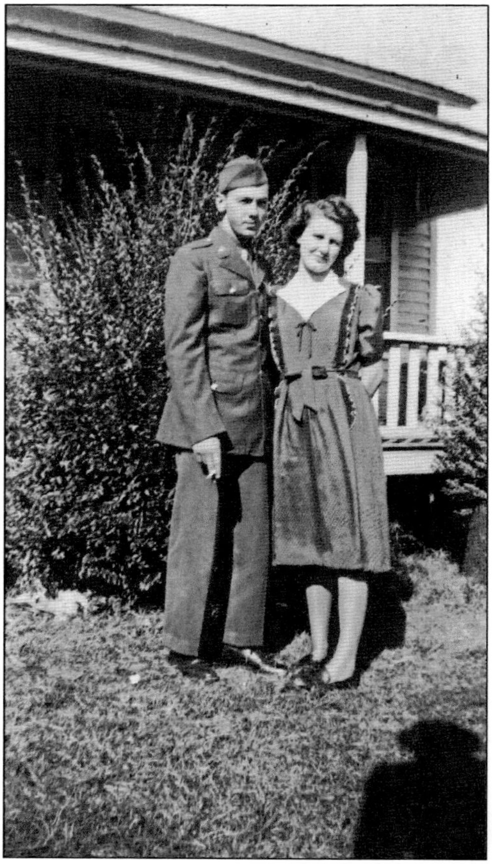

Frances and Crayton Hardin are dressed for Sunday church at Moore's Chapel Baptist Church in 1944. (Courtesy of Frances and Crayton Hardin.)

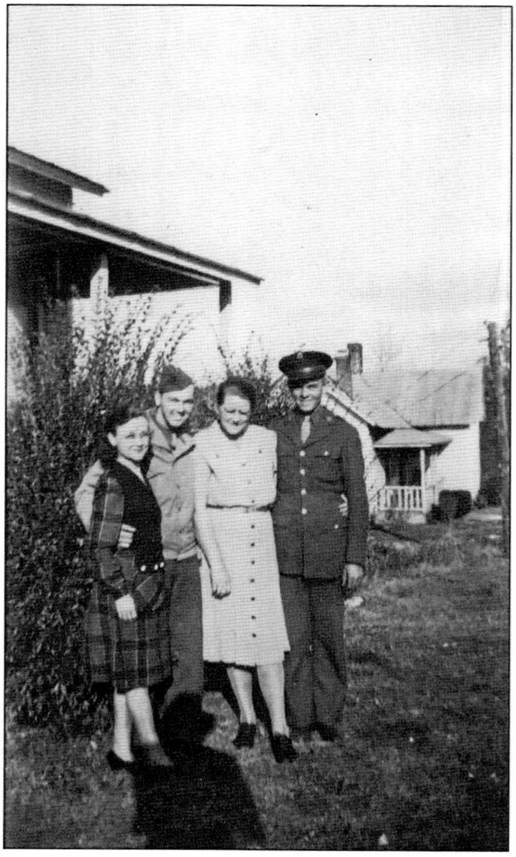

In 1944, from left to right, are Vaudie Hardin and her son Crayton Hardin; Frances Hardin's mother, Bertha Honeycutt; and Bertha's son L. A. Honeycutt. Frances was taking the photograph. (Courtesy of Frances and Crayton Hardin.)

Edgar Cashwell received a brand-new box camera in 1940. He and his friends gathered for a special friends photograph. Unfortunately, Edgar realized that he did not get to be in the photograph. From left to right are (first row) Doris Richardson Thompson, Eunicielle McBane, and Rena May Little; (second row) Rudolph Lloyd (a colonel in the air force), Geneva Braxton Foust, Frances Russell, and Wayne Lindley. (Courtesy of Edgar Cashwell.)

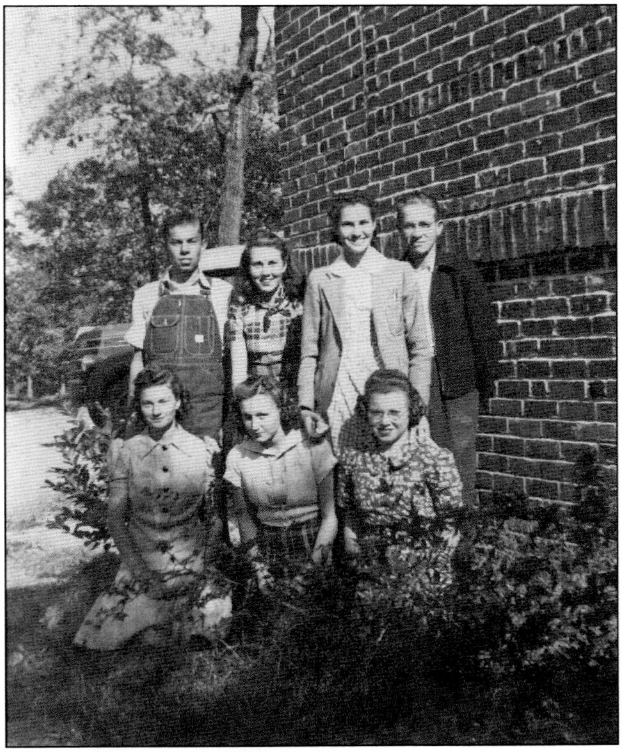

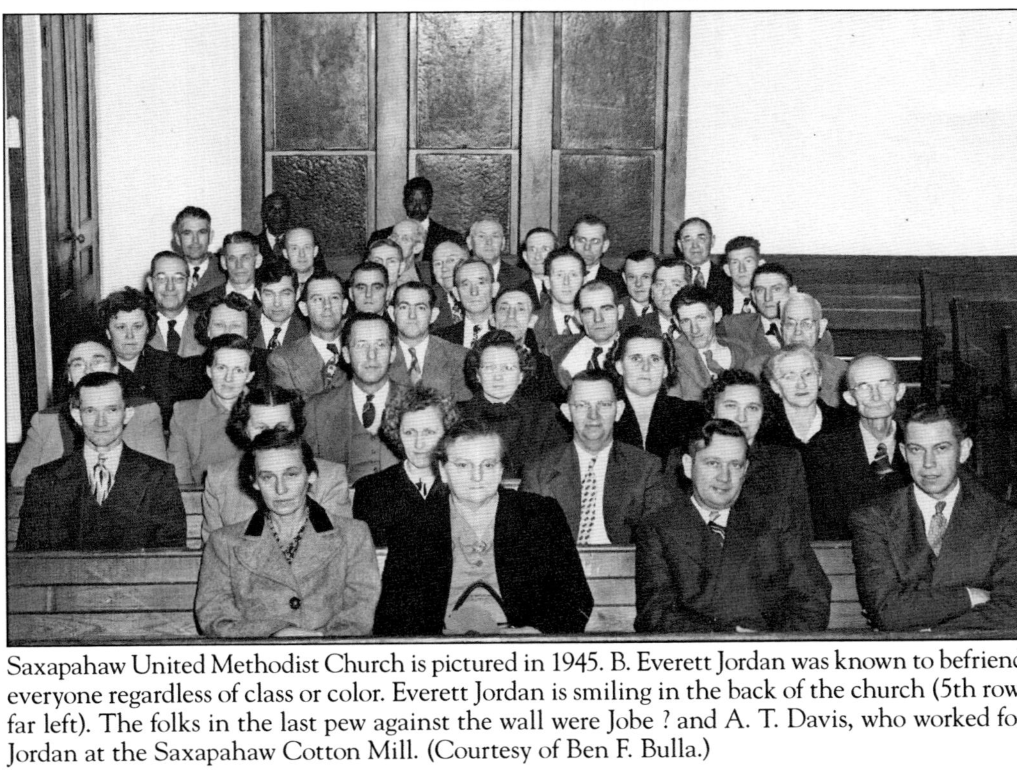

Saxapahaw United Methodist Church is pictured in 1945. B. Everett Jordan was known to befriend everyone regardless of class or color. Everett Jordan is smiling in the back of the church (5th row, far left). The folks in the last pew against the wall were Jobe ? and A. T. Davis, who worked for Jordan at the Saxapahaw Cotton Mill. (Courtesy of Ben F. Bulla.)

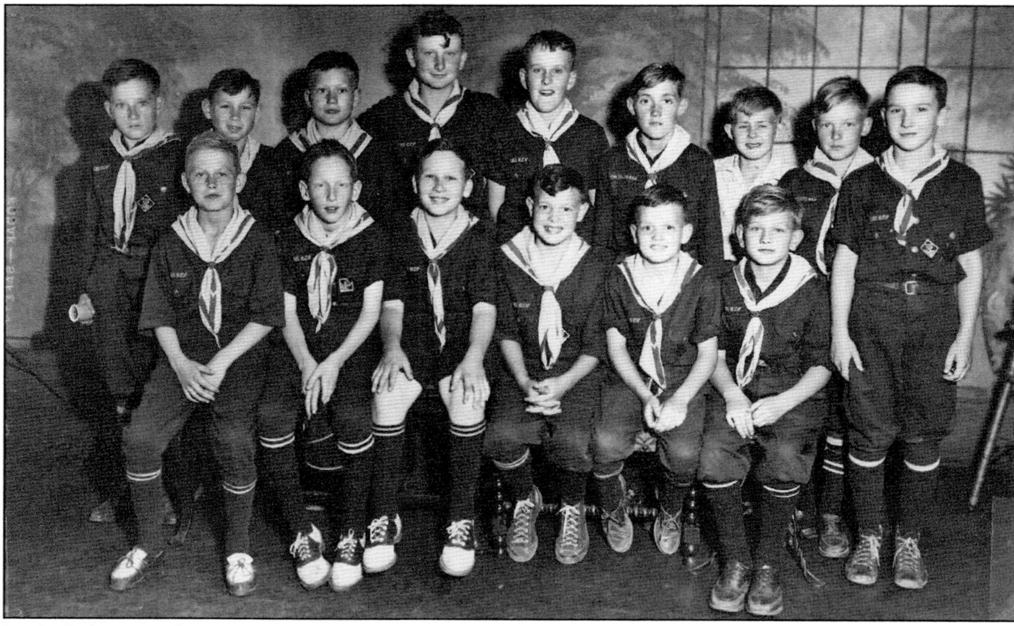

Included somewhere among the boys in this Saxapahaw Cub Scout photograph from the 1940s are Tippy Crisson, Delmer Crisson, and John Jordan. Katherine Jordan was the den mother. (Courtesy of John Jordan.)

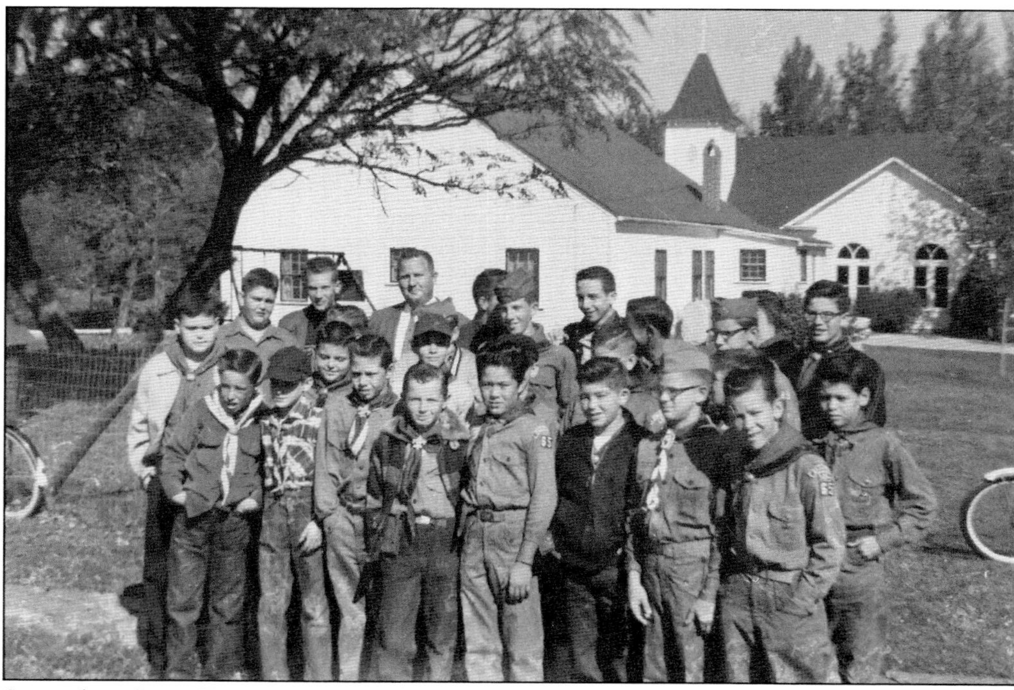

Saxapahaw Scout Troop No. 65 stands in front of the United Methodist Church on Saxapahaw Bethlehem Church Road. Although they cannot be individually identified, the photograph includes Steve and John Madden (sons of Leon Madden), Gregg Bulla (son of Ben F. Bulla), and Dan Cheek. (Courtesy of Edgar Cashwell.)

David Johnson and two unidentified friends celebrate May Day in 1956 at the original brick Saxapahaw Elementary school. (Courtesy of Gary Johnson.)

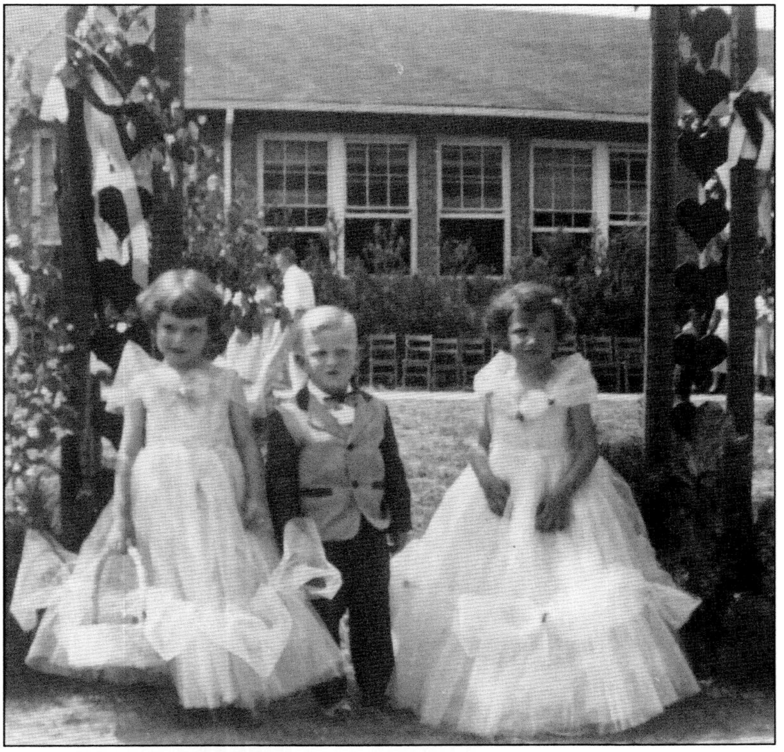

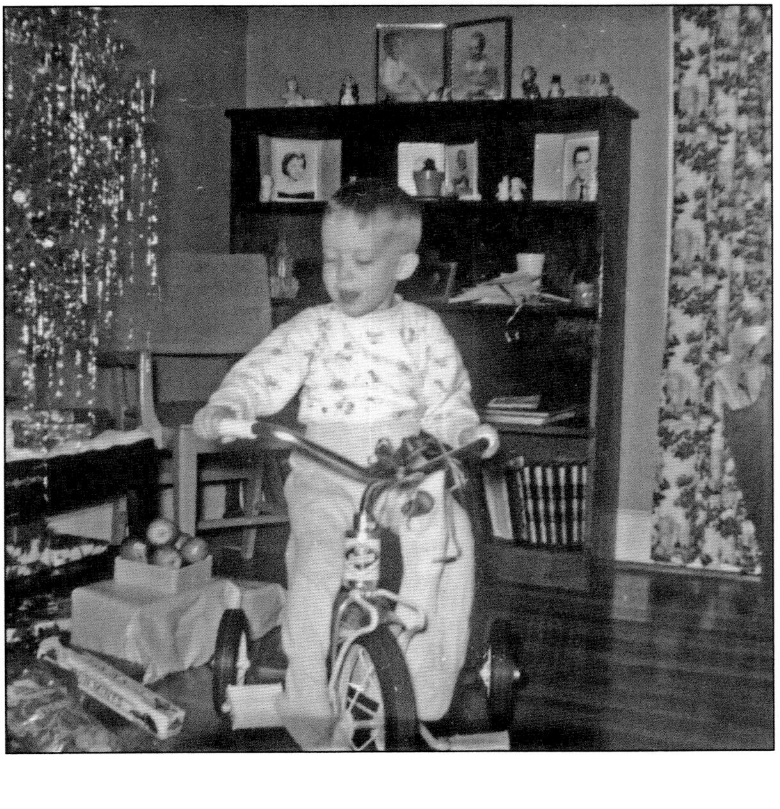

Gary Johnson, pictured in 1961, rode this bicycle until the wheels fell off and ran over people's feet at the Johnson store. At this age, Gary was at the Johnson store with his parents from 6:00 a.m. to 6:00 p.m. (Courtesy of Gary Johnson.)

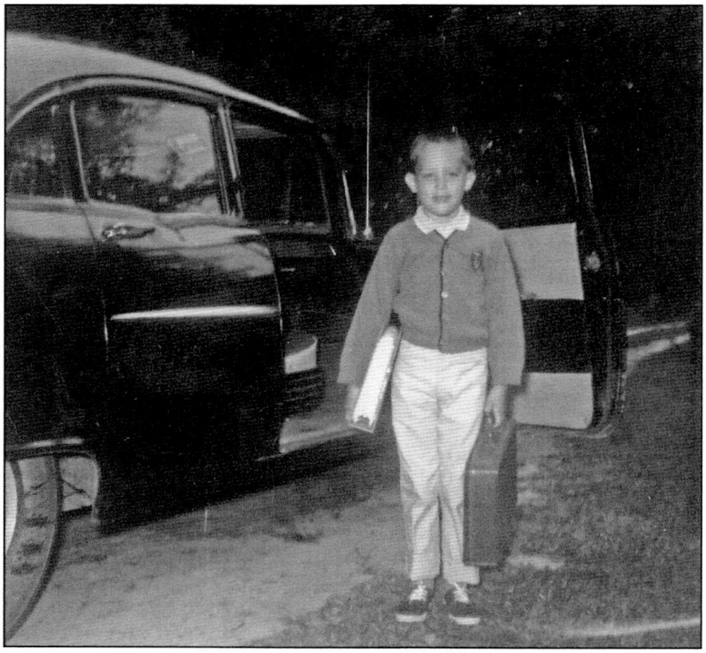

Gary Johnson (in September 1965) gets out of the car on his first day of school at Saxapahaw Elementary. Gary requested to have a briefcase instead of a school bag. It was no wonder Gary grew up to become an accountant. (Courtesy of Gary Johnson.)

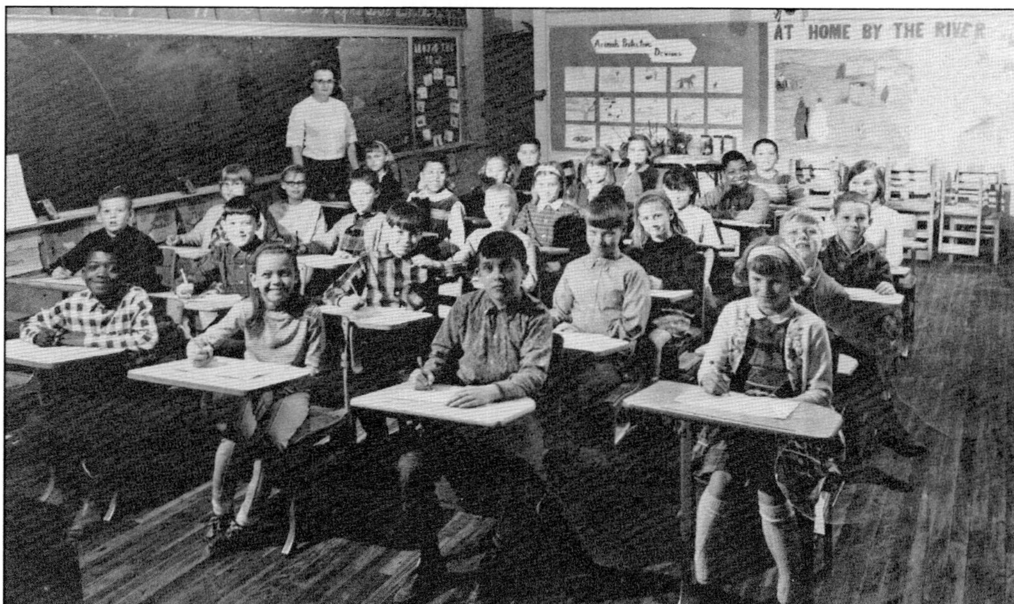

This was the last day at Saxapahaw Elementary in 1968. After this photograph was taken, the children walked out the door and into their new school at B. Everett Jordan Elementary (named after Senator Jordan). Teacher Mrs. Miller is seen with (in no particular order) Waden Quakenbush, Chris Braxton, Sammy Thompson, Vickie Watts, Terry Dover, James Dimuke, Debbie Bumgardner, Mary Wilson, Vernon Thompson, Doug Garnett, Cindy Knighten, Ricky Harnell, Randy Richardson, Angela McClure, JoAnn Brewer, Kathy Anderson, Craig Alston, Gary Johnson, Ann Williams, Lucille Bowden, Cathy Cartner, Johnnie Williams, Terry Knighten, Teresa Davis, Shelby Herring, and Pam Knighten. (Courtesy of Gary Johnson.)

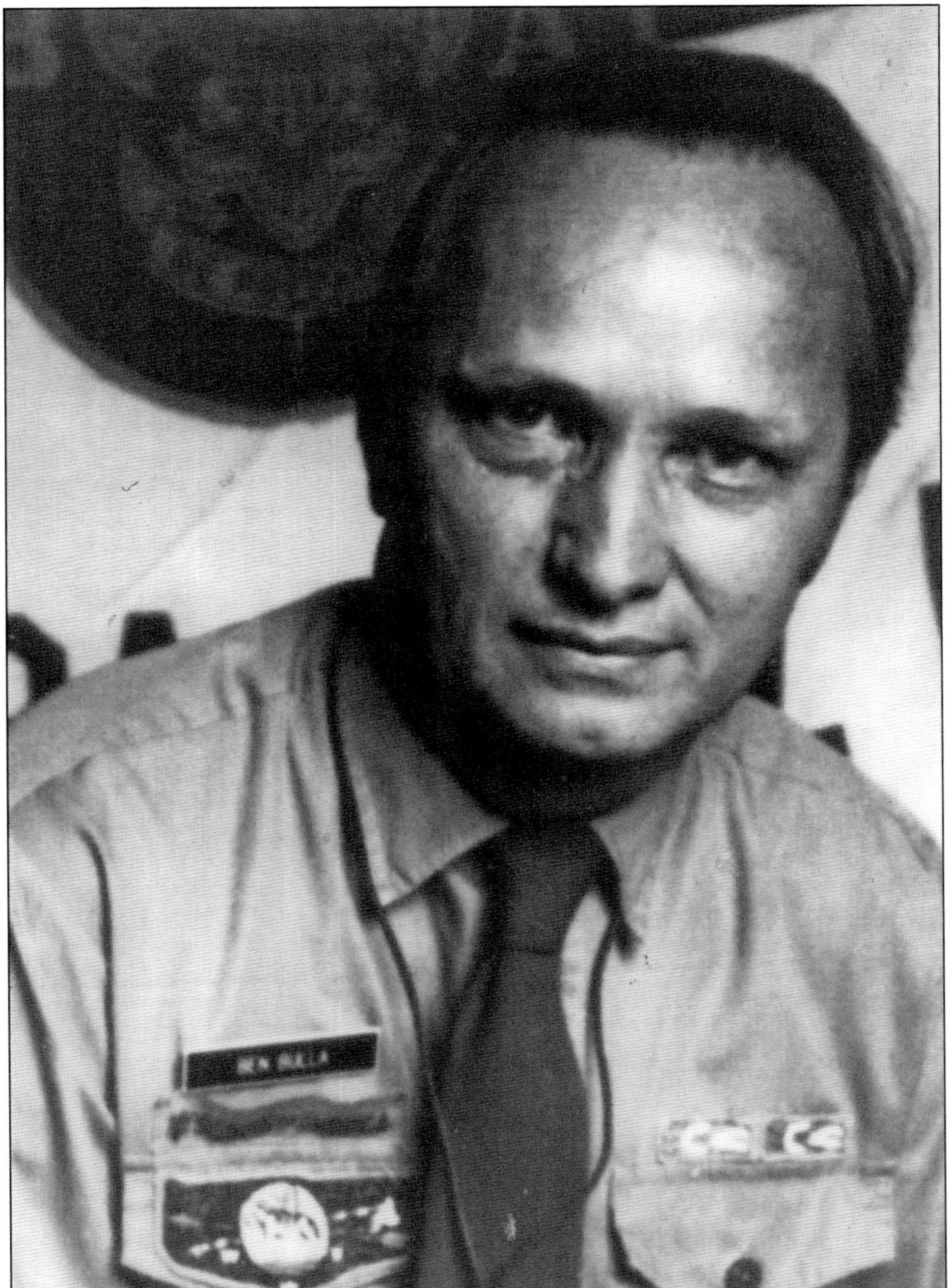

Ben F. Bulla was the Saxapahaw Scoutmaster of Troop 65. He planned and help build the Saxapahaw Scout cabin in 1964, developed Eagle Scout scholarships, and was instrumental in the development of the 1,140-acre Cherokee Scout Reservation. Ben F. Bulla married June Moore on August 2, 1946. Their son Gregg Bulla (Eagle Scout) married Cheri Fussel and had two daughters, Morgan and Courtney. Gregg's sister Beth married Bill Haney, and they had daughter Brooke. (Courtesy of Ben F. Bulla.)

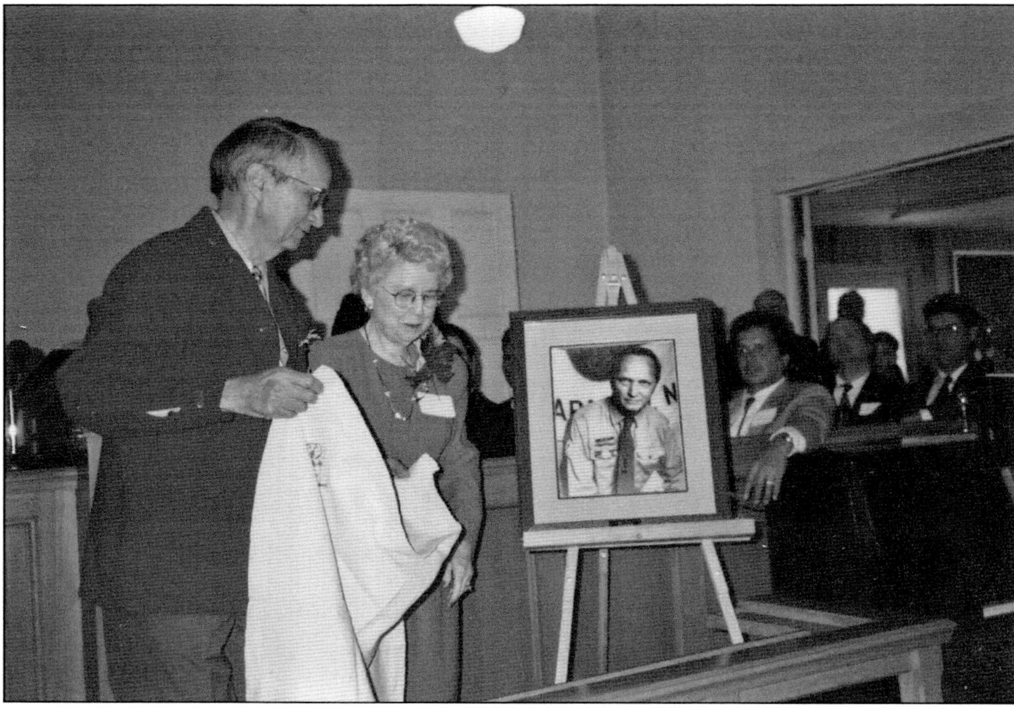

Ben F. Bulla was Scoutmaster for 33 years, from 1942 to 1975. This photograph was taken during the Scout cabin dedication to Ben F. Bulla. (Courtesy of Ben F. Bulla.)

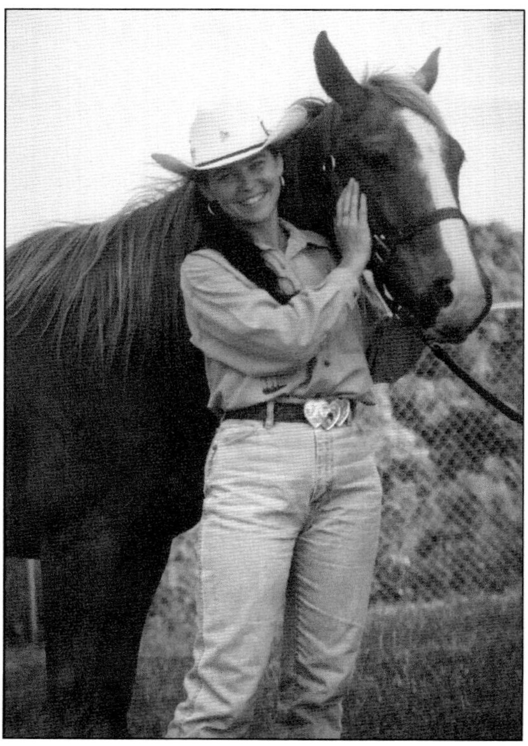

Shown here is Sandy Bradshaw (wife of Mark) of the Diamond B stud farm in Saxapahaw. Sandy is an accomplished equestrian and trainer. She won 17 awards in a single show. Sandy and Mark's daughter Rachel is also an accomplished and award-winning rider. Sandy continues to teach students to ride and show their horses in competition. (Courtesy of Austin Walker.)

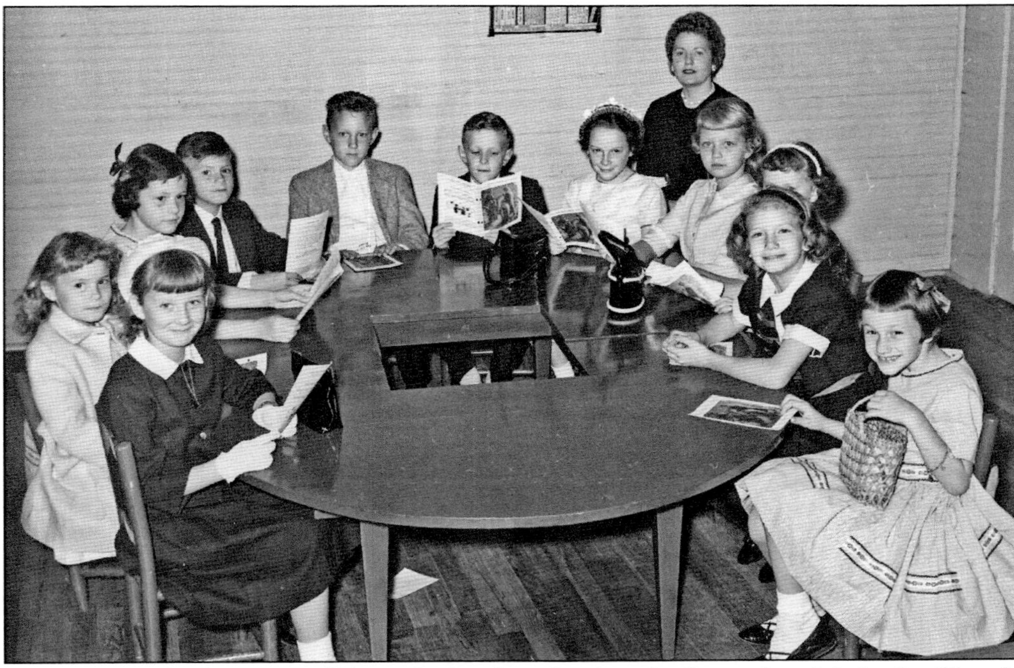

June Bulla (wife of Ben F. Bulla) taught Sunday school at the Saxapahaw Methodist Church. The children include, in unknown order, Beth Bulla, Cathy Jordan, Len Jordan, Doug Durham, Margie Newlin (now Dr. Margie N. Dickens), Vicky Neal, Judy Crutchfield, Judy Page, and the Walters children. (Courtesy of Ben F. and June Bulla.)

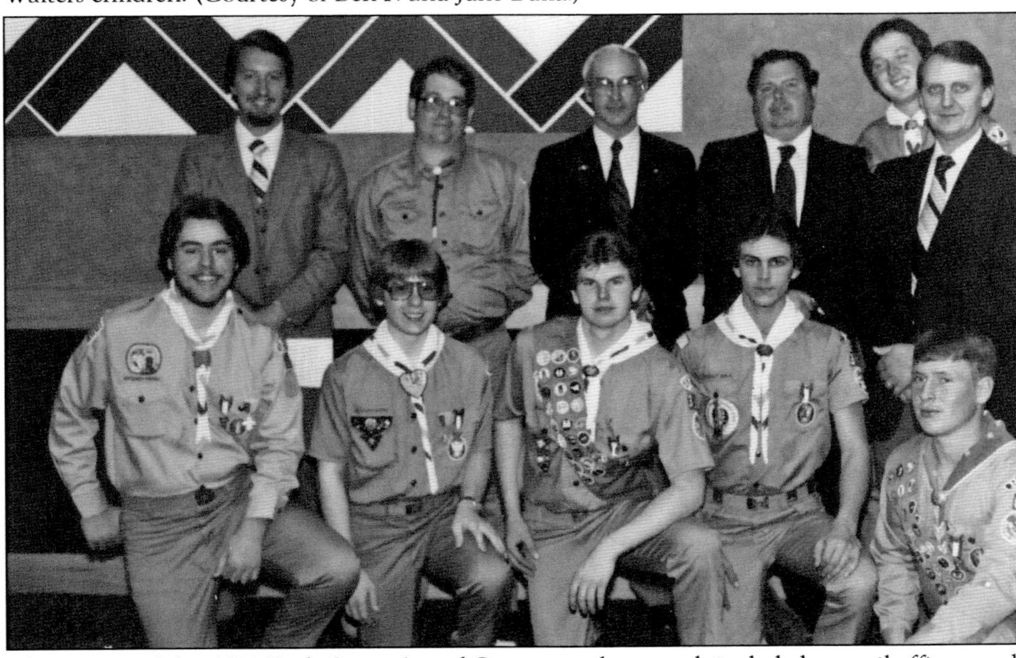

The top row of this 1981 Eagle Scout Award Ceremony photograph included council officers such as state representative John M. Jordan (center) and Ben F. Bulla (placement unknown). William Riley (far right) is the only identified Scout. (Courtesy of Jordan Properties Archives.)

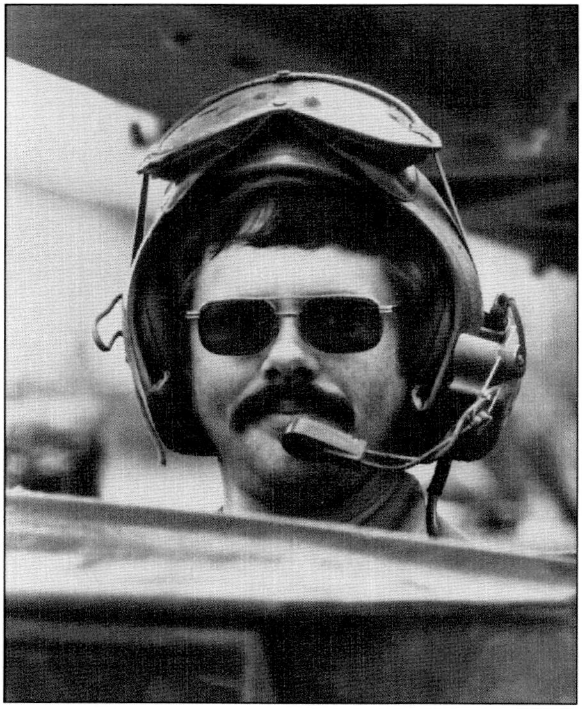

Gregg Bulla, son of Benjamin Bulla, was in the National Guard. (Courtesy of Ben F. and June Bulla.)

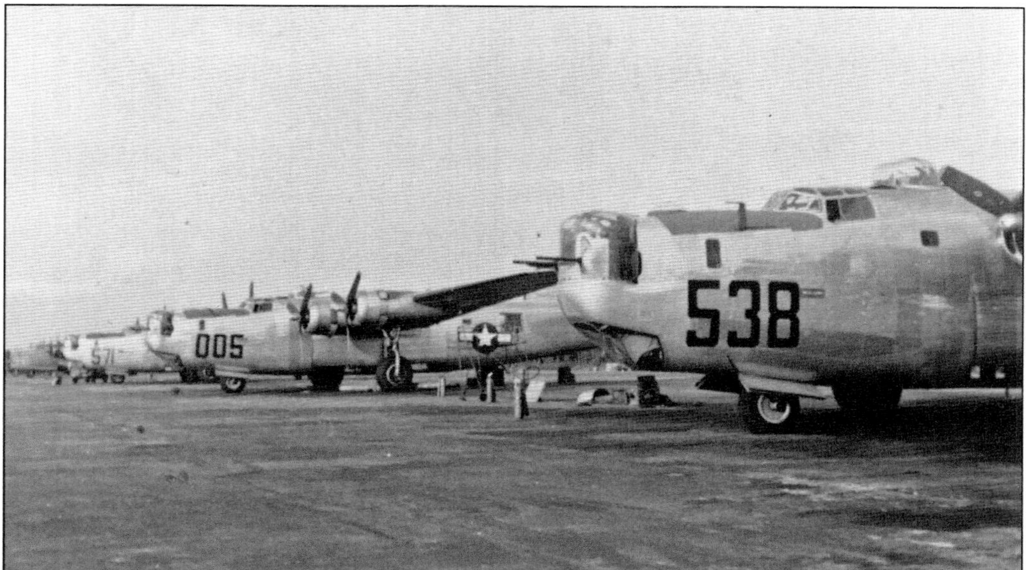


Leon Madden's family came to Saxapahaw in 1928 and at first moved into a house built by one of the sons of the original mill owners, the Newlins. Leon Madden began working at the Saxapahaw Cotton Mill in 1940. In 1942, he married Annie Ora Thompson and left for the air force a few months later. The B24 airplane on the right, shown in 1945, was the last plane Leon Madden restored while in the air force. This plane was his baby. After returning home from the air force, Leon continued to work at the mill until it closed its doors in 1994. (Courtesy of Leon Madden.)

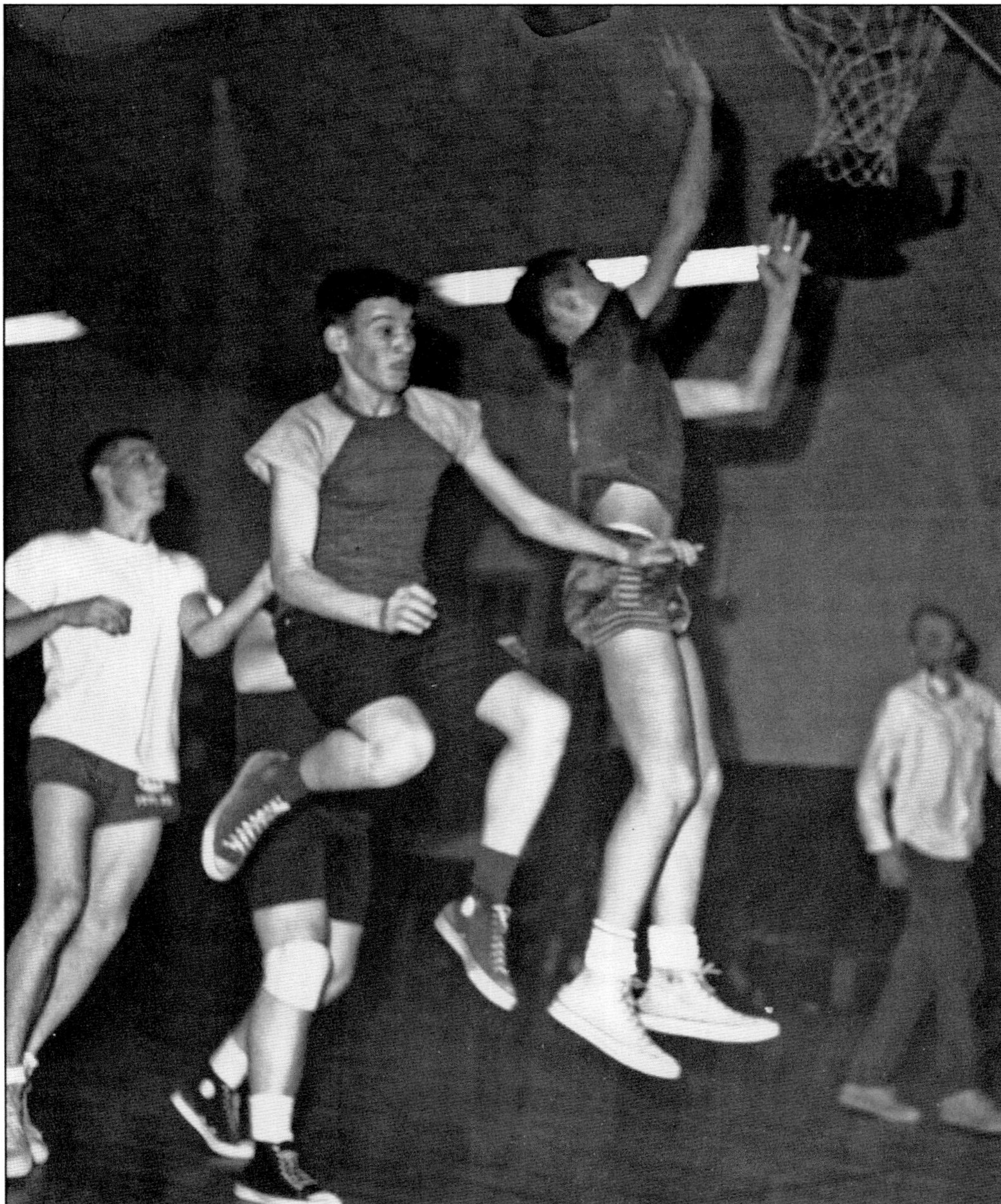

Buddy Paris (center) and Steve Madden (right) are in flight during a basketball game at the Buddy Collins Community Center. Robert Hubbard is pictured on the left. (Courtesy of Edgar Cashwell.)

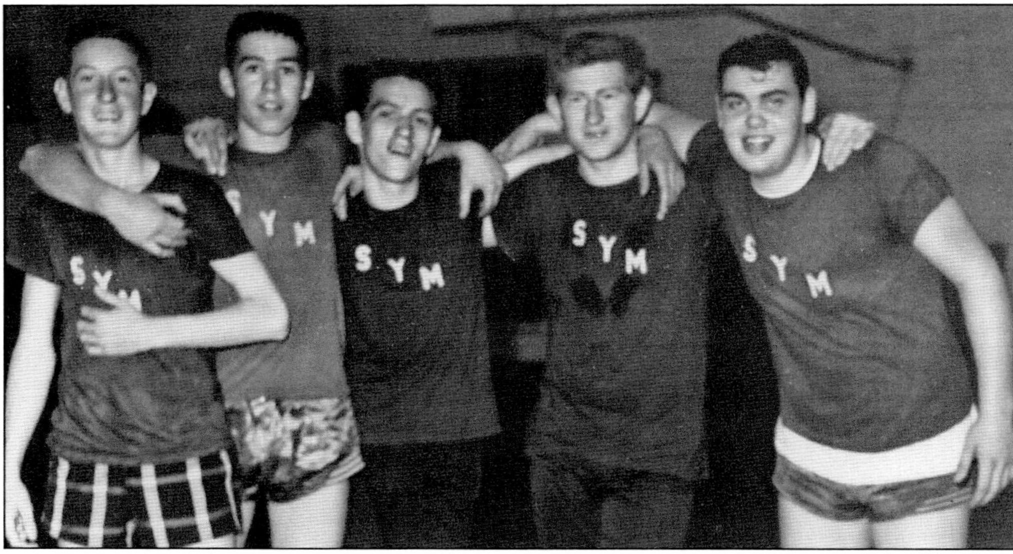


The Saxapahaw Young Men (or SYM) included, from left to right, Gene Barrett, Steve Madden (Leon Madden's son), Jackie Grumbles, Billy Gene Knighten, and Wayne Crisson. (Courtesy of Edgar Cashwell.)

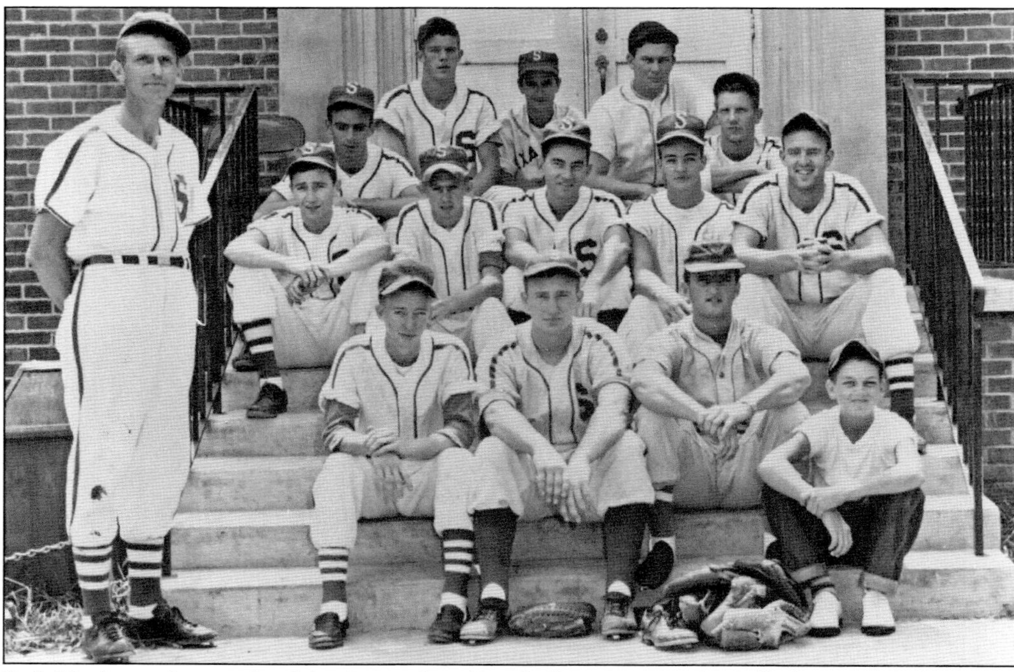

R. J. Neal was the coach of the Saxapahaw Baseball Team in 1954. Ball players included Byron "Big Barn" Guthrie, who was 6 feet, 7 inches and was signed to play with the Pittsburgh Pirates. A car ran into Big Barn while he was riding his motorcycle and destroyed his chances to ever play professionally again. Members of the team are, from left to right, (first row) Joe Boley, Van Dorn Crutchfield, Max Cortner, and Jerry Neal; (second row) Johnny Smith, Johnny Mae Haithcock, Henry Johnson, Billy Thompson, and Big Barn Guthrie; (third row) B. Neal, Melvin ?, Wade Dean, A. T. Blackstock, and Jack Hall. (Courtesy of Edgar Cashwell.)

On the right is Richard Craig Alston, son of Clara and Richard Alston, in 1958. Below, Clara and Richard leave for Sunday church. They had five children—Napoleon, Terry, Geneva, Cathy, and Craig. Richard was a large and muscular man and was able to give piggyback rides to three children at the same time. Richard did this almost every day until one day he laid on the floor, let the children climb on, and fell to the floor, begging for them to get off and realizing that the children had grown too much. Both Richard and Clara worked at the mill together for many, many years, although in different departments and different shifts. When Clara would go to work and pass her husband, he would pat her on the fanny when nobody was looking—until one day when John Jordan caught him. When Jordan asked what he was doing, Richard replied "getting her ready." (Both courtesy of Clara Alston.)

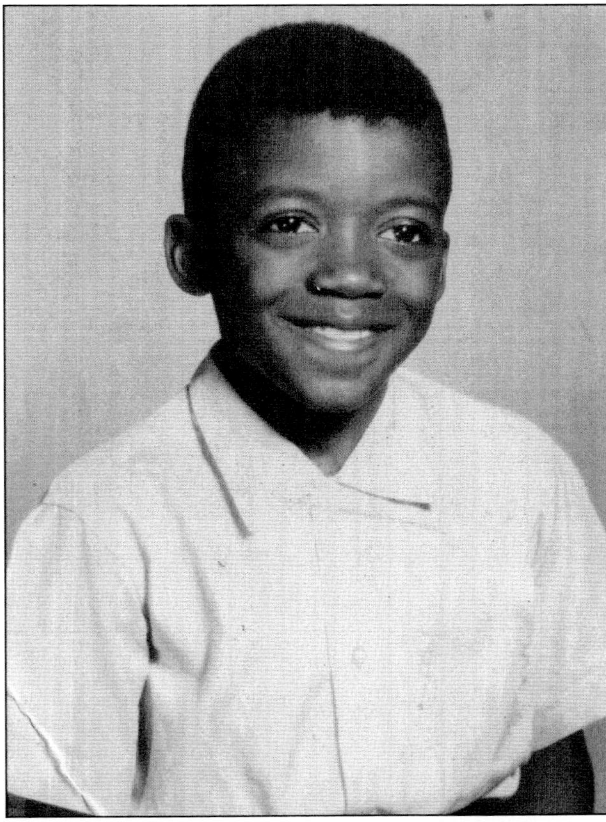

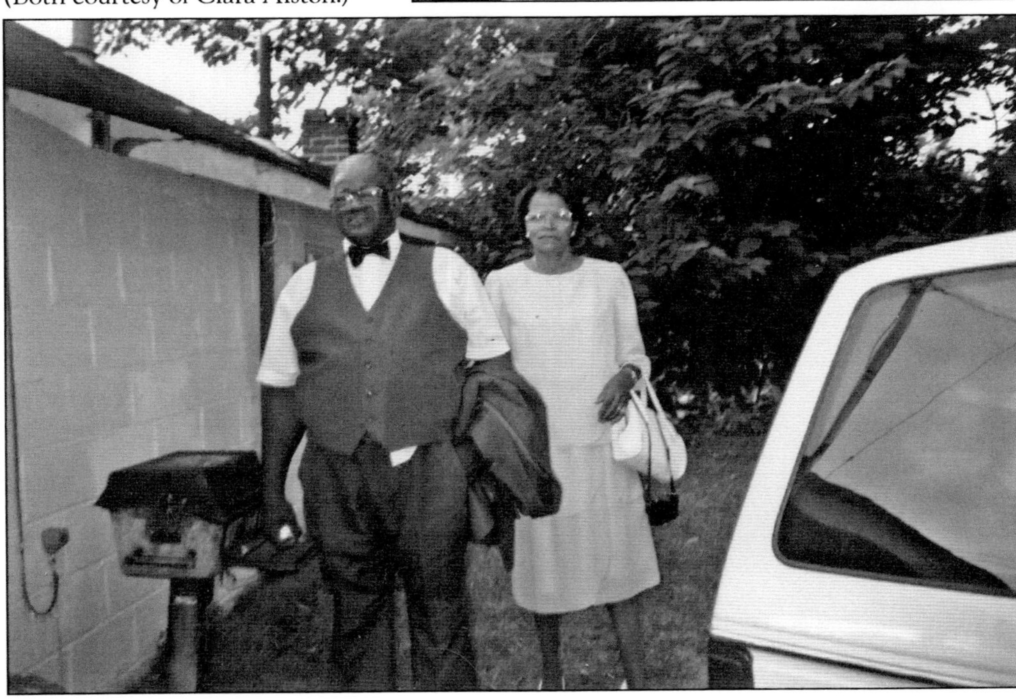

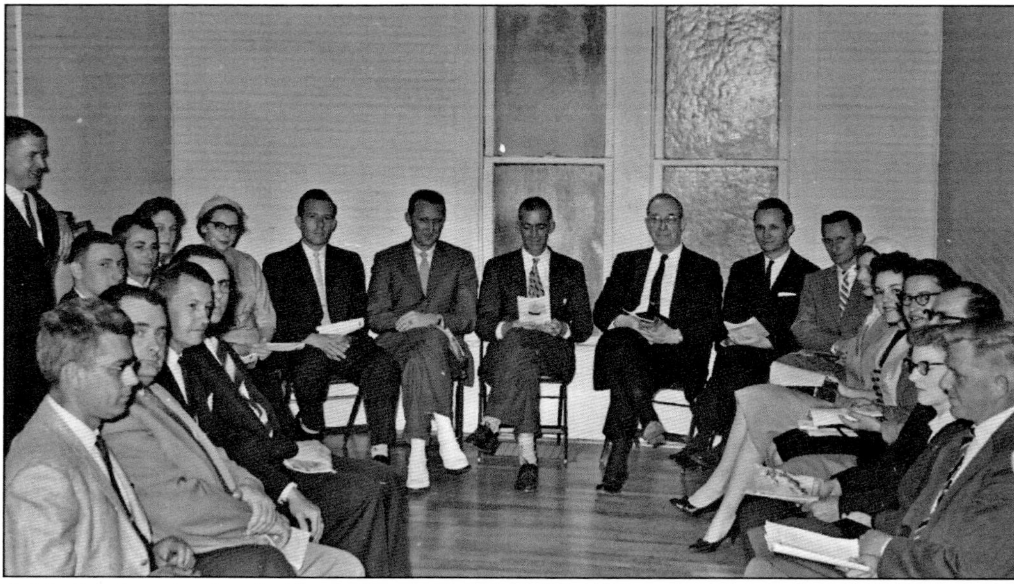

Adult Sunday school at the United Methodist Church in 1962 included, in no particular order, Leon Madden, Richard Stanford, Bruce Morten, Bobby Hardin, May Mclean, Vandoran Crutchfield, Ben E. Jr. and Ellen Jordan, Dan Montgomery, Hoover Dixon, Albert Neal, John Ray Madden, the Mcbanes, Ben F. Bulla, and Senator Jordan. (Courtesy of Ben F. Bulla.)

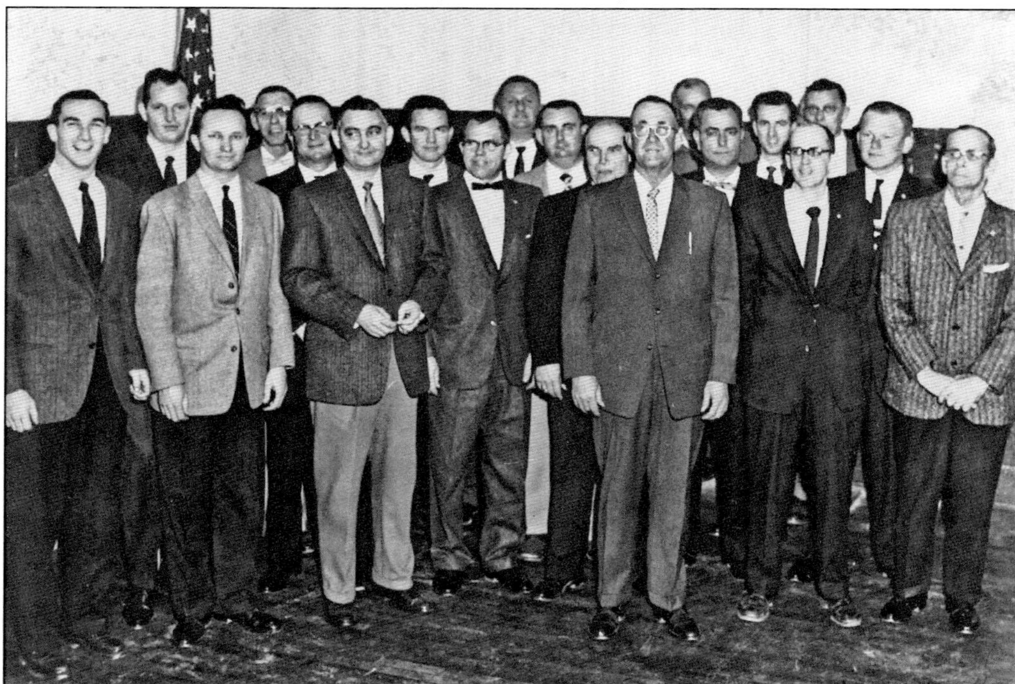

The Exchange Club of Saxapahaw in 1958 included Ben Freshwater (second from left), Edgar Cashwell (wearing bow tie), and in no particular order, John Jordan, Ben F. Bulla, Earl Johnson, Edgar Cashwell, Richard Stanford, Harvey Foust, Johnny Braxton, Ken Bailey, Raymond Braxton, Brooks Covney, Bob Gerrison, Alton Wilson, and Bill Arnette. (Courtesy of Ben F. Bulla.)

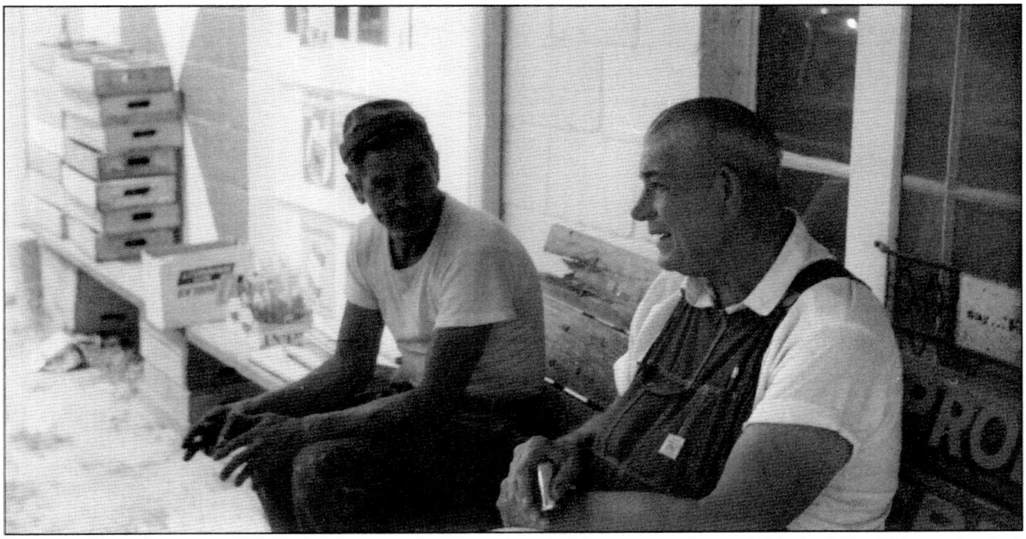

Everyone was fascinated with the "strongest man in Alamance County." "Big" Bud Foust (right) helped cut the ice from the Haw River in the winter. Some say he was able to carry a 300-pound block of ice under each arm. "Big" Bud would meet his wife, Pauline Herron, every day after work at a local service station store on Highway 87. On September 13, 1968, Foust was shot and killed at the store when he tried to stop a robbery. He was only 54 years old. Bud had 10 brothers and sisters. His father was Robert Lee Foust, and his mother was Mary Jane McPherson. Rowland Cole is pictured on the left. (Courtesy of Edgar Cashwell.)

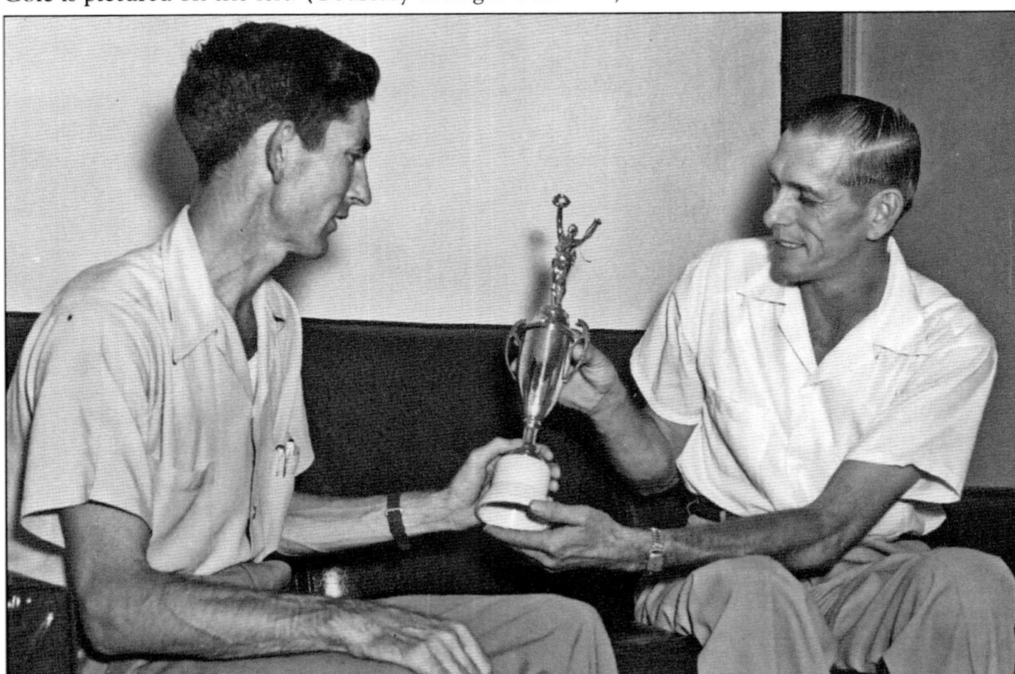

Saxapahaw Exchange Club (a civic organization) won yet another trophy. Pictured are Jake Miller (left) and Brooks Coveny. All of the trophies are on display in the Buddy Collins Community Center. (Courtesy of Edgar Cashwell.)

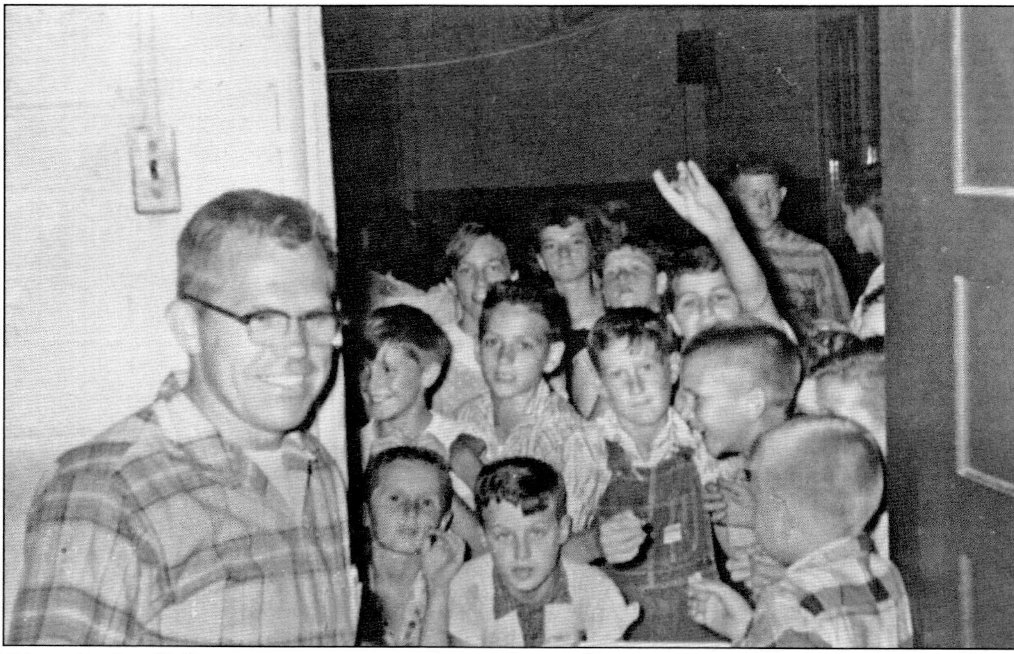

Edgar Cashwell (longtime community center director) is trying to distribute ice cream to the children. Ice cream was a big thing in Saxapahaw, constantly used as a reward and handed out on hot days. Although their placement is unknown, Gene Barrett and Billy Knighten are among the children in the doorway. The photograph is from the 1950s. (Courtesy of Edgar Cashwell.)

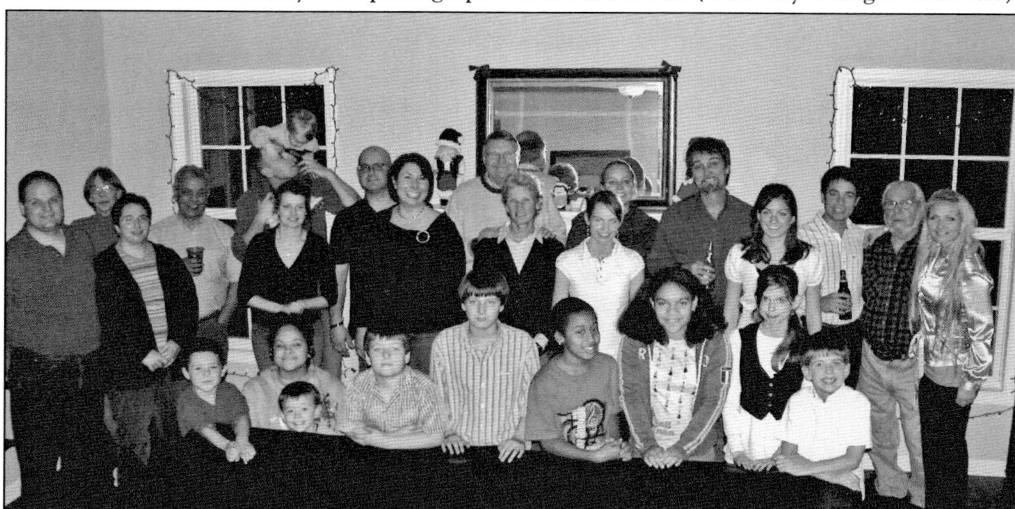

Shown here is the Haw Village Christmas Party at the Wallace's. From left to right are (first row) Connor Ramous, Saschya Williams (back), Michael Mues Jr., Zachary Weidemann, Nicholas Weidemann, Jocelyn ?, Tyese Williams, Julie Seals, and Justin Seals; (second row) Michael Weidemann, Emily Buker, Barbara Weidemann, Salim Benbahmed, Reaba and Mike Mues (with son Maverick on top), Jim and Jessica Ramous, John and Cheryl Treworgy, Angela Brehmer (back), Jessica Seals (front), Frankie Hayes, Jamie Seals, Nicholas Macaulay, Kenny Marsters, and Heather Wallace. (Courtesy of Chuck Brehmer.)

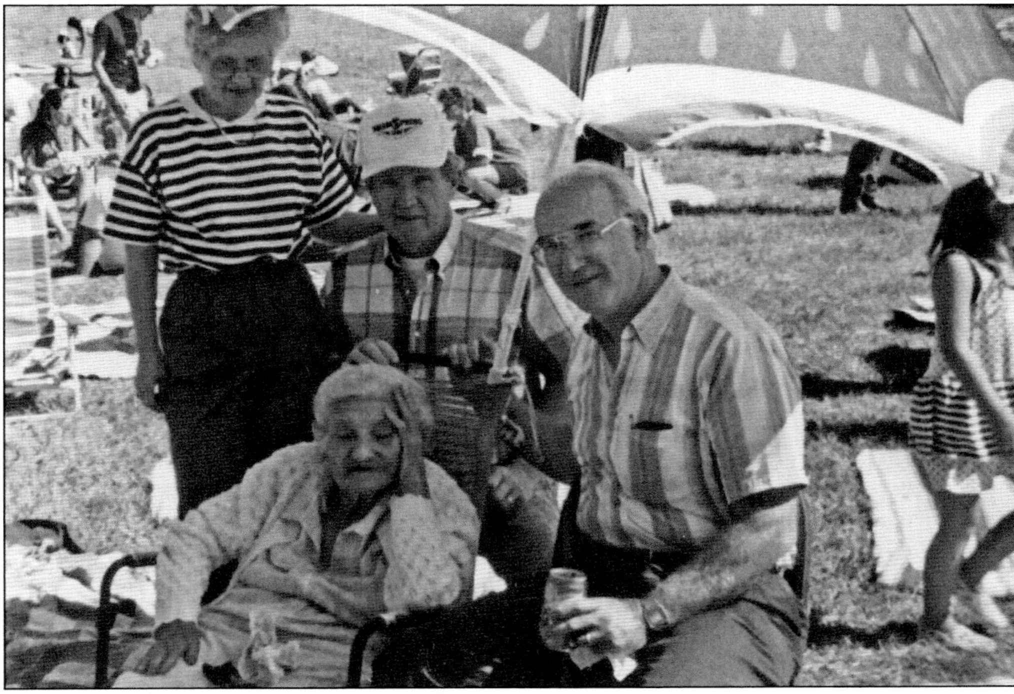

Meadowfest II, here in 1993, was an outdoor music festival planned by Mac Jordan to raise money for the Haw River Assembly. Wilma Phillips (standing) was John Jordan's secretary at the mill. Josie Grumbles, Luther's wife (seated), also worked at the mill. Josie was responsible for removing yarn from large wooden bobbins with her hands. In order to do her job quickly, she would grab box cutters and use them to remove the yarn. The box cutters would nick and destroy the wooden bobbins, so those bobbins could never be used again because they would snag future yarn. Josie continued to sneak box cutters and was finally let go from the mill. Josie and John (far right) remained friends. Harold Phillips is seen behind Josie. (Courtesy of John Jordan.)

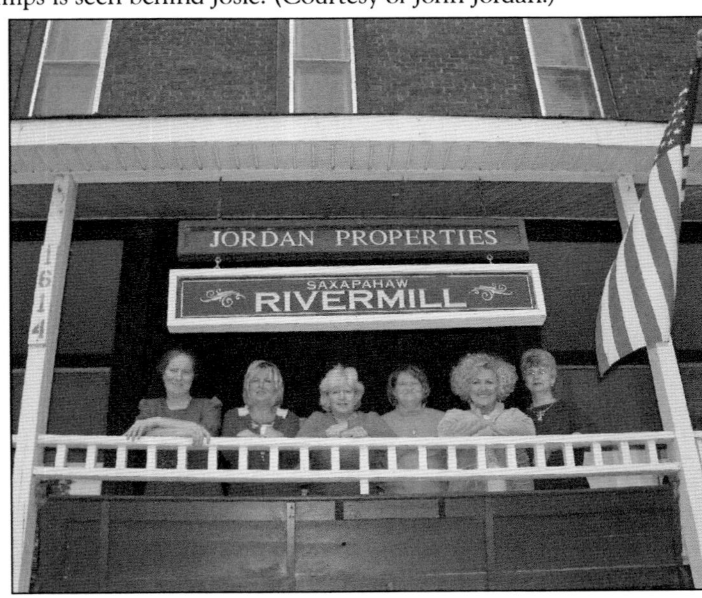


Pictured are the forever dedicated and southern belle–sweet ladies who work for the Jordan families. From left to right are Pam Aquino, Dana Sheffield, Dolores Apple, Sherry Martin, Sherry Graves, and Earlene Morris. Earlene, who recently retired, worked for the Jordans for many years. (Photograph by author.)

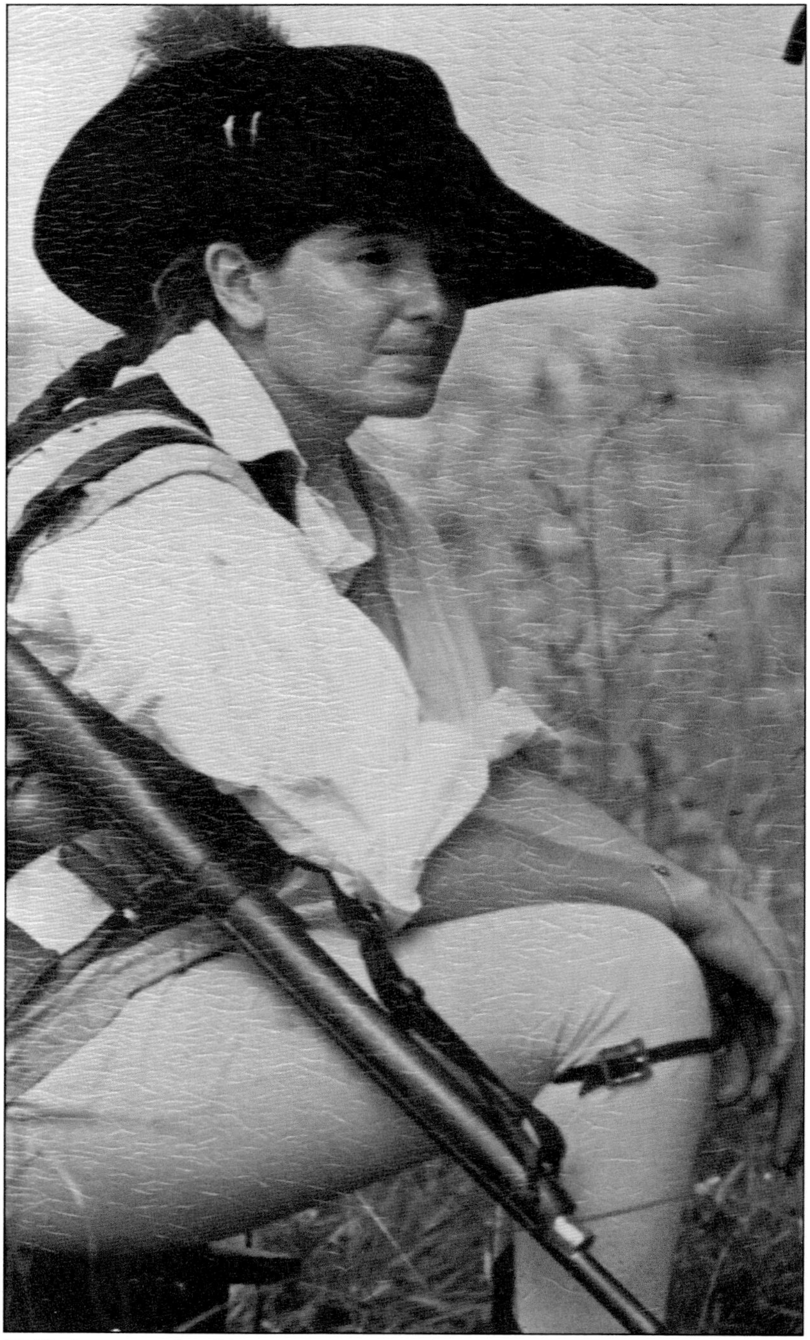

This is a 1977 photograph of Mary "Mary Sunshine" Glasgow. Mary attended a Civil War reenactment show during a 1976 bicentennial celebration. The following year, she became very involved in reenactment ceremonies. Mary attended East Carolina University, Atlantic Christian College, and Wilson Technical Institute and became a musician, playing the French horn. Mary switched her love to pottery after being taught by the famous Hiroshi Sueyoshi at Cape Fear Technical Institute. (Courtesy of Mary Glasgow.)

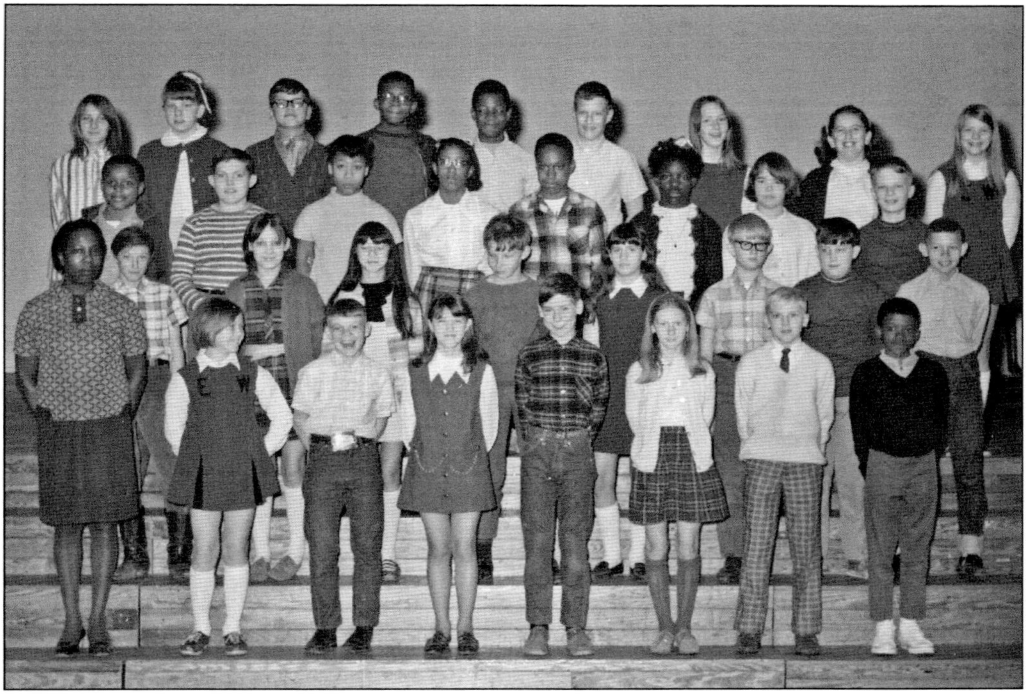

Eli Whitney's (possibly drama) class of 1971 includes Craig Alston and Gary Johnson. Their placement in the photograph is unknown. (Courtesy of Gary Johnson Archives.)

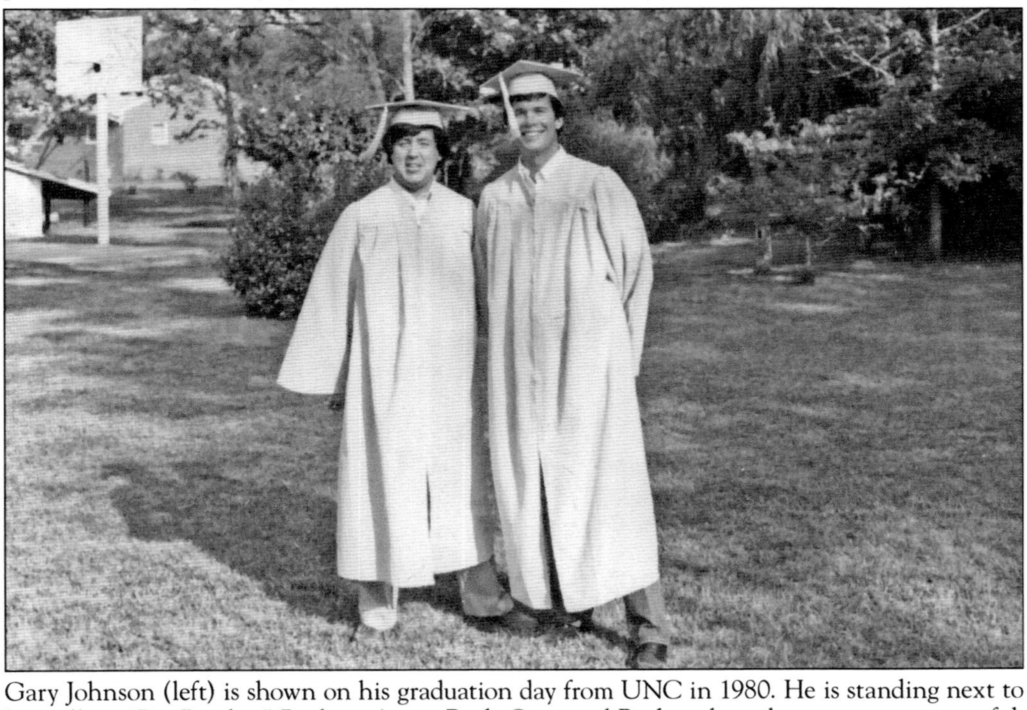

Gary Johnson (left) is shown on his graduation day from UNC in 1980. He is standing next to his college "Big Brother" Rodney Ange. Both Gary and Rodney have become very successful. (Courtesy of Gary Johnson Archives.)

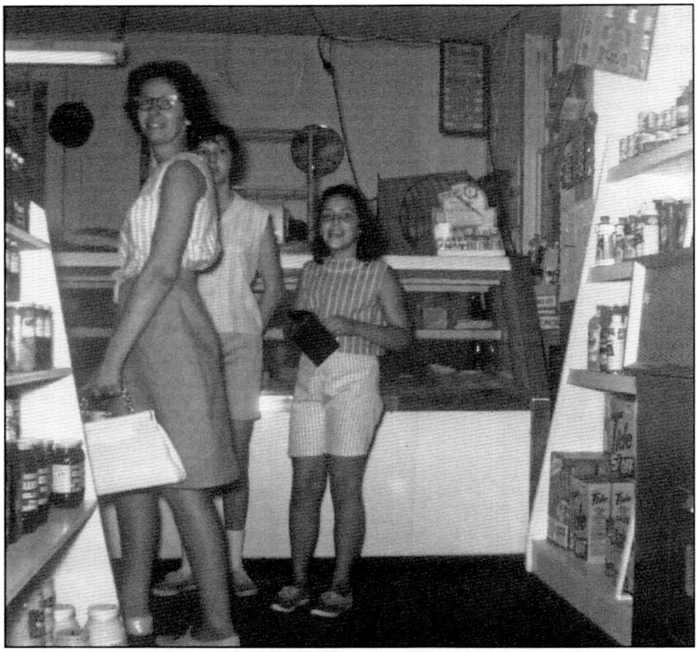

A photograph inside of the Johnson store in 1964 shows Nancy Keiser and two unidentified girls. Nancy and her husband, Melvin, were part of the Oriental Mission Society as missionaries. They both retired in Hong Kong. (Courtesy of Gary Johnson Archives.)

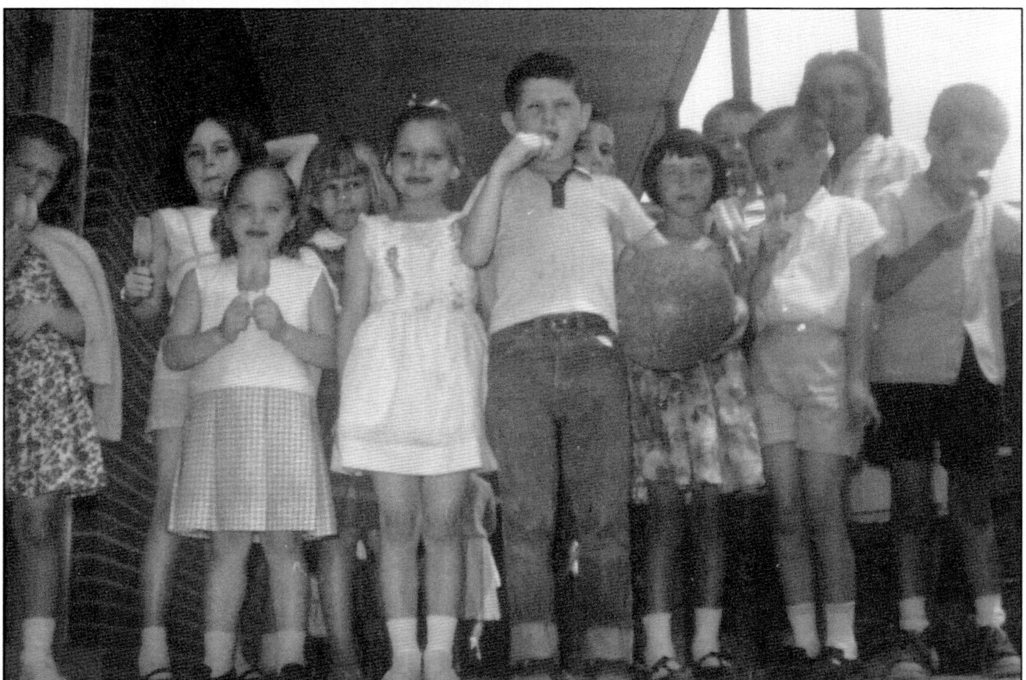

Olive Cashwell rewards her first-grade students with ice cream. Olive can be seen in the back on the right. Cathy Cartner, Olive's niece, is holding the ice cream with both hands; the girl behind the ball is Debbie Mcbane. The photograph also includes Gary Johnson, Lacy Rumley, and Renee Phillips, although their placement is unknown. The other children are unidentified. (Courtesy of Gary Johnson Archives.)

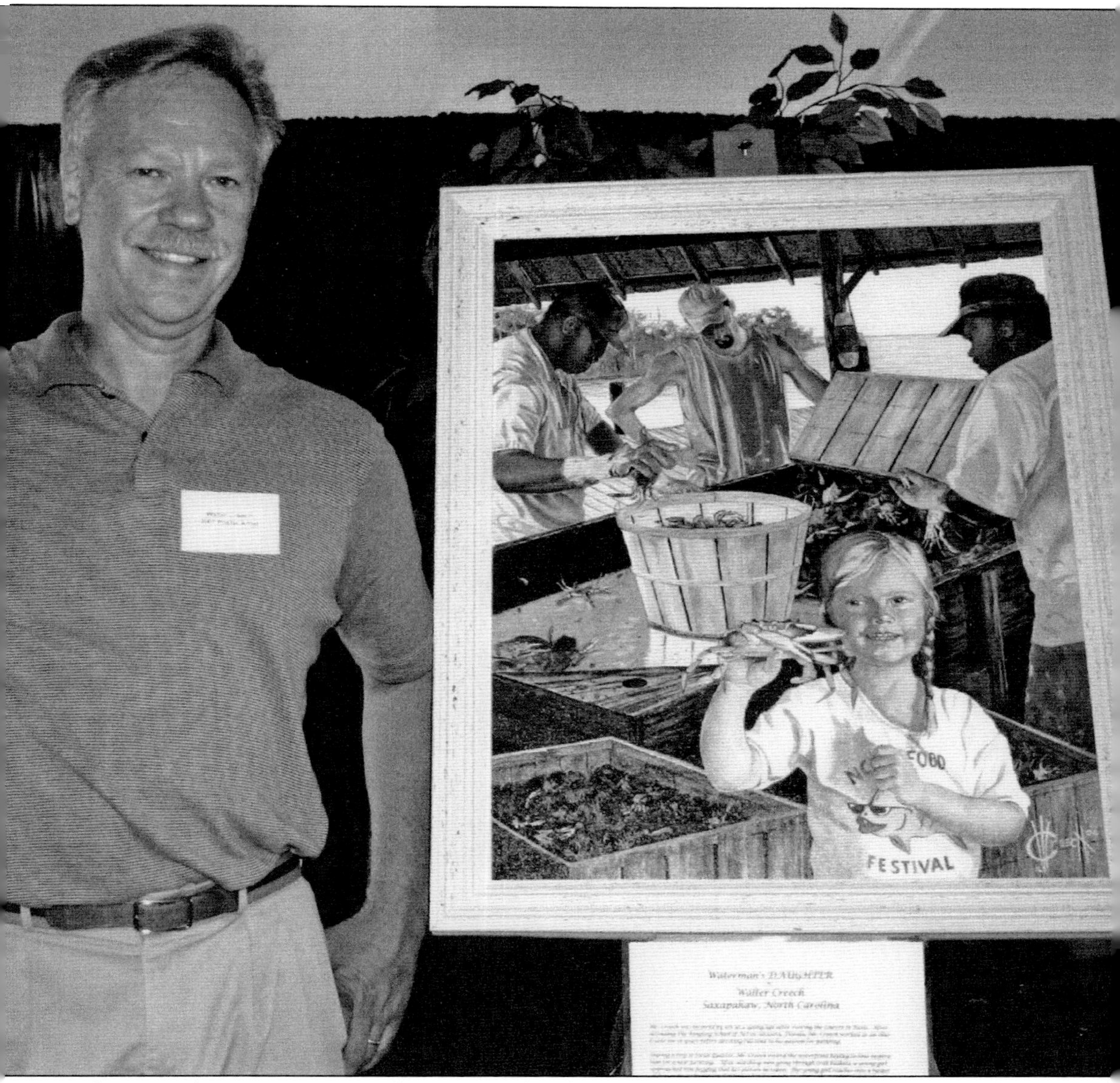


Walter Creech is an internationally recognized and award-winning artist. Walter is seen with his winning entry for the North Carolina Seafood Festival's poster contest in 2007. As a child born into a military family, while in the fourth grade, Walter went to the Louvre in Paris, where he saw some of the greatest artwork in the world. This made a profound impression on the young artist, who started drawing at a very early age. After graduating as an honor student from Ringling School of Art in Sarasota, Florida, in 1977, Walter worked as an illustrator for 18 years, always knowing he wanted to create his own art full time. In 2000, he started a new career as a full-time fine artist. His choice to take a road less traveled was a good one. Walter has been married for over 25 years to his wife, Ann. Ann Creech is Olive Cashwell's niece. They live with their three children, Zach, Rosa, and Sarah, in Saxapahaw. His address marker on the side of the road is made of a large easel. (Courtesy of Walter Creech.)

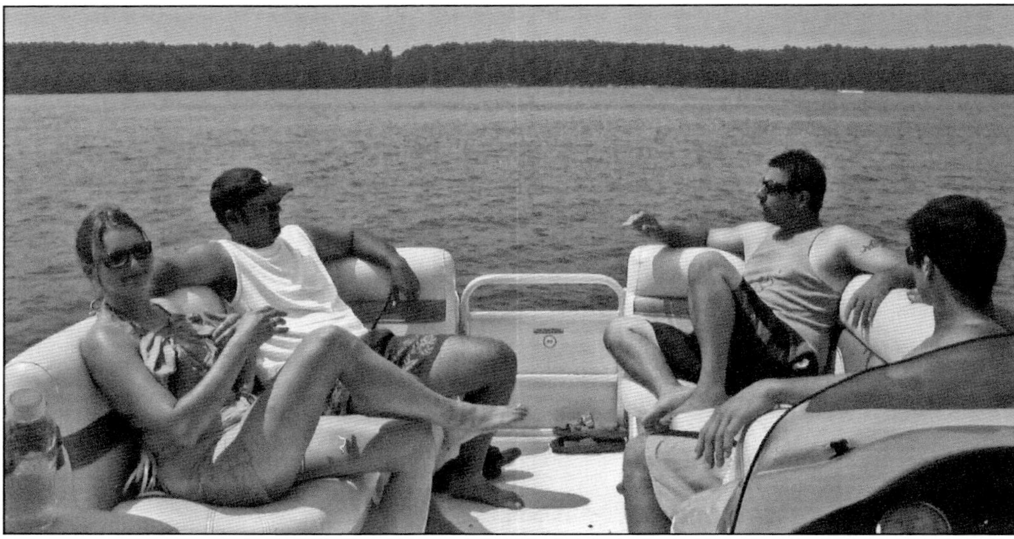

Senator Jordan's name lives on. Jordan Lake was originally called New Hope Lake in the 1960s during the construction by the Army Corps of Engineers. In 1974, after Senator Jordan's death, the lake project was renamed. The reservoir was finally flooded in 1983. The lake covers nearly 14,000 acres. The Jordan Lake Dam is 1,330 feet (405 meters) in length and has a top elevation of 266.5 feet (81 meters) above mean sea level. The Jordan Lake State Recreation Area totals 46,768 acres (189 square kilometers). The North Carolina Wildlife Resources Commission maintains a bald eagle observation platform located at the north end of the lake (just off Highway 751). It has been estimated that Jordan Lake is the largest summer home to the bald eagle. Above, Capt. Chris Matheus (not pictured), from the famed FOCM networking group, takes Haw Village residents for a tour of Lake Jordan to see the eagles. Clockwise are Rebecca and Shaun Kopczynski (owners of Kopps' Kandles), Jarod "Studly" Stelly, and Nicholas Macaulay. Below are sailboat races on Lake Jordan. (Above courtesy of Chris Matheus; below courtesy of Tonya and Bobby D'Angelo.)

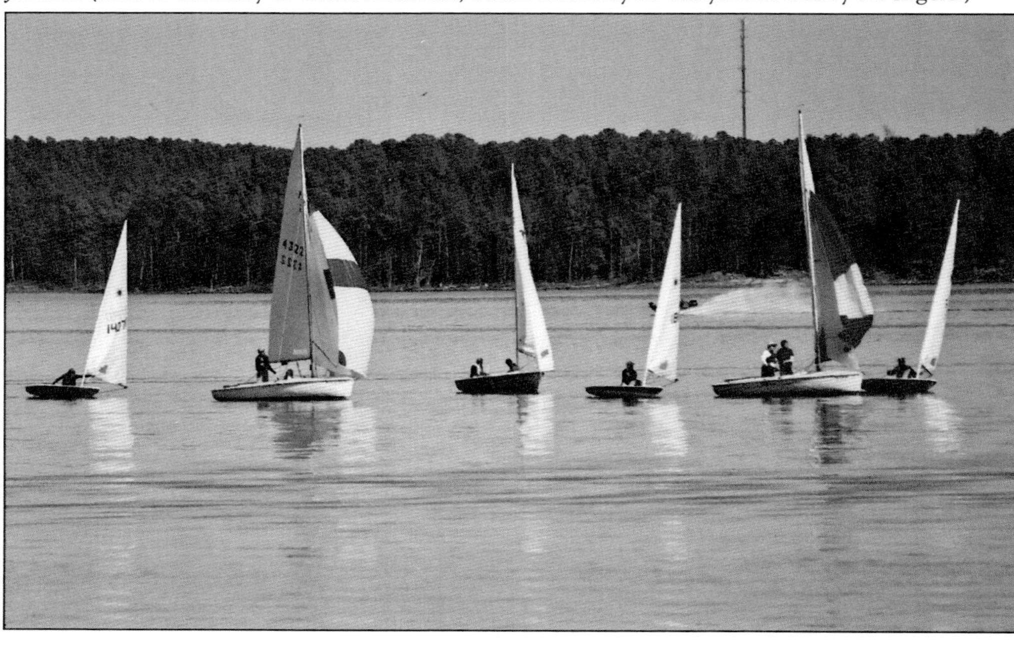

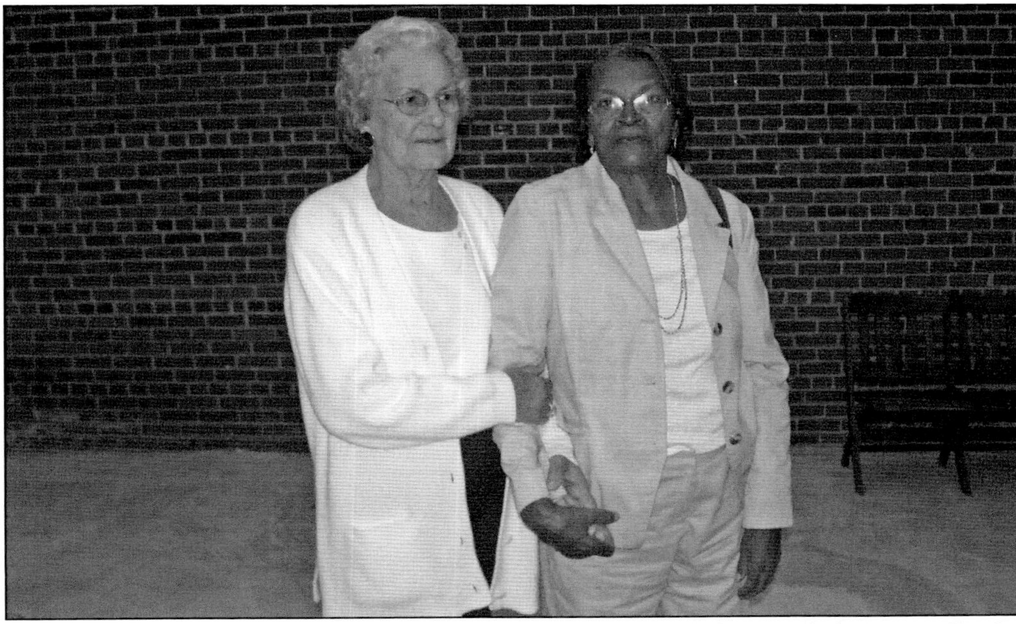

The lovely retired ladies of the Saxapahaw Cotton Mill pictured above include Frances Hardin (left) and Clara Alston. They are seen here holding hands during a mill tour given by Mac Jordan on Textile Heritage Day. Both Frances and Clara were discussing old times and were in shock over how beautifully the mill was restored, a place they knew almost as a second home. Below are Martha Wade (left) and Frances Hardin at the Textile Heritage Day Celebration Party held in the Puppethand Theater of Saxapahaw. Mill workers were like family with one another. There were strong feelings of respect and camaraderie among the coworkers at the Saxapahaw Mill. Everyone was treated equally. (Both photographs by the author.)

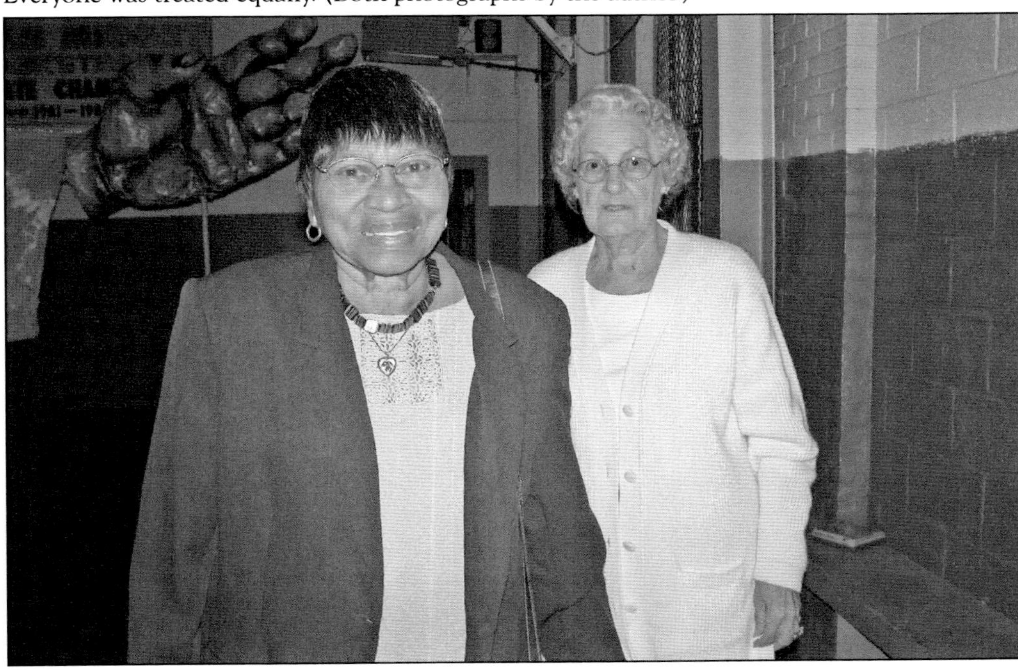

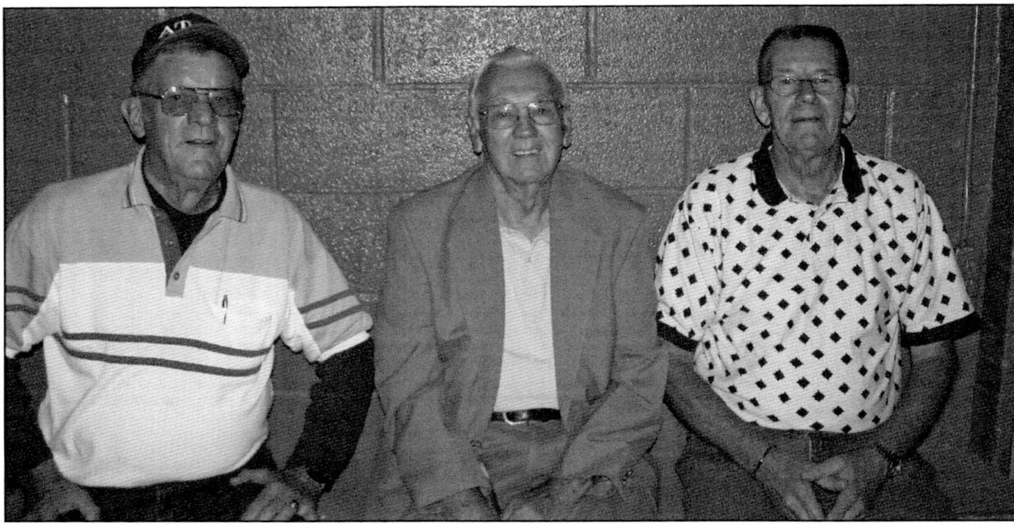

Above, Melvin Walters, Clayton Hardin, and O. D. Thrift, all former mill employees, celebrate Textile Heritage Day. Below, this gentleman picked up his own banjo and began to play music after hearing that the hired band could not make the celebration. The stage belongs to Saxapahaw's very own Paperhand Puppet Intervention who, according to their Web site, bring "many styles of puppetry and artistic expression" by way of "giant puppets, masks, stilt dancing, rod puppets, shadows or silhouettes, and anything else [they] might make at any time. [Their] vision is inspired by love for the earth and its creatures (including humans) as well as their belief in justice, equality, and peace." Donovan Zimmerman and Jan Burger are the original geniuses behind Paperhand and are supported by many. (Both photographs by the author.)

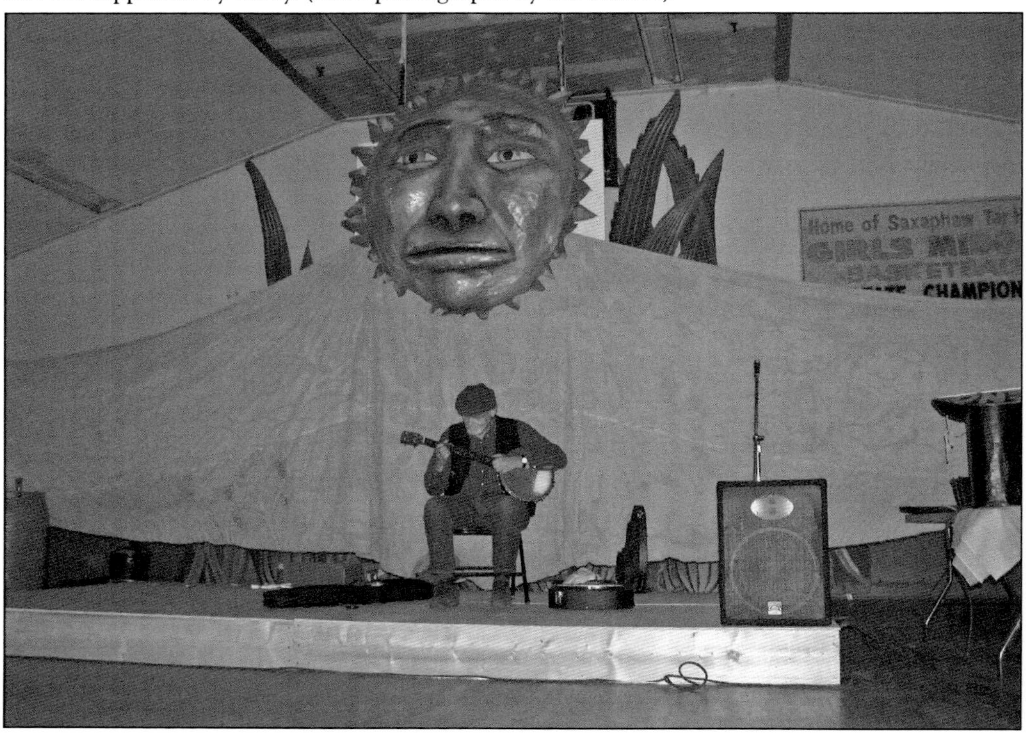

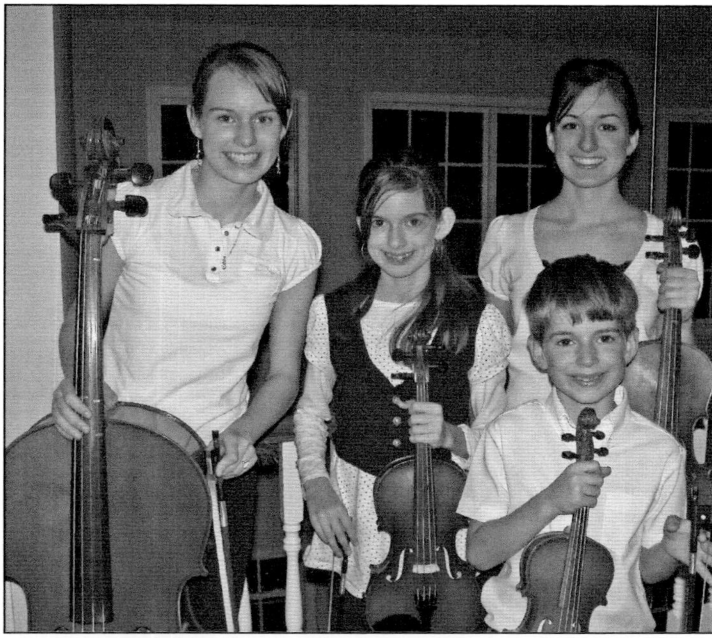

The Seals children of Saxapahaw's Haw Village are shown here. The whole family is musically gifted. From left to right are Jessica, who plays cello; Julie, who plays the mandolin and viola; Jamie, who plays violin; and Justin, who plays viola. They are available for professional performances. Their parents, Linda (who plays piano) and Jim (who plays guitar), have been home educating their children since 1995. Both Jamie and Jessica began taking college classes in the 11th grade. (Courtesy of Linda Seals.)

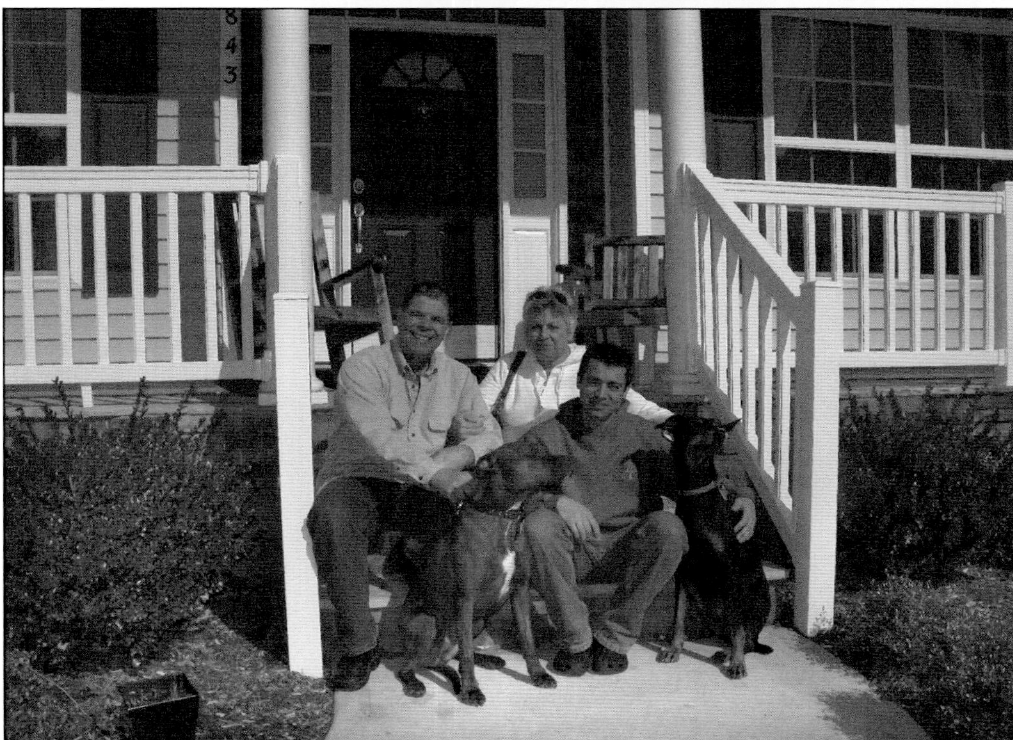

When Lorinda and Ronald Macaulay renovated their old farmhouse, they salvaged the wood from their bookcases and shelving to make bird houses, which they donated to the hillsides of Saxapahaw. Pictured from left to right are (first row) Chloe (the dog), Nicholas Macaulay, Jordan (the dog); (second row) Ron Macaulay and Lorinda Macaulay. (Courtesy of the Macaulays.)

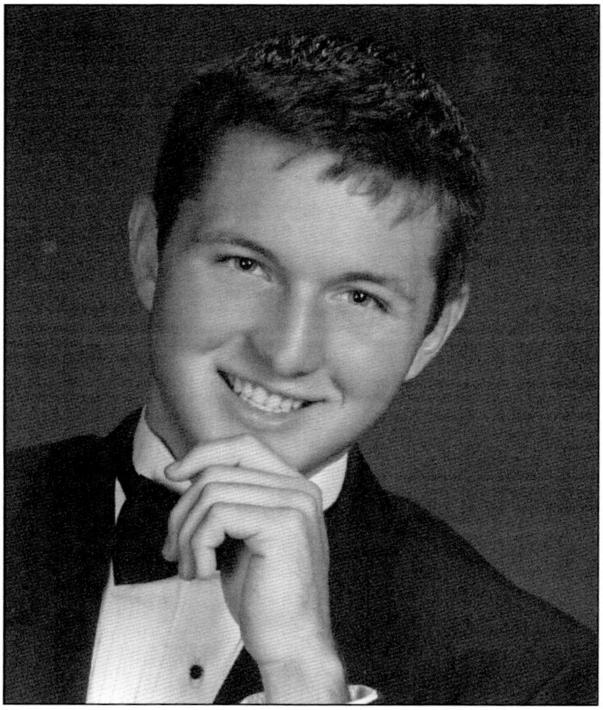

Keith Francis Kosman of Haw Village in Saxapahaw is the son of Heather Leigh Wallace. He was invited three times to the 3v3 Soccer National Championships held at Walt Disney World. Keith would like to be the U.S. secretary of defense one day or a vet if that doesn't work out. He loves waterskiing, tubing, eagle watching on Lake Jordan, and believes everyone should take time to "go to the beach." Keith is also a member of the Haw River Assembly. (Courtesy of Keith Kosman.)

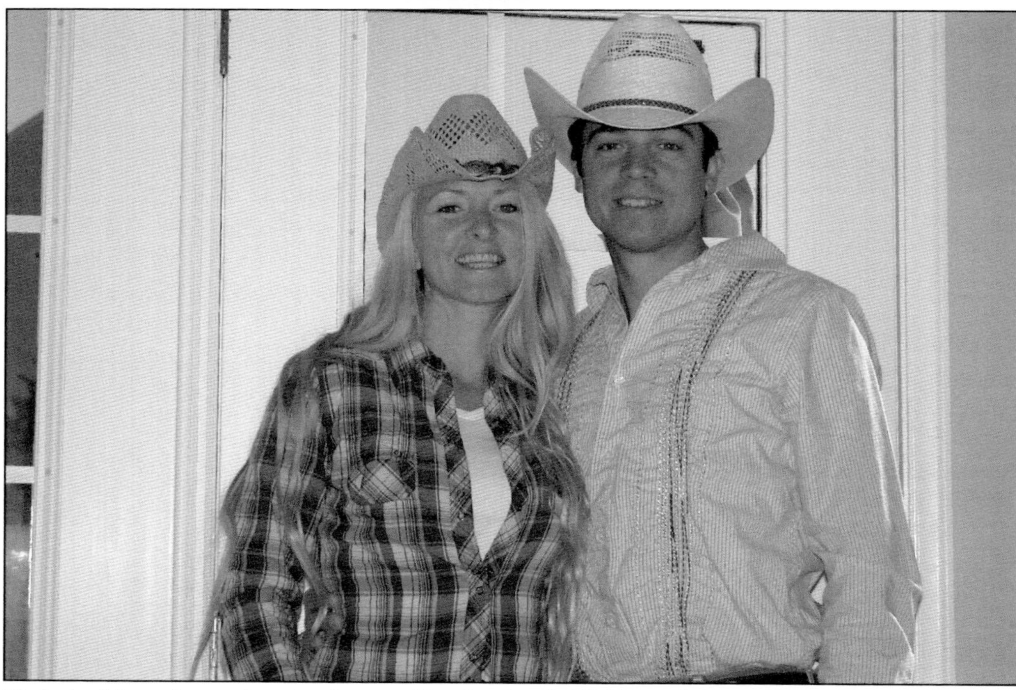

Nicholas Macaulay and medical writer Heather Leigh Wallace of Haw Village are pictured during one of their many trips to clean up the banks of the Haw River in Saxapahaw. They are both members of the Haw River Assembly and contribute greatly to wildlife conservation. (Courtesy of Nicholas Macaulay.)

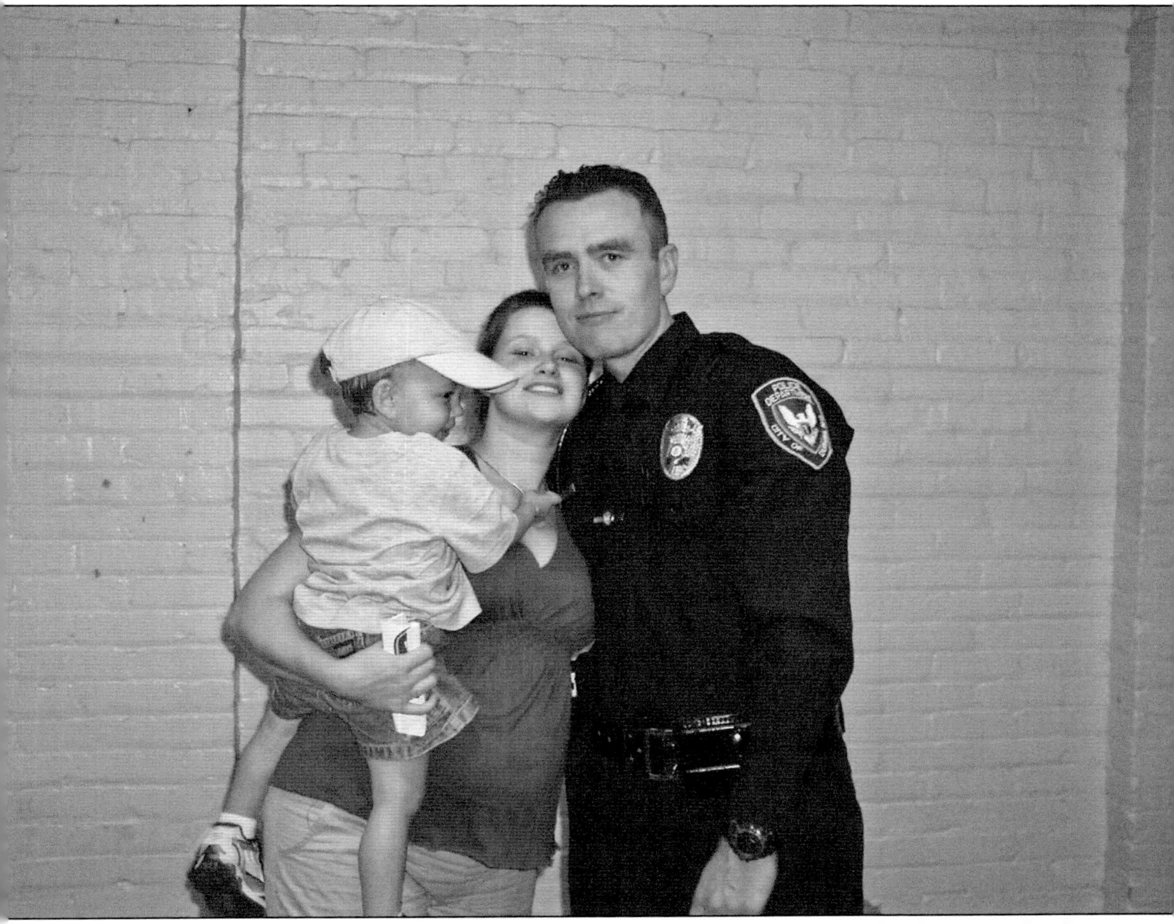

Haw Village residents Reaba and Michael Mues are shown with their son Michael Jr. at Michael's graduation from the police academy in Durham, North Carolina. Reaba, a medical writer, was pregnant at the time with their son Maverick. Mike was a fireman in the heart of New York City, and after having experienced September 11th firsthand, he brought his family to Saxapahaw, a place he felt safe to raise a family. Mike is a repeated recipient of Saxapahaw's Officer of the Year and Officer of the Month awards and was awarded the Distinguished Service Award by the Durham Jaycees in March 2009. New York City fireman Jim Ramous and his wife, Jessica, followed Michael Mues and his family to Saxapahaw. (Courtesy of Michael and Reaba Mues.)

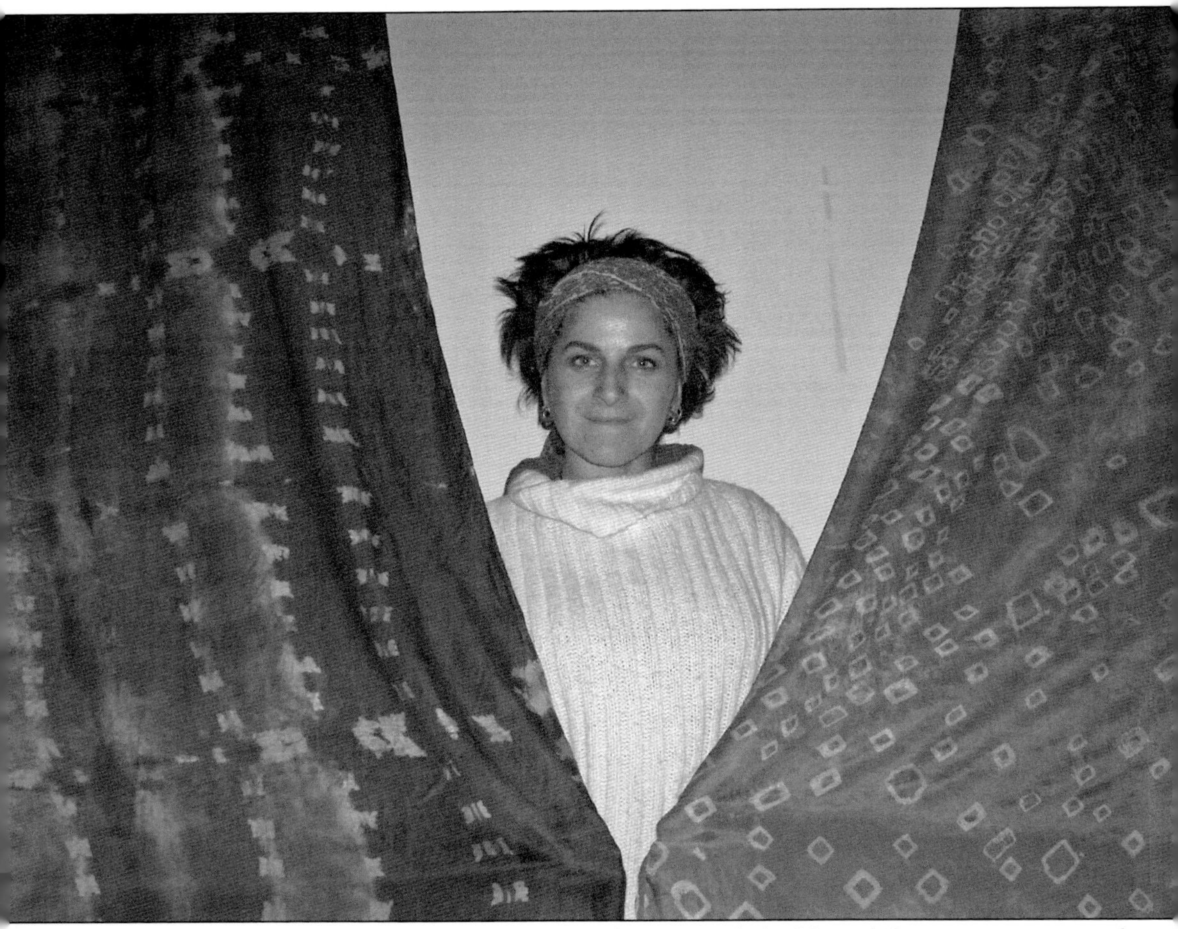

Monique de Latour from Melbourne, Australia, entered the United States as a person of "extraordinary talent" without needing visa sponsorship. According to Monique, "the aim of my art and design work is to generate a response with the visuals I create and to share my skills with others. Using textile design, graphic design, illustration, painting, or photography, the aim is always the same—to have the viewer *feel* something." Monique is a highly acclaimed art teacher at the private environmental high school of Saxapahaw called the Hawbridge School. Monique is photographed here with a silk shibori created with her students. (Photograph by the author.)

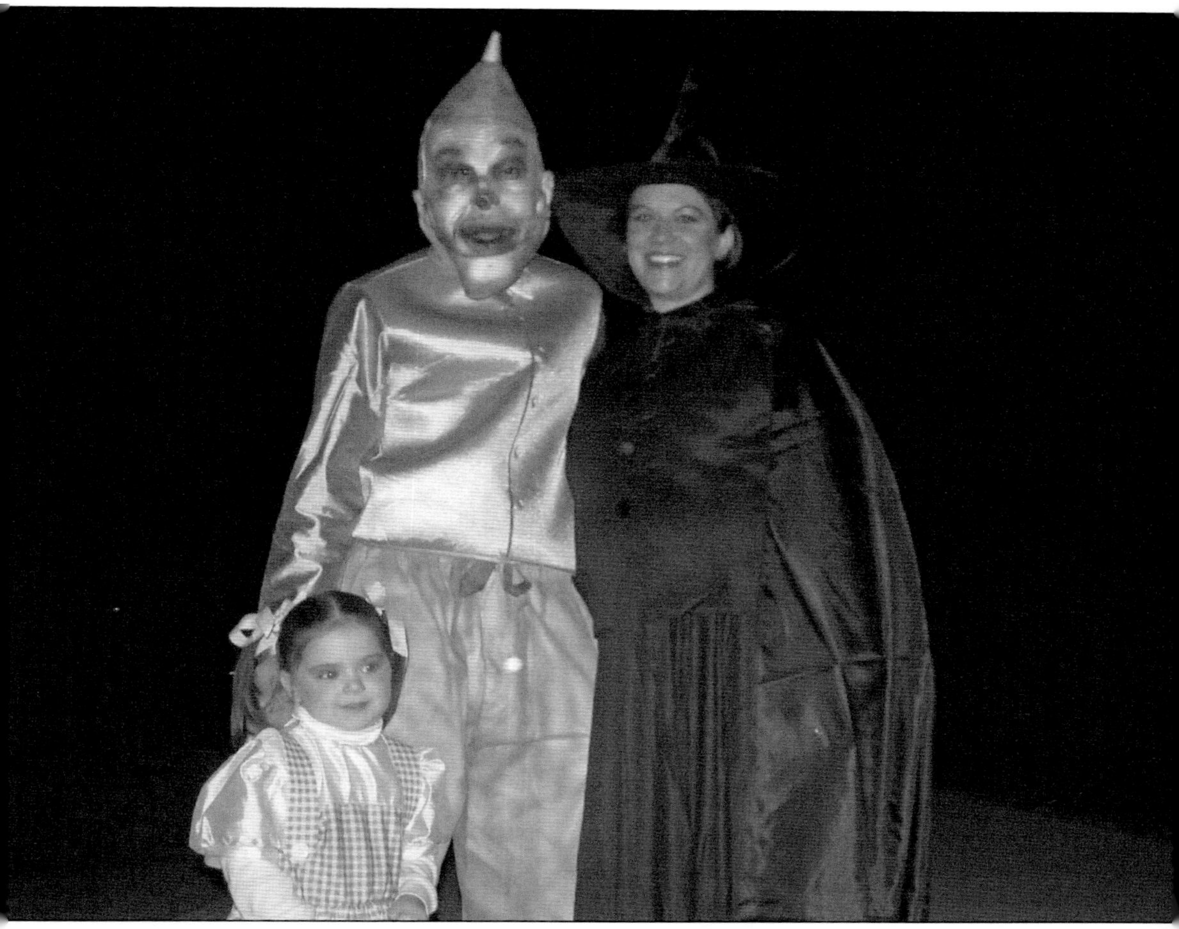

Residents of Haw Village in Saxapahaw are dressed up as the Tin Man (Efren Saenz), the Wicked Witch (Ashley Saenz), and their daughter Eva as Dorothy from *The Wizard of Oz*. They won the best family theme costumes. Ashley is pregnant here with their second child, Harrison. (Photograph by the author.)

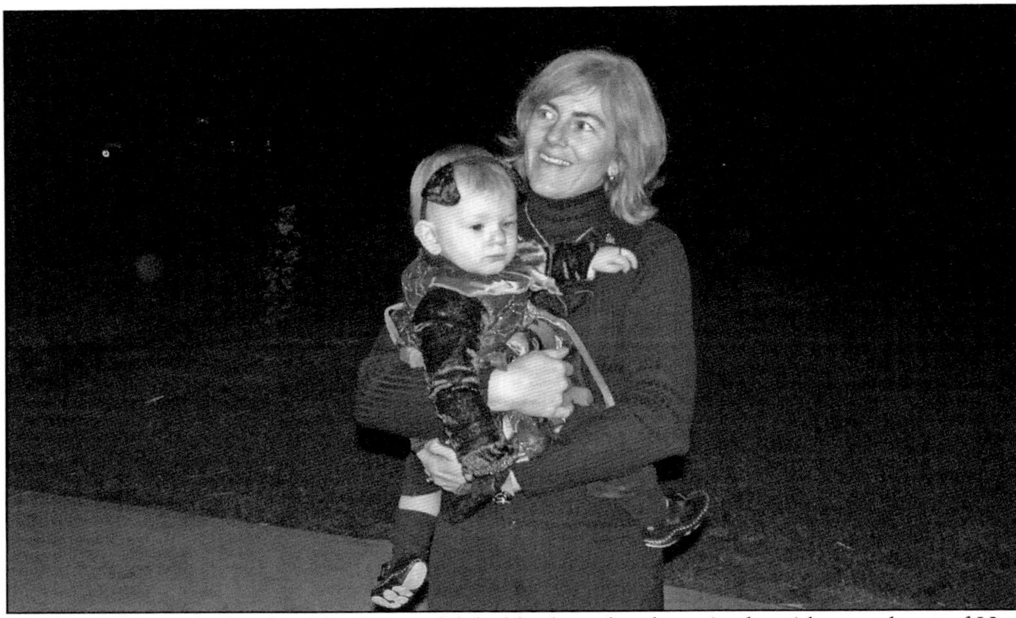

Tonya D'Angelo (wife of Bobby D'Angelo) holds their daughter Andie. Also residents of Haw Village in Saxapahaw, Tonya and Bobby both served in the U.S. military. Bobby was an F-4 pilot, and Tonya was a staff sergeant. (Photograph by the author.)

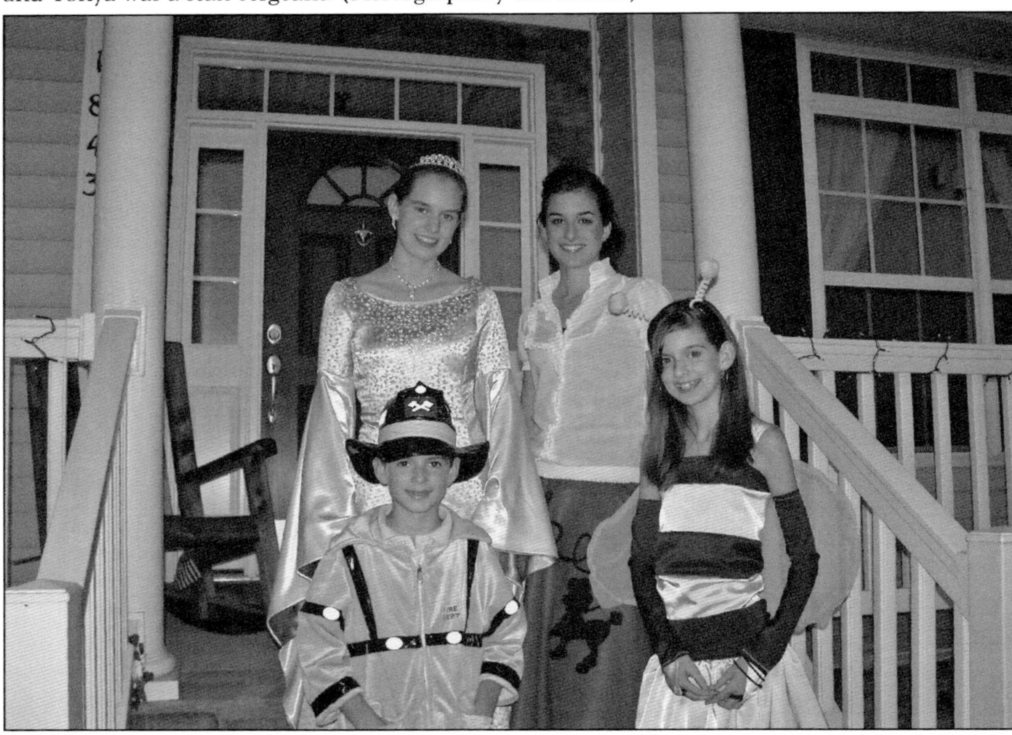

The Seals children of Haw Village are, from left to right, (first row) Justin and Julie; (second row) Jessica and Jamie. Jessica, Jamie, and Julie all handmade their costumes for Halloween. (Photograph by the author.)

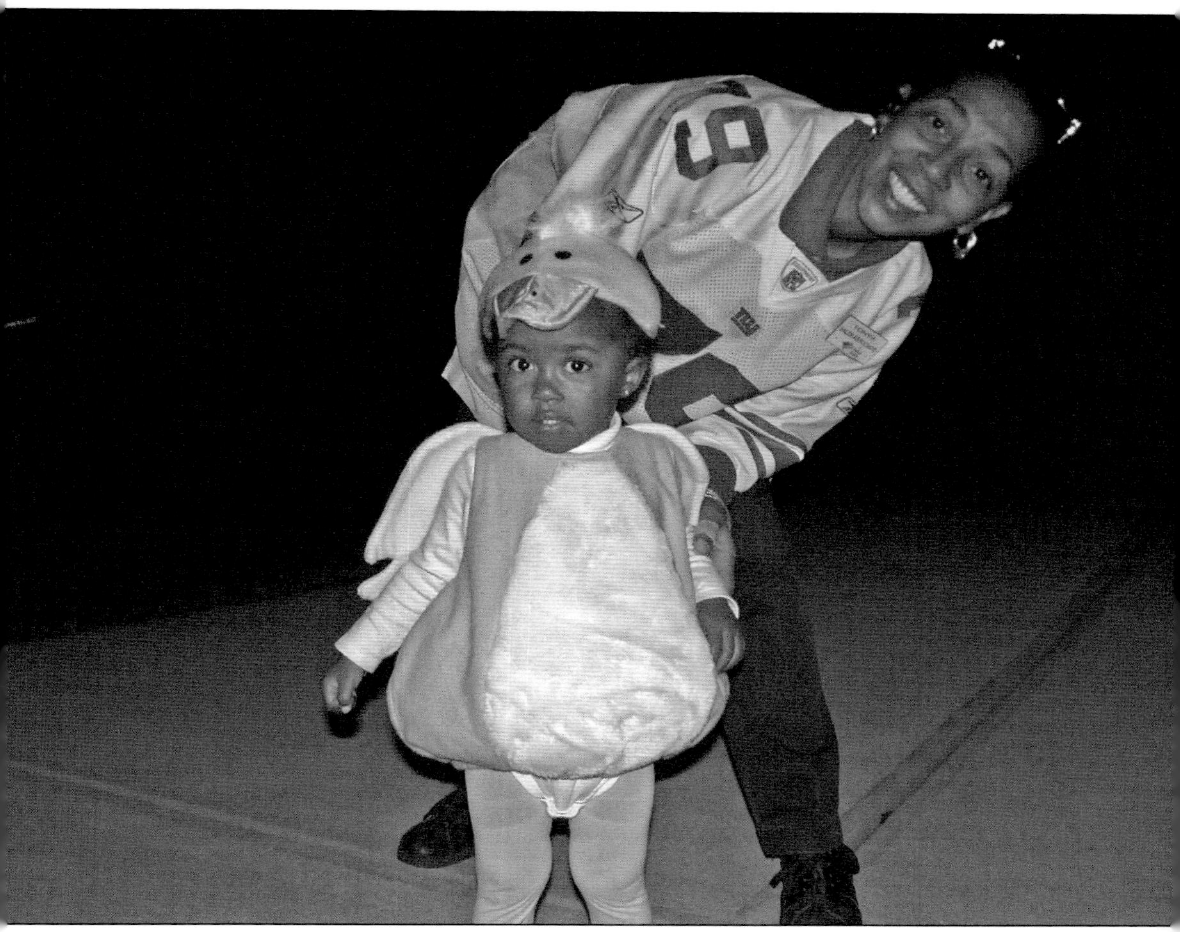

A Haw Village resident, Tonya Chase (wife of Don Chase) holds her daughter on the first Halloween she was able to trick-or-treat. (Photograph by the author.)

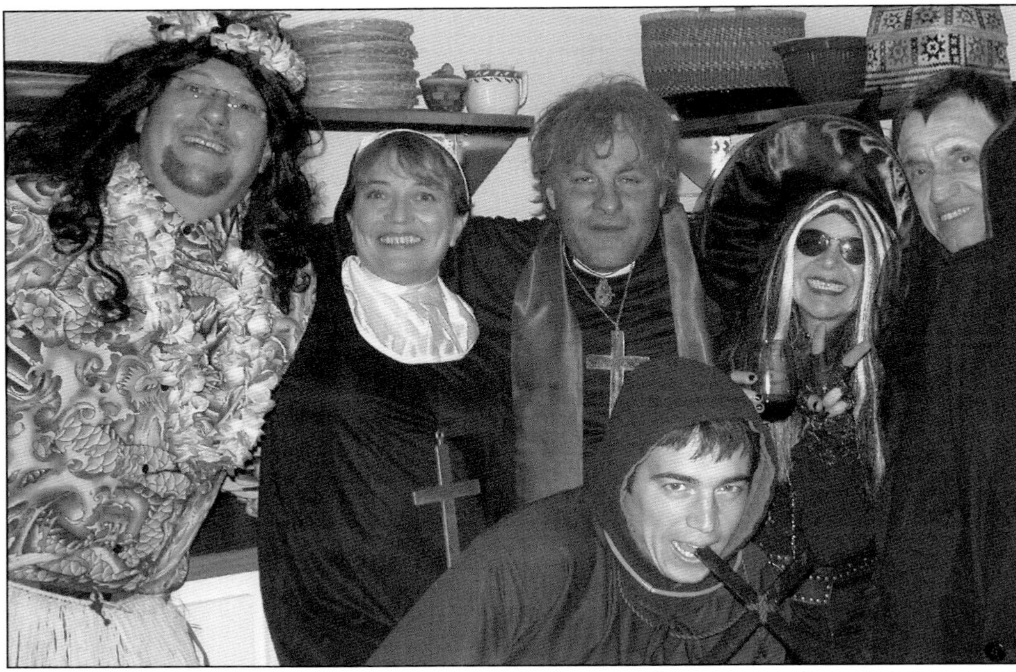

At the annual Saxapahaw Halloween Competition, these people are serious about their homemade costumes for hysterical ghoulish prizes. This evening event is used to raise money and collect food for the poor. The small village of Saxapahaw has 101 homes that were built prior to 1939 (many from the 1800s). These older-style Georgian and Victorian homes, with pocket windows, massive brick fireplaces, and expansive wooden staircases, create outstanding historic and charming atmospheres for Halloween parties. Halloween is celebrated in Saxapahaw just as much as Christmas. Above, Sue Dayton (giving the peace sign) holds a Halloween party with many Saxapahaw locals in her restored Georgian-style 100-year-old home. Below, Super Frankie (Frankie Hayes) is seen in the middle of the montage of locals. (Photographs by the author.)

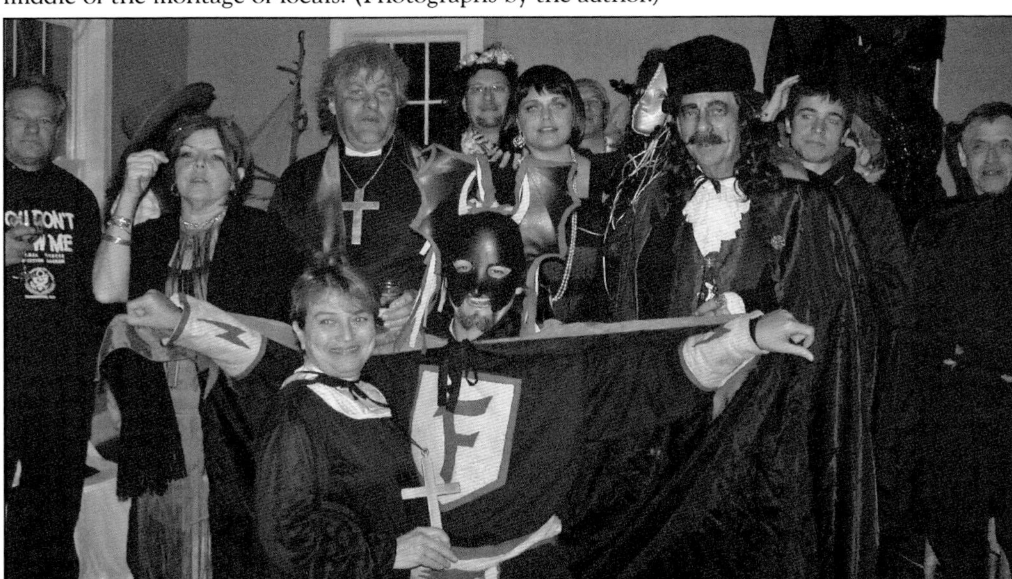

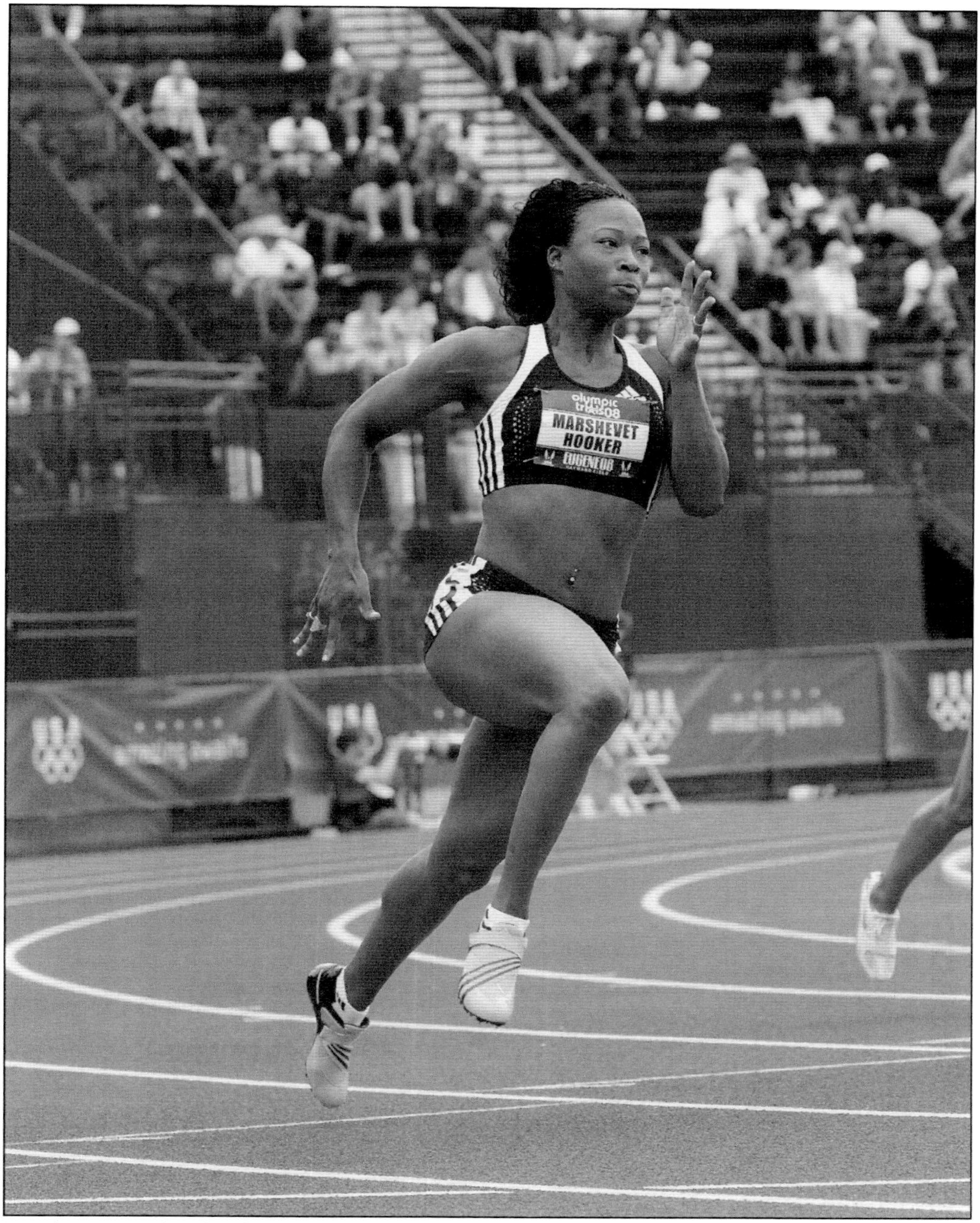


Marshevet Hooker finished fifth in the 200-meter race at the 2008 Beijing Olympics. Marshevet became the fifth-fastest woman in history; only Florence Griffith-Joyner, Marion Jones, Christine Arron of France, and Merlene Ottey of Jamaica have ever run faster than Hooker. Marshevet is the granddaughter of Connie Hooker. His home in Saxapahaw is where Marshevet has spent many fond summers. Her father, Ricky Hooker, is a former San Antonia Spurs basketball player, and her sister, Destinee, is a two-time NCAA champion in the high jump, in 2006 and 2007. (Courtesy of Cheryl Treworgy and www.prettysporty.com.)

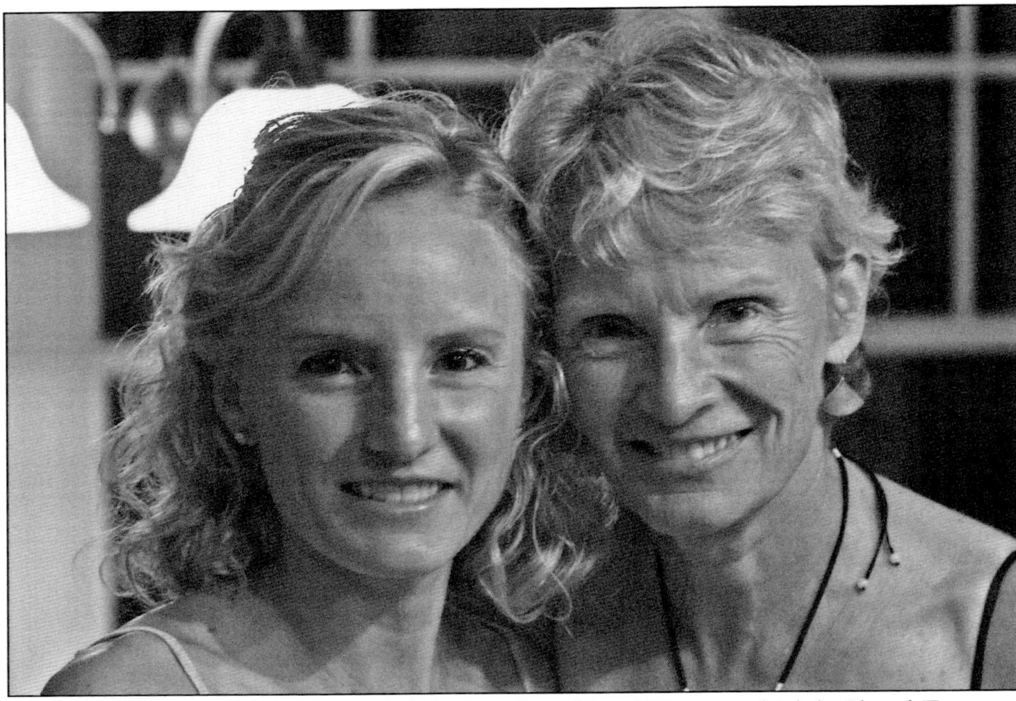

Shalane Flanagan (left) is shown with her mother, Cheryl Treworgy (right). Cheryl Treworgy, resident of Saxapahaw's Haw Village, is a former world-record holder in the women's marathon. She held the record before women were allowed to run more than 1,500 meters at the Olympics. As a working photographer at the Olympic trials, Cheryl watched her daughter earn an opportunity she had never been given. Cheryl, previously Cheryl Bridges, became the first woman in history to break 2:50:00 with a 2:49:40. She was also a five-time member of the U.S. team at the World Cross-Country Championships. (Courtesy of www.prettysporty.com.)

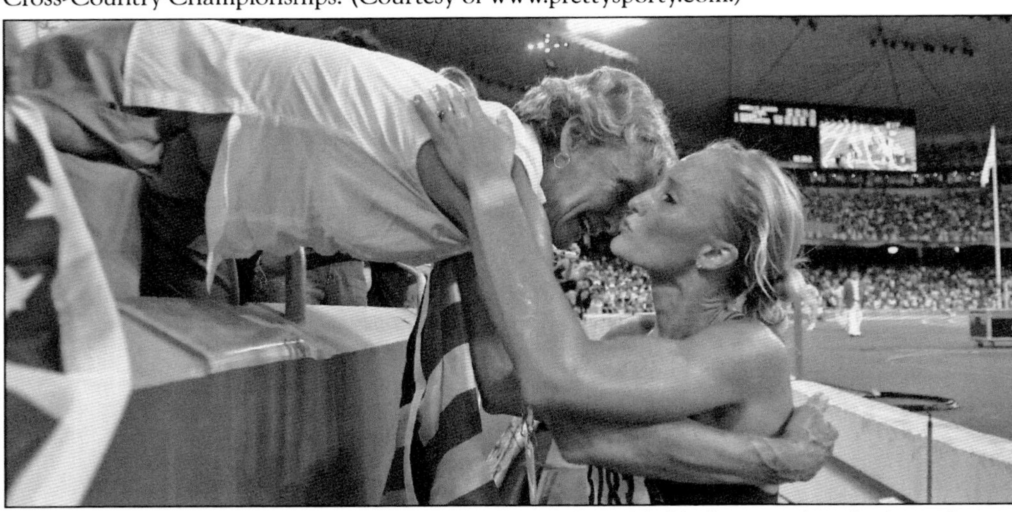

Shalane's mother, Cheryl Treworgy, professional track and field photographer, had an ultimate and emotional grandstand view of her daughter's Beijing Olympic 2008 winning event. Shalane is one of two American women to ever medal in the 10,000-meter. (Courtesy of Erich Schlegel and the *Dallas Morning News*.)

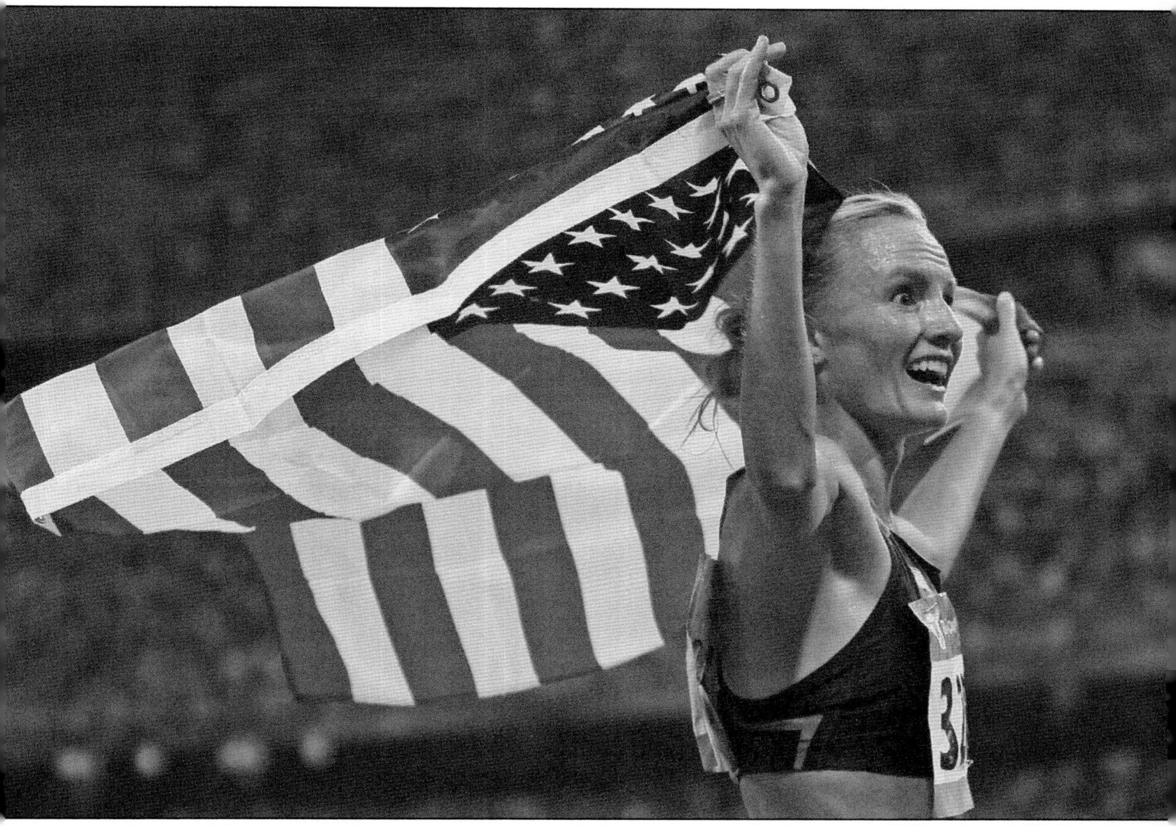


At the Beijing Olympics, Shalane Flanagan earned a bronze in the 10,000-meter. She was surprised by the finish, admitting she didn't know her place until after crossing the line. Shalane is a 2004 graduate of the University of North Carolina. Her collegiate career included being a 10-time NCAA All-American and two-time NCAA cross-country champion (2002 and 2003) as well as the 2003 NCAA indoor 3,000-meter champion. She turned professional in 2004 prior to graduation. At the Mount SAC Relays in 2007, Shalane won the 5,000-meter in 14 minutes, 44.80 seconds, breaking the American record. At the U.S. Outdoor Championships in 2007, she led the 5,000 meter from wire-to-wire, winning in 14:51:75, the fourth-fastest time ever by an American. If you look closely, that jogging person in Saxapahaw passing you by might be Shalane Flanagan or her mother, Cheryl Treworgy. (Courtesy of Erich Schlegel and the *Dallas Morning News*.)